Reader in Qualitative Methods in Migration Research

Reader in Qualitative Methods in Migration Research

Edited by

Ibrahim Sirkeci, Theodoros Iosifides,

Carla DeTona, Annalisa Frisina

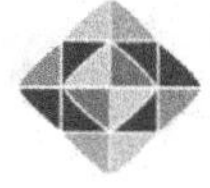

TRANSNATIONAL PRESS LONDON

2019

Reader in Qualitative Methods in Migration Research
Edited by Ibrahim Sirkeci, Theodoros Iosifides, Carla DeTona, Annalisa Frisina

First Published in 2019 by TRANSNATIONAL PRESS LONDON in the United Kingdom, 12 Ridgeway Gardens, London, N6 5XR, UK.
www.tplondon.com

Paperback
ISBN: 978-1-912997-10-7

Cover Design: Gizem Çakır
Cover Photo: By Panek - Own work, CC BY-SA 4.0,
https://commons.wikimedia.org/w/index.php?curid=20304235

www.tplondon.com

CITATION INFORMATION

Chapter 1:

DeTona, C., Frisina, A., & Ganga, D. (2010). Research Methods in Ethnic and Migration Studies. *Migration Letters*, 7(1), 1-6.

Chapter 2:

Iosifides, T. and Sporton, D. (2009). Biographical methods in migration research. *Migration Letters*, 6(2), 101-108.

Chapter 3:

Wray, S., & Bartholomew, M. (2010). Some reflections on outsider and insider identities in ethnic and migrant qualitative research. *Migration Letters*, 7(1), 7-16.

Chapter 4:

Cliggett, L., & Crooks, D. L. (2007). Promoting Multi-methods Research: Linking Anthropometric Methods to Migration Studies. *Migration Letters*, *4*(2), 159-169.

Chapter 5:

Moskal, M. (2010). Visual methods in researching migrant children's experiences of belonging. *Migration Letters*, *7*(1), 17-31.

Chapter 6:

Scheibelhofer, E. (2010). Gendered differences in emigration and mobility perspectives among European researchers working abroad. *Migration Letters*, *7*(1), 33-41.

Chapter 7:

Bertozzi, R. (2010). A Participatory Approach to Research with Migrant Working Adolescents. *Migration Letters*, *7*(1), 57-67.

Chapter 8:

Scheibelhofer, E. (2011) Potential of qualitative network analysis in migration studies-Reflections based on an empirical analysis of young researchers' mobility aspirations. *Migration Letters*, *8*(2), 111-120.

Chapter 9:

Boyles, J. (2016). Overcoming Challenges of International Migration Research: A Case Study Approach in Southern Mexico. *Migration Letters*, *13*(1), 131-143.

Chapter 10:

Kühner, A., & Langer, P. C. (2010). Dealing with Dilemmas of Difference-Ethical and Psychological Considerations of "Othering" and "Peer Dialogues" in the Research Encounter. *Migration Letters*, *7*(1), 69-78.

Chapter 11:

Psoinos, M. (2010). Forced migration and psychosocial health: meaning-making through autobiographical narratives in the UK. *Migration Letters*, *7*(1), 79-90.

Chapter 12:

Gray, B. (2009). Migration, life narratives, memory and subjectivity: Reflections on an archival project on Irish migration. *Migration Letters*, *6*(2), 109-117.

Chapter 13:

Bjarnesen, J. (2009). A Mobile Life Story Tracing Hopefulness in the Life and Dreams of a Young Ivorian Migrant. *Migration Letters*, *6*(2), 119-129.

Chapter 14:

Clark-Kazak, C. (2009). Power and politics in migration narrative methodology: Research with young Congolese migrants in Uganda. *Migration Letters*, *6*(2), 131-141.

Chapter 15:

Christou, A. (2009). Telling Diaspora Stories: theoretical and methodological reflections on narratives of migrancy and belongingness in the second generation. *Migration Letters*, *6*(2), 143-153.

Chapter 16:

Xenitidou, M. (2011). National identity and otherness in Greek speakers' talk about immigration: Methodological and transdisciplinary reflections. *Migration Letters*, *8*(2), 121-131.

EDITORS

Ibrahim Sirkeci is Professor of Transnational Studies, Director of Regent's Centre for Transnational Business and Management, Head of Marketing Subject Cluster, and Associate Dean for Research (Interim) at Regent's University London. Previously he worked at the University of Bristol, Atilim University, Hacettepe University and Bilkent University. He earned his PhD from the University of Sheffield. His research focuses on migration, integration, labour market outcomes, remittances and transnational marketing. He has founded *Migration Letters* journal with Jeffrey Cohen and Elli Heikkila in 2003 and has been chief editor or associate editor of several other journals including *Remittances Review*, *Transnational Marketing Journal*, and *Goc Dergisi*. He has chaired the Migration Conference series since 2012.

Theodoros Iosifides is Professor of Social Science Methods at the Department of Geography, University of the Aegean, Greece and teaches Human Geography at the Hellenic Open University. He is a sociologist and human geographer, studied Sociology and Regional Development in Panteion University of Athens, Greece and holds a D.Phil. in Geography from the University of Sussex, UK. For the last 19 years he teaches social science methods, human/social geography and migration studies at the University of the Aegean, Greece and at the Hellenic Open University. He has written extensively books, journal papers and book chapters on social science methodology and epistemology, qualitative methods, migration and human geography and participated in several international and research projects.

Carla De Tona is an independent researcher, with expertise in the field of international migration, gender, race/ethnicity/diaspora, memory and narratives, race and education, qualitative research methodologies. She has published extensively on these issues and has worked in Ireland, the UK, Germany and Italy. She has a PhD in Sociology from Trinity College Dublin and has worked as Research Associate/Lecturer in Trinity College and as a Research Associate/Fellow at the University of Manchester. Since 2012, as an independent researcher she has collaborated with various organisations including IPRS, Italy and Griffith College, Ireland. She is currently an editor of Migration Letters Journal and member of International Advisory Group for EU research projects.

Annalisa Frisina is Associate Professor of Sociology at the Department of FISPPA, University of Padua, Italy. She has extensive research experiences in youth studies, migration studies, religious studies, with a special expertise on visual and collaborative/participatory research methods. She is co-founder of InteRGRace (Interdisciplinary Group on Race and Racisms and the research group SLAN.G. on Social Control, Labour, Racism and Migration. She is committed to researching/contrasting different forms of racisms (mainly islamophobia, anti-black racism and antiziganism) through cultural work with young people. She is in the Editorial Board of the international journals of *Visual Ethnography* and *Migration Letters.* She is also member of the RC57 of Visual Sociology of the International Sociological Association (ISA), of the International Visual Sociology Association (IVSA). She has published in peer-reviewed journals including *Rassegna Italiana di Sociologia, Mondi Migranti, Journal of Ethnic and Migration Studies, Journal of Intercultural Studies, and Migration Letters.*

CONTENTS

ON QUALITATIVE METHODOLOGIES IN MIGRATION RESEARCH

Ibrahim Sirkeci, Theodoros Iosifides, Carla DeTona, Annalisa Frisina

Transnational Press London launched this *Reader In* series of reprints of articles published in the journals portfolio to extend the reach and life of studies and scholarship produced in various social science disciplines. *Reader in Qualitative Methods in Migration Research* is the first volume in the series.

This edited volume aims to offer a collection of articles on qualitative research methodologies employed in research on migration from various disciplinary perspectives by researchers from around the world. In this framework, *Reader in Qualitative Methods in Migration Research* is likely to offer insights and answers to many theoretical and practical questions to researchers and students interested in researching migrants, migration and related topics.

In the last decade, we have witnessed an exponential growth of research in migration studies. This growth, however, has not been accompanied with a matching growth in training opportunities and there is a mismatch between the need for research in this field and the skilled and trained people who can deliver quality research. Therefore there is an increasing need to nurture this field of research with more theoretical and methodological knowledge and experience sharing. *Reader in Qualitative Methods in Migration Research* aims to contribute to filling this gap.

The chapters included in this book was originally published in regular issues and two special issues of *Migration Letters* journal from 2009 onwards. These special issues were guest edited by Carla De Tona, Annalisa Frisina and Deianira Ganga in 2010 and by Theodoros Iosifidis and Deborah Sporton in 2009. We have regrouped and ordered these studies to enhance the flow and transition in the book. The first six chapters look into more general issues and debates in migration research methodologies, while chapters seven to ten offer cases studies on alternative qualitative methodologies and then the final six chapters focus on narratives and challenges of the narrative methodology applied in migration studies.

As was the case in the last decade, when these papers were originally published, the chapters included here deal with significant challenges and authors hoped to offer a ground for "reflection and exchange in the quest for a common vocabulary and ethical research practices" (DeTona et al., 2010:4).

Chapter 1 titled "Research Methods in Ethnic and Migration Studies" by

DeTona, Frisina and Ganga, the guest editors of that special issue offer a framework to discuss the complexities and underline that reflective role of sharing these articles on methods in migration research. Another guest editorial is Chapter 2 titled "Biographical methods in migration research" by Iosifides and Sporton (2009) focuses on the discussion and utility of biographical methods which are more widely used in migration research.

Chapter 3 by Wray and Bartholomew (2010) tackles the outsider and insider identities dilemma in qualitative research. They argue that "insider and outsider status shifts constantly throughout the research". It is followed by Cliggett and Crooks (2007) favourable take on multi-methods research bringing in the use of Anthropometric Methods in Migration Studies. Moskal's (2010) work was quite novel then and still valuable as we are seeing more and more use of visual methods particularly in researching migrant children's experiences. She shows the need for children's participation in research on migrant children's experiences of transnationalism. Chapter 6 by Scheibelhofer (2010) explores the European researchers' gendered perspectives in doing research abroad. She argues that "a better understanding of the gendered importance of social relations for the future mobility aspirations of scientists working abroad" can be gained.

The three chapters following bring us three cases; of participatory approach by Bertozzi (2010), of qualitative network analysis by Scheibelhofer (2011), and case study approach by Boyles (2016).

The last part of the collection focuses on narrative methodologies and brings insights from the field as well as conceptual discussions. Kühner and Langer (2010) in "Dealing with Dilemmas of Difference-Ethical and Psychological Considerations of "Othering" and "Peer Dialogues" in the Research Encounter" argue that "strategies of recognition of the "other" - seen as a reflexive agent - have to be developed systematically as an ethical precondition of socially responsible research".

In Chapter 11, Psoinos (2010) investigates the way refugees make sense of their migratory experience and their psychosocial health using narrative methodology. Breda Gray (2009) in her contribution titled "Migration, life narratives, memory and subjectivity: Reflections on an archival project on Irish migration", discusses an archival project focused on the life narratives of those who witnessed mass out-migration from 1950s Ireland.

Bjarnesen (2009) in chapter 13, presents a "life story" case focusing on the experiences of a young Ivorian migrant. He argues that "the mobile life story is intended to guide the exploration of the subjective experiences of migrants at various stages of a migrant trajectory". Clark-Kazak (2009) in the following chapter expands the discussion into power and politics using narrative methodology. She argues that ethical and methodological issues of representativity, ownership, anonymity and confidentiality all come into play as professional and personal boundaries become blurred.

The last two chapters by Christou (2009) and Xenitidou (2011) in this collection coincidentally look into Greek experiences regarding migrancy, belongingness, national identity and otherness.

References

Bertozzi, R. (2010). A Participatory Approach to Research with Migrant Working Adolescents. *Migration Letters*, *7*(1), 57-67.

Bjarnesen, J. (2009). A Mobile Life Story Tracing Hopefulness in the Life and Dreams of a Young Ivorian Migrant. *Migration Letters*, *6*(2), 119-129.

Boyles, J. (2016). Overcoming Challenges of International Migration Research: A Case Study Approach in Southern Mexico. *Migration Letters*, *13*(1), 131-143.

Christou, A. (2009). Telling Diaspora Stories: theoretical and methodological reflections on narratives of migrancy and belongingness in the second generation. *Migration Letters*, *6*(2), 143-153.

Clark-Kazak, C. (2009). Power and politics in migration narrative methodology: Research with young Congolese migrants in Uganda. *Migration Letters*, *6*(2), 131-141.

Cliggett, L., & Crooks, D. L (2007). Promoting Multi-methods Research: Linking Anthropometric Methods to Migration Studies. *Migration Letters*, *4*(2), 159-169.

De Tona, C., Frisina, A., & Ganga, D. (2014). Editorial: Research methods in ethnic and migration studies. *Migration Letters, 7*(1), 1-6.

Gray, B. (2009). Migration, life narratives, memory and subjectivity: Reflections on an archival project on Irish migration. *Migration Letters*, *6*(2), 109-117.

Iosifides, T. and Sporton, D. (2009). Biographical methods in migration research. *Migration Letters*, 6(2), 101-108.

Kühner, A., & Langer, P. C. (2010). Dealing with Dilemmas of Difference-Ethical and Psychological Considerations of "Othering" and "Peer Dialogues" in the Research Encounter. *Migration Letters*, *7*(1), 69-78.

Moskal, M. (2010). Visual methods in researching migrant children's experiences of belonging. *Migration Letters*, *7*(1), 17-31.

Psoinos, M. (2010). Forced migration and psychosocial health: meaning-making through autobiographical narratives in the UK. *Migration Letters*, *7*(1), 79-90.

Scheibelhofer, E. (2010). Gendered differences in emigration and mobility perspectives among European researchers working abroad. *Migration Letters*, *7*(1), 33-41.

Scheibelhofer, E. (2011). Potential of qualitative network analysis in migration studies-Reflections based on an empirical analysis of young researchers' mobility aspirations. *Migration Letters*, *8*(2), 111-120.

Wray, S., & Bartholomew, M. (2010). Some reflections on outsider and insider identities in ethnic and migrant qualitative research. *Migration Letters*, 7(1), 7-16.

Xenitidou, M. (2011). National identity and otherness in Greek speakers' talk about immigration: Methodological and transdisciplinary reflections. *Migration Letters*, *8*(2), 121-131.

CHAPTER 1

RESEARCH METHODS IN ETHNIC AND MIGRATION STUDIES

Carla DeTona, Annalisa Frisina, Deianira Ganga

Abstract

The acceleration and diversification of the movement across borders of millions of people have recently implied a heightened relevance of topics such as ethnicity, race and migration in the social sciences. Nevertheless, being migration a highly interdisciplinary and complex issue, the diverse national academic traditions and methodologies of investigation currently existing have up to now hindered the development of a clear framework for the understanding of the phenomenon. Through this special issue, HERMES (European Researchers in Migration and Ethnic Studies) attempts to provide a dedicated arena offering European researchers the opportunity to disseminate the results of their investigations in the field of migration and, in particular, of reflecting on fieldwork and/or methodological issues. The eight articles presented here all contribute – in their own ways – to the provision of a reflexive ground for the understanding of methodological choices and options and, hopefully, to the creation of a shared understanding of such issues across disciplines and research traditions.

Methods and research practice

The study of ethnicity and migration is a prominent subject in the social sciences since the 1960s. Its relevance has been proven and heightened in more recent years with the acceleration, globalisation and differentiation of international migration (Castles and Miller, 2003). Ethnic and migration studies remain however 'a rag-tag field', as Piaras Mac Éinrí claims, 'a ragged field of study, not an intellectually unified discipline' (Mac Éinrí, n.a.). Drawing from a range of disparate and sometimes competing disciplines, different paradigms have emerged. However, we still lack a set of clear and dominant theories and approaches to help make sense of this complex phenomenon. Moreover, there is a 'tendency for all paradigms to outlive their usefulness, and the specific historical circumstances which produced them in the first place may by now be helping to obscure fundamental underlying changes' (Mac Éinrí, n.a.).

In this context, migration and ethnic studies have been largely preoccupied with formulating and devising appropriate theories and often competing with each other. Far less structured and critical has been the engagement with methodological questions and the quest for appropriate and sophisticated methods. Clearly, the accumulation of data must be guided by broader theoretical formulations but at this stage, our understanding of fieldwork remains underdeveloped and our empirical work often a provisional, tentative and isolating task. The process is largely carried out borrowing methods developed in other fields, trying to fit and refine them *ad hoc*. While there are many and illuminating accounts from scholars and researchers working in the field (Booth 2003; Babbie 1998; Clifford 2003; Gerber and Chuan 2000; Gupta and Ferguson 1997; Johannes 2001; Marcus 1998; Sanjek 1990), there is still limited space and interest for fruitful exchange and confrontation. Furthermore, due to the diverse nature of the disciplines and European academic traditions involved, there is the need of critically analyzing the consequences of methodological choices on the research process and outcomes.

For Stephen Castles, some basic methodological principles for a critical sociology of migration and ethnicity include interdisciplinarity and comparative studies that can increase awareness of general trends and alternative approaches. He argues that researchers in this field need to take a holistic approach and needs to investigate the human agency of migrants, employing participatory research methods, which give an active role to migrants and other persons affected by migration in research processes (Castles, 2007: 367). Castles also notes that migration and ethnic studies must often use 'information-collection methods that correct frequent practices of exclusion based on class, gender or race' (Castles, 2007: 366).

Reflections from the field

As a network of early stage researchers working in various European institutions, often engaged first-hand in the design and application of research methods in the field, we have been informally and formally reflecting on these issues since 2004, when we set out to form and consolidate *HERMES, European Researchers in Migration and Ethnic Studies*. HERMES was born out of our need to facilitate communication and cooperation among European researchers. At present, HERMES operates as an inclusive and non-hierarchical network, offering the possibility to explore and learn from the differences of disciplines, cultures and research traditions inside – and, recently, also outside - the EU (http://www.hermes-researchers.net/).

Our initiatives have been largely concerned with the reflection on methodological issues, often driven by intellectual curiosity and practical necessity. Since 2005, we have coordinated various Research Streams at the European Sociological Association conferences on research methods in Ethnic and Migration Studies; we implemented the IMISCOE/HERMES Training Messenger and, in 2006, we edited a Special Issue on "Qualitative Migration Research in Contemporary Europe" published on *Forum Qualitative*

Socialforschung (http://www.qualitative-research.net/index.php/fqs).

The rationale for this special issue of *Migration Letters* emerged out of the Research Stream 9 within the research network Qualitative Research of the 2009 ESA Conference in Lisbon, entitled 'Research Methods in Ethnic and Migration Studies'.

The conference hosted more than 30 papers over three days divided into clear-cut sessions, ranging from the use of new approaches in migration research, to the analysis of the challenges of qualitative research to the identification of power structures in doing fieldwork.

The variety and the level of the papers presented, the liveliness of the discussions that followed, and the sense of having created a group of people enthusiastic for each other's work were such that a special issue of Migration Letters including some of the articles presented at the conference was felt as a necessary step.

References

Babbie, E. (1998). The Practice of Social Research. 8th Edition. USA: Wadsworth.

Booth, W., et al. (2003). The Craft of Research. Chicago: University of Chicago Press.

Castles, S. and M. Miller. (2003). Age of Migration. London: Palgrave.

Castles, S. (2007). 'Twenty-first century migration as a challenge to sociology'. *Journal of Ethnic and Migration Studies* 33(3): 351-71.

Clifford, J. (2003). 'Interviewer: Alex Coles London/Santa Cruz'. In On the Edges of Anthropology. Chicago: Prickly Paradigm Press.

Gerber R. and Chuan G. K. (Eds). (2000). Fieldwork in Geography: Reflections, Perspectives and Actions. USA: Springer.

Gupta, A. and Ferguson J, ed. (1997). Anthropological Locations: Boundaries and Grounds of a Field Science. Berkeley and Los Angeles: University of California Press.

Heath S., Brooks R., Cleaver E. and Ireland E. (2009). Researching Young People's Lives. London: Sage.

Johannes, F. (2001). Remembering the Other: Knowledge and Recognition. In Anthropology with an Attitude: Critical Essays. Stanford: Stanford University Press.

Mac Éinrí, P. (n.a). 'States of Becoming: Is there a "here" here and a "there" there? Some reflections on home, away, displacement and identity'. UCC, Irish Centre for Migration Studies [http://migration.ucc.ie/statesofbecoming.htm; date accessed 18/10/2007]

Marcus, G. (1998). 'Ethnography in/of the World System: The Emergence of Multi-Sited Ethnography'. In Ethnography Through Thick and Thin. Princeton University Press, Princeton.

Sanjek R. ed. (1990). Fieldnotes: The makings of anthropology. Cornell University Press, Ithaca.

CHAPTER 2

BIOGRAPHICAL METHODS IN MIGRATION RESEARCH

Theodoros Iosifides & Deborah Sporton

Biographical methods and research practice

During the last decades, qualitative biographical/narrative methods gained a prominent position within the spectrum of social science methodology and research practice, mainly due to a reaction to the positivist-empiricist dominance and associated views of social reality. After an initial interest to biographical methods, which followed the edition of 'The Polish Peasant in Europe and America (1919-1921)' by Thomas and Znaniecki (1958), biographical and generally qualitative research methods gave way to empiricist-quantitative approaches and only since the end of 1960 the positivist domination begun to be unsettled (Halfacree and Boyle 1993; Findlay and Li 1997; Tsiolis 2006).

Empiricism reduces social reality to a series of observable and discrete, highly atomistic entities (events, behaviours etc.), which may be allegedly categorized and measured with the use of 'objective' quantitative methods by more or less 'neutral' social scientists (Iosifides 2008). The purpose of this, is the discovery of empirical, 'law like' regularities between variables, which are considered to exhaust both social processes and causal relations (Iosifides and Spyridakis 2006; Iosifides 2008). Against this a view of social reality as consisted by meaningful actions and social interaction gives great emphasis on individual meanings and interpretations and moves human subjectivity and social inter-subjectivity from the periphery to the center of social inquiry. Instead of variable-oriented law like explanations, such a view adopts an understanding (verstehen) approach to social phenomena, granting qualitative methods (including biographical/narrative approaches) an indispensable position in social research practice (Iosifides 2008). In-deed biographical approaches aim at the reconstruction of life trajectories of research participants and of the ways of making sense of the world, of their conceptualizations, meanings and representations of it. We would add to those, the investigation of their practices, actions, interactions, the influence of socio-economic and cultural context and the role of the personal, familial and social material conditions and circumstances (Iosifides 2008).

Biographical methods in the social sciences lead to an increased appreciation of the role of agency and subjectivity in producing and reproducing social reality, of the ways of mediation of broader social structures by an active human agency and of the efforts of constructing coherent biographies through different and diverse experiences, conceptualizations and events (Katrivesis, 2004; Tsiolis 2006; Apitzsch and Siouti 2007; Creswell 2007). As regards research practice, the biographical interview differs considerably from other types of interviewing, for example from the more focused in-depth qualitative interviewing. The main difference lies to the special role of the researcher as an 'active listener' of the life story/biographical narrative of participant which is the result of a well designed and carefully formulated 'generative question' (Tsiolis 2006). The main purpose of the biographical interview is the production of a detailed biographical narrative with the least possible interventions by the researcher. After the narration phase, a more active interaction between the participant and the researcher, in the form of classical qualitative interviewing, may follow (Iosifides 2008). Thus, biographical research, aims at the production of a reconstruction of the biography/life history of the participants, which may be simultaneously characterised by elements such as narratives of efforts for the realisation of personal plans, interactions with institutional and societal rules and demands, biographical experiences of powerlessness and weakness, phases of rapid and unforeseeable change and biographical ruptures and the multi-dimensional relations between events, societal influences, meanings, representations, decision making processes and the continuing struggle to formulate and maintain a sense of biographical coherence over time (Tsiolis 2006, 2007; Iosifides 2008). There is probably no other social phenomenon which marks personal biographies with almost all the above ways than migration. For this reason the next sections turn to a more analytic debate of some key issues in biographical migration research.

Biographical methods in migration research

The study of migration phenomenon was, for a long time, dominated by empiricist-positivist approaches, concerning mainly with the process of migration decision making and modeling aspects of the phenomenon as determined by a series of discrete, interrelated variables, either at the levels of the individual and small groups (i.e. family, household etc.) or at the macro level such as country or regional development performance, unemployment rate etc. The call to incorporate biographical/narrative methods in studying migration aims at overcoming the limitations of empiricist approaches in a series of ways (Halfacree & Boyle 1993; Findlay & Li 1997). The first is related to placing agential intentionality and meaning making processes at the centre of migration research practice and thus moving away from deterministic and law-like causal explanations. The second is related to paying attention to the importance of 'practical consciousness' along with the unconscious and the discursive, that is paying attention to the ways which agents act in everyday life without reflecting thoroughly or plan upon their actions. Finally, other ways include the detailed investigation of the multiplicity and multi-dimensionality of subjective migration experiences and the attention on the cultural dimension of processes related to migration phenomena.

Nevertheless, in many instances, reaction to empiricism in migration studies took, the form of exaggerations as regards the role of agency and subjectivity in producing and reproducing social reality, leading to neglect of broader structural factors, voluntarism and an almost total replacement of efforts to discover and analyze social causation processes with 'interpretative understanding' through lay discourses. In this paper, we adopt a more balanced position as regards the role of biographical methods in migration studies. We view those methods as extremely useful devises for understanding and causally explain the complex interplay between meaningful action and structural/cultural context (Laoire 2000; Iosifides 2004).

Key issues in biographical migration research

The quality-quantity debate

Qualitative methods and in particular biographical methods can enrich our understanding of the complex and multidimensional phenomenon of migration as compared mainly to the traditional positivist employment of quantitative techniques to migration studies. This employment entails methodological individualism, a utilitarian ontology of the self and uniform concept of rationality (Boswell 2008: 552). On the contrary, biographical and qualitative methods in general, may help to take into account the social and cultural context of any 'rational' decision making and the meanings and interpretations that actors ascribe to their actions and to the actions of others. Some of the most well-known strengths of biographical, and to some extent of almost all qualitative methods, are the in-depth and holistic understanding of phenomena and processes, the avoidance of imposing commonsensical or the researcher's categories to actors, subtlety, detail and the avoidance of the limitation of the discourses of actors to some (usually pre-selected) quantitative variables (Rubin and Rubin 2005). One example, showing the potentially valuable role of biographical and qualitative methods in general, in researching various aspects and dimensions of migration phenomenon, is related to the different meanings, that some migrants within certain contexts, attach to 'friendship' and in particular to 'friendship with natives'. For them, 'friendship with natives' means 'superficial friendly contact' and not 'more or less stable relations of reciprocity and solidarity'. So the positive response to a question about whether migrants have native friends refers to the former concept of friendship and not to the latter (Iosifides et al. 2007). Thus, only the in-depth investigation of the life course of immigrants and their biographical experiences of social relations in the host country may highlight the reasons for the adoption of this particular meaning of 'friendship with natives' rather than other alternative meanings and interpretations.

Biographical methods in migration studies may be applied to a series of specific domains related to different aspects of biographical migratory experiences such as for example migration decision making and motivation, identity formation and change (see for example Kazmierska 2003), the role of social capital and social networks, processes of social integration and/or exclusion, political/social participation and mobilization etc. Biographical methods can lead to thorough investigation of the above aspects of migratory processes mainly because they place temporality, sequenciality, trajectory paths, and personal and/or collective memory at the center of social inquiry (Apitzsch and Siouti 2007). Furthermore, biographical methods may lead to detailed and comprehensive reconstructions of linking chains between events, meanings/interpretations, actions and practices. As regards practices, the examination of their genealogy and evolution may result in theoretical propositions of embeddedness within broader social structures which function quite independently of interpretations of actors. To give but one example, individual reasons and interpretations of migrants for the acceptance of specific kind of jobs need not have any direct relation to the functioning of 'ethnic specialization' systems in the labour market, which often result in channeling migrants of specific ethnic background or gender to certain economic and labour market niches, irrespective of educational and other skills (Iosifides et al., 2007). This last remark leads us to the examination, in the next section, of the relation between agency and structure, and how this relation can be incorporated in or highlighted from biographical migration research.

The relation between agency and structure

Generally, the relation between agency and structure is probably the most important issue of interest for sociological theorizing, addressed implicitly or explicitly in almost every theoretical and methodological strategy in the social sciences. There has been a quite powerful tendency in social theory either to reduce agency to structure (structuralism) or structure to individuals or interactions between individuals (methodological individualism and situationism) (Mouzelis 1991, 1995; Archer 1995). Efforts to resolve the 'paradox' of structure – agency relations include conceptualizations of structure and agency as mutually constitutive, granting to structure a 'virtual existence' coming into being through the social practices of actors (structuration theory) (Archer 1995). Finally, discursive analytic approaches to social theorizing tend to fall either in methodological individualism/situationism or macro-constructionism (Burr 2003).

A thorough critique of the above approaches exceeds the scope of the present paper. Nevertheless it has to be noted that biographical approaches are usually viewed and applied as part of the micro-sociological paradigm in the sense that the existence and influence of structural factors on individuals or social groups are undervalued and the powers (intentional and through discourse) of actors are exaggerated. Problems associated with those approaches may be resolved subject to a different conceptualisation of the relations between agency and structure. This conceptualisation entails a view both of agency and structure as existent in a separate way (analytic dualism), holding distinct characteristics and powers irreducible to one another and being in a constant interplay (Archer 1995). In this way biographical methods may contribute in a significant way not only to the investigation of the ways that individual or social interpretations and discourses produce results such as social action but also of the ways broader societal factors and structures condition meanings and interpretations (Sims-Schouten et al. 2007). Returning to the example of immigrant social networking and 'ethnic specialisation' (see previous section), a biographical approach may highlight in great detail the life trajectories of immigrants resulting in social networking along with the associated in depth examination of immigrant's meanings and interpretations related to crucial decisions and actions. But, equally importantly, biographical approaches may contribute to our understanding of how broader contextual and structural features of immigrant's social networks, condition (constrain or enable) actions and meaning making processes (see also Archer 2000, 2003).

The realism-relativism debate

The crucial question about the way of conceptualisation and interpretation of the biographical narrative, about its usefulness and its relation to broader social processes, introduces us inevitably to some form of the realism-relativism debate. Relativist positions, mainly those of the strong version of social constructionism, stress that biographical narratives are the mere product of the communicative interaction between the researcher and the research participant in the present (that is at the time of interaction), and cannot be used in order to highlight the impacts and role of any 'real' processes (see Tsiolis 2006). Thus, a narrative of an immigrant about her trajectory of spatial and social mobility in the host country, about passing different stages and phases resulted in modified social situation and relations, have value only as 'accounts' that is as interpretations or discourses. As those accounts or interpretations/discourses exhaust the domain of the social, they cannot inform us about any 'reality' behind the told story (Steensen n.d.a.).

The problems of strong versions of social constructionism and relativism in general, are manifold. Those versions cannot lead to satisfactory explanations of how discourses are produced and changed and on why some discourses are characterized by more durability and impact than others. This is because strong social constructionism does not acknowledge the dialectical interplay between discursive and extra-discursive elements and factors, falling to a form of 'discursive reductionism' (Sims-Schouten et al. 2007). Furthermore, those versions of constructionism tend to ignore social hierarchies and the positioning (or conditioning) of discourses within hierarchical social and organisational systems and sub-systems (Mouzelis 1991). Thus, the discourses of migration policy officials, employers, immigrant community leaders and immigrants with different social characteristics do not 'construct' social reality in the same way and to the same extend. Whose constructions matter, when and why, is not a feature of discourse alone but of extra-discursive factors as well (social hierarchies, systems of material recourse and power distribution, structured positions systems etc.).

Those points remind us the centrality of interpretative/action power of human agency along with the fact that those powers are always exercised within given circumstances and structures, are characterized by unintended consequences and influenced by the intentions and unintended outcomes of actions of others (Iosifides 2008). Especially in the field of migration studies, biographical narratives may lead to deeper understanding of social processes and inform policy making, subject to their conceptualisation not just as 'stories', but as reconstructions of the complex and dialectical interplay between agency action and meaning making with certain structural and systemic conditions, constrains and enablements (Archer 1995, Iosifides 2008).

References

Apitzsch, U. and Siouti, I. (2007) *Biographical Analysis as an Interdisciplinary Research Perspective in the Field of Migration Studies. Frankfurt am Main: Research Integration,* Johann Wolfgang Goethe Universität, University of York.

Archer, M. (1995). *Realist Social Theory: The Morphogenetic Approach.* Cambridge: Cambridge University Press.

Archer, M. (2000). *Being Human. The Problem of Agency.* Cambridge: Cambridge University Press.

Archer, M. (2003). *Structure, Agency and the Internal Conversation.* Cambridge: Cambridge University Press.

Bauman, Z. (2001) *The Individualized Society*, Cambridge: Polity.

Beck, U., and Beck-Gernsheim, E. (2002) *Individualization.* London: Sage.

Boghossian, P. (2006) *Fear of Knowledge. Against Relativism and Constructivism.* Oxford: Oxford University Press.

Boswell, C. (2008) 'Combining economics and sociology in migration theory', in *Journal of Ethnic and Migration Studies*, 34 (4): 549-566.

Burr, V. (2003) *Social Constructionism. Second Edition.* London: Routledge.

Creswell, J.W. (2007) *Qualitative Inquiry and Research Design, Choosing Among Five Approaches. Second Edition.* Thousand Oaks, CA: Sage.

Findlay, A.M. & Li, F.L.N. (1997) 'An Auto-Biographical Approach to Understanding Migration: The Case of Hong Kong Emigrants' in, *Area*, 29(1): 34-44.

Halfacree, K.H. & Boyle, P.J. (1993) 'The challenge facing migration research: the case for a biographical approach', in Progress in *Human Geography*, 17 (3): 333-348.

Iosifides, T. (2004) "Relativist approaches in social sciences: impacts and critique", in *Theseis*,

86: 57-67 (in Greek).

Iosifides, T. (2009) Review of the book 'The Cultures of Economic Migration: International Perspectives' edited by Suman Gupta and Tope Omoniyi, Aldershot: Ashgate, 2007, 226 pp. *Journal of Ethnic and Migration Studies*, 35 (3): 510-511.

Iosifides, T. (2003) "Qualitative migration research: some new reflections six years later", in *The Qualitative Report*, 8 (3): 435-446. www.nova.edu/ssss/QR//QR8-3/iosifides.pdf.

Iosifides, T. (2008) *Qualitative Research Methods in the Social Sciences (revised edition)*. Athens: Kritiki (in Greek).

Iosifides, T. and Spyridakis, M. (2006) (Eds.) *Qualitative Social Research. Meth-odological Approaches and Data Analysis*. Athens: Kritiki (in Greek).

Iosifides, T., Lavrentiadou, M., Petracou, E., Kontis, A. (2007) Forms of social capi-tal and the incorporation of Albanian immigrants in Greece, in *Journal of Ethnic and Migration Studies*, 33 (8): 1343-1361.

Katrivesis, N.S. (2004) *Sociological Theory. Contemporary Currents of Sociological Thought*. Athens: Gutenberg (in Greek).

Kazmierska, K. (2003) 'Migration experiences and changes of identity: an analysis of a narrative', in *Forum: Qualitative Social Research*, 4 (3), Article 21.

Laoire, C.N. (2000) 'Conceptualising Irish rural youth migration: a biographical approach', in *International Journal of Population Geography*, 6: 229-243.

Mouzelis, N.P. (1991) *Back to Sociological Theory. The Construction of Social Orders*. London: Macmillan.

Mouzelis, N.P. (1995) *Sociological Theory – What Went Wrong? Diagnosis and Remedies*. London: Routledge.

Rubin, H.J. and Rubin, I.S. (2005) *Qualitative Interviewing. The Art of Hearing Data. Second Edition*. Thousand Oaks: Sage.

Sayer, A. (2004) Realism and Social Science. London: Sage.

Sims-Schouten, W., Riley, S. C. E. & Willig, C. (2007) Critical Realism and Dis-course Analysis. A Presentation of a Systematic Method of Analysis Using Women's Talk of Motherhood, Childcare and Female Employment as an Example. *Theory and Psychology*, 17 (1), 101-124.

Steensen, J. (no date available) Biographical Interviews in a Critical Realist Perspective. Department of Education, Learning and Philosophy, Aalborg Uni-versity, Denmark (uit.no/getfile.php?PageId=8315&FileId=31, accessed 28.05.2009)

Thomas, W. and Znaniecki, F. (1958) The Polish Peasant in Europe and America (1919-1921). New York: Dover.

Tsiolis, G. (2006) *Life Histories and Biographical Narratives. The Biographical Ap-proach in Sociological Qualitative Research*. Athens: Kritiki (in Greek).

CHAPTER 3

SOME REFLECTIONS ON OUT-SIDER AND INSIDER IDENTITIES IN ETHNIC AND MIGRANT QUALITATIVE RESEARCH

Sharon Wray and Michelle Bartholomew

Abstract

This article explores some of the methodological issues relating to outsider and insider identities in ethnic and migrant qualitative research. It draws up-on two qualitative research studies that set out to examine older (55-75 years) migrant African Caribbean women's experiences of health and age-ing in the UK. An aim is to problematise the conceptualisation of insiderness and outsiderness as polarised and discrete, and provide some examples of how these identities might overlap and intersect. The article takes issue with the argument that it is both possible and desirable to 'match' the ethnic background of researcher and participant.

Introduction

A number of writers have commented on the methodological issues arising from biographical differences between researcher and research participant's when undertaking qualitative research (for example, Maynard 1994; Edwards 1996; Bhopal 2001; Gunaratnam 2003; Clingerman 2008). This has included discussion of specific aspects of identity, for example those relating to ethnicity, socio-economic class and gender, and how these interact to generate feelings of insiderness and outsiderness. It has also provided insight into reflexive methodological approaches that engage with questions of identity, power, and how ethnic differences in the backgrounds of researcher and research participant shape the research process (e.g. Stanley & Wise 1990; Bahvnani 1991; Edwards 1996; Gunaratnam 2003; Ramji 2008). In this work, the importance of researcher reflexivity is emphasised as a central component of research methodology. It is also argued that within research 'one's self can't be left behind', and crucially, 'our consciousness is always the medium through which research occurs' (Stanley and Wise 1993: 157-161).

In this article, we reflect on some of the insider and outsider issues arising from two research studies examining older (55-75 years) migrant African Caribbean women's experiences, of health and ageing in the UK. Insiderness and outsiderness are conceptualised as overlapping interconnected status positions (Merton 1972; Clingerman 2008). Throughout the discussion the authors are referred to as researcher A and researcher B. Researcher A identifies her ethnic background as white British[1] and researcher B as British African Caribbean. The parents of researcher B migrated to England in the 1960s from Grenada in the Caribbean. In contrast, the parents of researcher A were born in England and have never lived anywhere else. Both researchers describe their socio-economic upbringing and background as working class, which was similar to the majority of their research participants. With regard to religious belief, researcher A does not have a strong affiliation and describes herself as agnostic. In contrast, researcher B describes herself as a practicing Roman Catholic. In terms of age, researcher A was 38 years old and researcher B was 33 years old when their research with older African Caribbean migrant women took place. Thus, there were similarities and differences in background between the two researchers, and between the researchers and their research participants.

Insiderness and Outsiderness in Ethnic and Migrant Research

Interest in insider and outsider status has a long history that can be traced back to the work of sociologists such as for example Merton (1972) and Schutz (1976). Merton's influential work continues to provide an important backdrop to debates on the significance of what it means to be an insider and/or outsider, and the 'matching' of researcher and participant in order to increase the accuracy of research findings (e.g. Labaree 2002; Clingerman 2008). Merton (1972) identifies important issues that are relevant to current methodological debates and the arguments presented in this article. These include; the theorisation of outsider and insider identities as interactive and unstable rather than polarised and discrete, the problems arising from assuming that similarity of background between researcher and participant means they will share similar values, beliefs, and experiences.

Since Merton's (1972) paper, researchers have sought to examine the epistemological and methodological significance of insiderness, outsiderness and the processes of 'othering' that may accompany them (e.g. Reinharz 1997; Hill-Collins 2000; Acker 2001; Sherif 2001; Labaree 2002; Sin 2008). Some researchers have focused on the significance of 'insiderness' (Bhopal 2001; Sherif 2001; Labaree 2002; Papadopoulos & Lees 2002) whilst others have examined 'outsiderness' (Edwards 1996; Pitman 2002; Reed 2005). Yet this positioning of insider and outsider identities as opposites is problematic because it does not take into account the ways in which identities interconnect, and 'are marked by the multiplicity of subject positions that constitute the subject' (Brah 1996: 123). Thus identities are not static and fixed but are fragmented and subject to constant alteration (Hall 1990; Bauman 1996). Moreover, as Hall suggests, 'identities are the names we give

[1] Here whiteness is defined as an ethnic category as discussed by Frankenberg (1993). The authors recognize the heterogeneity of the categories of 'white' and 'African Caribbean'.

to the different ways we are positioned by, and position ourselves within, the narratives of the past' (1990: 223). The process of identity disruption and re-formation is an integral part of the research. For example, when researcher and participant discuss and compare their different 'narratives of the past', previously held understandings and perceptions that construct aspects of insiderness and outsiderness are often disrupted.

The fluctuating rather than static nature of ethnic identities has been explored by some researchers (e.g. Naples 1997; Sherif, 2001; Gunaratnam 2003; Clingerman 2008); however these are notable exceptions[2]. One main point of contention is whether it is possible or desirable to 'match' researcher and participant backgrounds, and the extent to which this increases the authenticity and validity of qualitative research (Bhopal 2001; Papadopoulos and Lees 2002). For example, Bhopal argues her insider status, as a South Asian woman, meant that she 'was able to empathise with these women in a way perhaps white women were not' (2001: 284). She goes on to add that white researchers undertaking research with Asian and black participants 'may have preconceived ideas about the particular group they study, which will be rooted in their own whiteness and their own ethnocentricism' (Bhopal 2001: 284).

Others have argued that the greater the ethnic similarities between researcher and research participant the more likelihood there is of accessing information and developing trust and rapport (Edwards 1990; Papadopoulos and Lees 2002). Nevertheless, such approaches tend to essentialise characteristics of ethnic and cultural identity as distinct and fixed. This effectively recreates whiteness as the 'norm' and minority ethnic as the 'Other' (Frankenberg 1993; Moreton-Robinson 2004). Additionally, this perpetuates whiteness as the 'norm' from which difference becomes constructed as the 'Other' (Said 1978).

Our reflections on access and trust in the research process

This section explores the extent to which our different ethnic backgrounds influenced access to our participants and the development of trust. Researcher A negotiated access to the group through a gatekeeper, a white British health promotion community worker. In contrast, researcher B had worked with older women in the Black community for a number of years and was able to contact potential participants personally. Although initially, it seemed that gaining access would be easier for researcher B this was not always the case, as she comments:

From the beginning, I felt my insiderness would mean that all the women

[2] Researchers have tended to focus on either the significance of 'insiderness' (Bhopal 2001; Labaree 2002; Papadopoulos & Lees 2002) or 'outsiderness' (Edwards 1996; Pitman 2002; Reed 2005). This binary positioning of insiderness and outsiderness does not take into account the fluidity of these identities ands statuses.

would accept and participate in the research. I felt an insider because we shared similarities in ethnic, cultural, and social class backgrounds and all had a similar religious affiliation. However, two of the women declined to participate.

One of these potential participants did not meet the inclusion criteria. The second refused to participate because she did not want to be involved in a focus group discussion with women from the same community. For researcher B, belonging to the 'same community' raised issues about anonymity and confidentiality. There was concern that information from the interview would not remain confidential. This highlights how perceived insiderness may become an obstacle to the recruitment of participants.

In contrast, researcher A's participants all agreed to be interviewed despite what might have been regarded as her 'outside' ethnic status. Here, similarities between the researcher and potential interview participants were important in determining her status within the group as both insider and outsider:

As I got to know the participants, both similarities and differences emerged between us that did not simply place us as 'outsider' or 'insider'. Some of my experiences connected with theirs, particularly in relation to class background. I often find myself occupying insider and outsider status positions at the same time. For example, certain aspects of my identity and biographical details, such as ethnicity and age mark me as 'outsider', whilst others such as class background, gender, and parental status define me as 'insider'. However, these markers of identity status are also subject to continual re-interpretation. This means that my insider and outsider statuses constantly fluctuate and interconnect to produce unexpected effects (Research diary, researcher A).

Thus, although there were ethnic and cultural differences between researcher A and the participants, there were also similarities of experience based on motherhood, social class, gender, and previous occupation. The age difference between the participants and researcher A and B also influenced the power dynamics that ensued in a similar way (Thapar-Bjorkert 1999). Age was regarded as a marker of status, so that older age denoted wisdom and was viewed with respect by the participants generally. Interestingly, the younger age of the two researchers did not increase their outsider status as expected. Unexpectedly it meant that the participants described their experiences of past events in more detail because they assumed the researchers were too young to have first hand experience of them. As such, the data that was generated was perhaps more in-depth than it would have been if the participants and researchers had been of a similar age.

Initially being a member of the community enabled researcher B to gain access and contributed to levels of trust (Haniff 1985; Bhopal 2001).

However, this development of trust may also have been influenced by her 'outsider' status as a University researcher:

I think access was gained easily because I shared the same ethnic status and was known to the women. Also, I had already established initial levels of trust. However, maybe access was gained because of my outsiderness because the participants are interested in the research and want to be involved, or maybe they have their own 'agenda'? (Researcher B).

It is interesting that although there are similarities in ethnic and cultural background between researcher B and her participants, her ability to gain access may also have been influenced by her perceived professional 'stranger' identity (Shutz 1976; Agar 1980). This highlights the ways in which presumed outsiderness and insiderness intersect to create unexpected effects. It also means that it is unclear whether this initial trust was influenced by researcher B's perceived insider ethnic status, or simply a consequence of the participants existing trust in the gatekeeper who had recommended the research to them.

(…) I have got participants for the interviews. I think they trust me, otherwise, knowing them, they would have said no, or maybe it's because of the trust they have in the person that recommended the research to them? (Research diary, researcher B)

It seems likely that the participants would not have agreed to participate had they not had some degree of trust in researcher B (Clingerman 2008). Nevertheless, sharing similar ethnic backgrounds was not the only factor in establishing access and trust; the existing relationship of trust between the gatekeeper, who recommended the research to the participants, and the participants was also an important factor.

Researcher A also commented on how getting to know the participants enabled trust to develop:

Empathy and trust between us developed as we shared stories about our different life experiences. I realised that it was only through spending time together that any sort of trust could be established. Trust is earned and cannot be presumed on the basis of any perceived similarities and differences between us (Research diary).

Through this process of swapping stories about different life experiences ethnocentric 'insider outsider' identities were disrupted and challenged (Lorde 1984; Brah 1996). Additionally, because researcher A's white ethnic identity was situated in difference to the African Caribbean identities of the participants its visibility as an ethnic category was increased (Frankenberg 1993; Brah 1996).

Differences emerged between researcher A and B regarding the type and depth of information gained from the participants in relation to ethnic background and cultural rules about privacy. Researcher B did not ask her participants to self-define their ethnic identities because she felt that the participants assumed that she did not need to ask, due to her similar ethnic background. Additionally, with regard to privacy researcher B was aware of 'cultural rules' about the appropriateness of discussing matrimonial matters outside of the immediate family, this made her feel uneasy about discussing what might be construed as private matters in an interview setting.

Further, we found that because researcher A did not share the same ethnic background the participants were more likely to elaborate on issues relating to history and tradition. In contrast, the shared ethnic background and culture created problems for researcher B because participants would often assume that she had knowledge, passed to her generationally, of Black experiences in the UK. However at times her participants also assumed that her knowledge and experiences of life in the Caribbean would differ, due to her age and the Caribbean island her parents had originated from. Consequently homeland island identities and age could be used as markers of difference to disrupt researcher B's insider status and place her as insider and outsider simultaneously. This example highlights how the process of 'Othering' may still occur regardless of presumed similarities between the ethnic background of researcher and participant (Said 1978; Thapar-Bjorkert 1999).

Researcher B's similar ethnic background meant that her participants assumed she had knowledge of their experiences. Sometimes this meant they did not elaborate on particular issues but instead would say 'you know what I mean don't you'. This was especially apparent when examples of racism were discussed.

No concerns with discussing racism. The women were very open and I felt comfortable with discussing these issues. At times they would say 'you know what I mean don't you' and expect me to know the full details of their negative experiences. I had to ask them to fully explain. Our experiences were similar, but also different (Research diary, researcher B).

Researcher B and her participants had a shared understanding of experiences of racism and she found herself personally empathising with their experiences (Bhopal 2001). However although researcher B's knowledge and experience of racism positioned her as insider, the participants' discussion of ethnic and cultural knowledge could quickly move to include topics that she knew nothing about, at these times she felt like an outsider. Subsequently, researcher B often occupied insider and outsider positions simultaneously as her cultural knowledge about the participants ethnic experiences varied throughout the interviews. At times, the participants tended to assume that she had greater knowledge of their lives and experiences than she did; this sometimes meant that they did not elaborate on particular issues.

Her experiences highlight the fluid and unstable nature of ethnic identity construction and insider outsider positions, moreover, why it is unrealistic to assume that the identities of researcher and participant can somehow be 'matched' (Hall 1991; Khan 1998; Gunaratnam 2003; Clingerman 2008). Instead, our experiences suggest that ethnic and cultural differences between researcher and research participant do not simply have a negative or positive effect on the research process. Moreover, the assumption that researcher and participant should be ethnically matched is problematically based on the idea that ethnic identities are *essentially* and categorically different (Gunaratnam 2001, 2003). A potential consequence of this is the reproduction and reification of those ethnocentric ideologies that are divisive and likely to create, rather then challenge misunderstandings (Lorde 1984).

Constructing whiteness as 'Other'

In subtle ways researcher A was constructed as the 'Other' during interview discussion. It is interesting to reflect on the processes through which this occurred. For example, participants inadvertently referred to their own ethnic status as 'other' to the researchers'. This was particularly evident when researcher A asked the participants about their ethnic identity and how they viewed this. Despite this being a sensitive question, all of the participants answered and explained their affiliation to different Caribbean islands and why this was important to them. However, the participants did not ask the researcher about her own white ethnic identity, but they did sometimes allude to in response to other questions. For example, when discussing the topic of menopause Jane commented on how Black women experienced this differently to white women:

'We' don't have one. I didn't have anything. At home, it's so hot…we don't notice hot flushes. We just carry on. Here it's the same we don't let it stop us doing anything we ignore it.

Interestingly, although researcher A is not identified as 'white' in an overt way, by Jane or Marie, there is a presumption that she does not belong to the 'we' category. Marie and Jane also referred to skin colour as symbolic of cultural differences between themselves and Researcher A:

(…) you find that 'our' skin is really….might be darker but you hardly find a lot of wrinkles in 'our' faces. People say 'blimey you haven't got a lot of wrinkles', and you find that white people have a lot of wrinkles. The skin that 'we' get…the skin that 'we' have… (Marie). 'Cause 'we' don't go out in the sun you know…? (Jane) Well, black people don't sit in the sun (Marie).

These quotations reveal the momentary and understated ways in which the process of othering may occur. In these examples, researcher A is constructed as the 'Other' due to her white identity (Said 1978). Thus, being white was sometimes read as symbolic of other differences such as tradition and history. Nevertheless, it was equally apparent that researcher A's 'insiderness', her working class background her experiences of motherhood and gender, overlapped and merged with issues associated with outsiderness. Moments like this are important in research because they make visible those differences that construct experiences of otherness, insiderness and outsiderness (Lorde 1984:112). They also reveal the subtle ways in which ethnic identities shift and reconfigure, making it possible to occupy insider outsider positions simultaneously.

Concluding comments

We set out to examine issues relating to researcher insiderness and outsiderness. One aim was to problematise the conceptualisation of insiderness and outsiderness as polarised and discrete and provide examples of how they might overlap and intersect (Naples 1997 Gunaratnam 2003). We have shown that similarity of the background between researcher and participant may be less important than the identification, scrutinisation and destabilisation of those power relations that maintain insiderness and outsiderness and the essentialised categories that re/inscribe the 'Other'. It is this reflexive engagement with the difference that serves as a vehicle for social and political change. As Lorde puts it: "Difference must not be merely tolerated but seen as a fund of necessary polarities between which our creativity can spark like a dialectic" (1984:111).

It is perhaps only through this type of reflexive engagement with notions of difference or 'outsiderness' that we might move beyond notions of identities and outsider insider positions as static and challenge the false ethnocentric categories these inevitably (re) affirm and (re) create.

References

Acker, S. (2001). "In/out/side: Positioning the researcher in feminist qualitative research" (1) *Resources for Feminist Research.* http://www.accessmylibrary.com/comsite5/bin/aml-landing-tt.pl

Agar, M. (1980). *The Professional Stranger: An Informal Introduction to Ethnography*, New York: Academic Press.

Bhavnani, K.K. (1991). "Tracing the contours: Feminist research and feminist objectivity", *Women's Studies International Forum,* 16 (2): 95-104.

Bauman, Z. (1996). "From pilgrim to tourist – or a short history of identity', in S. Hall and P. du Gay (eds) *Questions of Cultural Identity,* London: Sage.

Bhopal, K. (2001). "Researching South Asian women: Issues of sameness and difference in the research process", *Journal of Gender Studies*, 10 (3): 279-286.

Brah, A. (1996). *Cartographies of Diaspora: Contesting Identities*, London and New York: Routledge.

Clingerman, E. (2008). "An insider/outsider team approach in research with migrant farmworker women", *Family & Community Health,* 0 (1): 75-84.

Edwards, R. (1996). "White woman researcher-Black women subjects", in, S. Wilkinson and

C. Kitzinger (eds) *Representing the Other: A Feminism and Psychology Reader,* London: Sage

Frankenberg, R. (1993). *White Woman, Race Matters: The Social Construction of Whiteness*, London: Routledge.

Gunaratnam, Y. (2001). "Eating into multiculturalism: hospice staff and service users talk food, 'race', ethnicity, culture and identity", *Critical Social Policy* 21 (3): 287-310.

Gunaratnam, Y. (2003). *Researching 'Race' and Ethnicity*. London: Sage.

Hall, S. (1990). "Cultural identity and diaspora", J. Rutherford (ed) *Identity: Community, Culture, Difference,* London: Lawrence and Wishart.

Haniff, N. (1985). "Toward a native anthropology, methodological notes on a study of successful Caribbean women by an insider", *Anthropology and Humanism Quarterley*, 10: 107-113.

Hill-Collins, P. (2000). *Black Feminist Thought. Knowledge, Consciousness and the Politics of Empowerment*, New York: Routledge Keegan Paul.

Khan, S. (1998). "Muslim women: negotiations in the third space", *Signs: Journal of Women in Culture and Society*, 23 (2): 464-494.

Labaree, R. V. (2002). "The risk of 'going observationalist': negotiating the hidden dilemmas of being an insider participant observer", *Qualitative Research*, 2 (1):97-122.

Lorde, A. (1984). *Sister Outsider: Essays & Speeches,* CA: The Crossing Press Feminist Series.

Maynard, M. (1994). "Methods, practice and epistemology: The debate about feminism and research", in M. Maynard and J. Purvis (eds) *Researching Women's Lives from a Feminist Perspective,* London: Taylor and Francis.

Merton, R. K. (1972). "Insiders and outsiders: a chapter in the sociology of knowledge", *The American Journal of Sociology*, 78 (1): 9-47.

Moreton-Robinson, A. (ed) (2004). *Whitening Race: Essays in Social and Cultural Criticism.* Canberra: Aboriginal Studies Press.

Naples, N. A. (1997). "A feminist revisiting of the insider/outsider debate: The "outsider phenomenon" in rural Iowa", in R. Hertz (ed) *Reflexivity and Voice,* London: Sage.

Papadopoulos, I. and Lees, S. (2002). "Developing culturally competent researchers"', *Journal of Advanced Nursing,* 37 (3): 258-64.

Pitman, G.E. (2002). "Outsider/insider: the politics of shifting identities in the research process", *Feminism & Psychology*, 12 (2): 282-288.

Ramji, H. (2008). "Exploring commonality and difference in in-depth interviewing: a case-study of researching British Asian women", *The British Journal of Sociology*, 59 (1): 99-116.

Reed, K. (2005). "Dealing with differences: researching health beliefs and behaviours of British Asian mothers", *Sociological Research Online,* 4 (4) http://www.socresonline.org.uk/4/4/reed.html

Reinharz, S. (1996). "Who am I? The need for a variety of selves in the field", in R. Hertz (ed) *Reflexivity and Voice*, London: Sage Publications.

Said, E. (1978). *Orientalism.* London: Penguin.

Sherif, B. (2001). "The ambiguity of boundaries in the fieldwork experience: establishing rapport and negotiating insider/outsider status", *Qualitative Inquiry*, 7 (4): 436-447.

Schutz, A. (1976). "The stranger", in G. Bowker & J. Carrier (eds) *Race and Ethnic Relations,* London: Hutchison.

Sin, C. H. (2007). "Ethnic matching in qualitative research: reversing the gaze on 'white others' and 'white' as 'other", *Qualitative Research*, 7 (4): 477-499.

Stanley, L. and Wise, S. (1990). "Feminist praxis and the academic mode of production: an editorial introduction", in L. Stanley (ed.) *Feminist Praxis: Research, Theory and Epistemology in Feminist Sociology,* London: Routledge.

Stanley, L. and Wise, S. (eds) (1993). *Breaking Out Again: Feminist Ontology and Epistemology,* London: Routledge.

Thapar-Bjorkert, S. (1999). "Negotiating otherness: dilemmas for a non-western researcher in the Indian sub-continent", *Journal of Gender Studies*, 8(1): 57-69.

CHAPTER 4

PROMOTING MULTI-METHODS RESEARCH: LINKING ANTHROPOMETRIC METHODS TO MIGRATION STUDIES

Lisa Cliggett & Deborah L. Crooks

Abstract

The experience of migration includes costs and benefits to migrants and sending communities. In the tradition of a "letters" type discussion, this paper presents a synthesis of recent work from a longitudinal study from Zambia, Africa that used a mixed-methods approach to investigate the experience and outcomes of migration among the Gwembe Tonga. In this ethnographic study, we argue that including anthropometric methods in migration studies enhances our ability to empirically assess the impacts of mobility to better understand the experience of migration. In this particular African context we see, on average, a beneficial outcome for mi-grants' nutritional status, and livelihoods.

Introduction

Scholars frequently examine the positive and negative effects of migration on those moving, and those left behind. We know that remittances can contribute to cultural renaissance and community level economic improvements in sending communities, and increased economic and educational opportunities for migrants themselves (e.g. Cohen 2001; Massey et al., 1998; Trager 2005). We also know that migration can lead to improvements in environmental circumstances that translate to greater growth and improved nutritional status for migrant children (Boas, 1912; Bogin 1999). Evidence also exists for less positive outcomes of migration, such as increased infant mortality in communities with high rates of outmigration (e.g. Kanaiupuni et al., 1999), and increased psychosocial stress with implications for chronic disease in some groups of migrants (e.g., Brown 1981; Pearson et al., 1993).

The preliminary findings we report here utilize a mixed-method approach to the study of migration in which we conduct fine-grained ethnographic analysis while also collecting anthropometric measures of height, weight, and arm circumferences to measure well-being within the migrant community (Crooks et al. 2007). This approach allows us to ascertain how well (or not) migrants are faring in their new communities, compared to their families and neighbours in sending communities where loss of labour and regular income have broad impacts on households and livelihoods.

By collecting anthropometric data on children as both household members (in the context of household surveys) or as community members (in the context of school "measuring days"), we can see children's growth and nutritional status as a proxy for the well-being of the household and the communities more generally (Schell 1986). By combining these data with data that reflect the changing ecological and economic circumstances of migrants, we are able to gain insight into the particular aspects of change that contribute to or detract from health and well-being

Our project is on-going and our data analysis still preliminary. Thus, this paper presents a synthesis of preliminary data from one aspect of the on going study of the Gwembe-Tonga people (Zambia), with a focus on the voluntary migrants to the frontier farming region outside of the original Zambezi valley homeland (Cliggett et al., 2007). In addition to producing important empirical findings, the ongoing research project demonstrates the high value of collaborative research programs which join a range of research methods to interrogate questions of migration and mobility. In the case of the current research, joining longitudinal qualitative data and previously collected anthropometric data on child growth and development which are part of the 50-year Gwembe Tonga Research Project described below, with contemporary survey and ethnographic data and recent anthropometric data, produces findings that clearly document ways in which voluntary migration benefits a particular rural African population. The research also offers a model to other qualitative researchers seeking a way to empirically measure costs and benefits of migration for other populations, with attention to change over time.

Background to the project

The Gwembe-Tonga Research Project (GTRP) began as a "before and after" study of the impact of the large-scale Kariba Dam development project (Colson, 1960, 1971; Scudder, 1962). Following displacement from their homeland due to the construction of the Kariba Hydroelectric Dam on the Middle Zambezi River in 1957, over 57,000 Gwembe-Tonga people (in Zambia and Zimbabwe) were forcibly resettled onto land that was inadequate to support their needs. As a consequence, their economic, nutritional and overall well-being was compromised (Colson 1971; Scudder and Colson 2002). In addition, social conflict increased in the Gwembe Valley, which added to material insecurity both within and between households (Cliggett, 2000). Because of these difficult conditions, which continued to worsen over time, many Gwembe-Tonga chose to migrate to a newly-opened frontier zone on the plateau to the north and west of the valley.

The research we report here is on-going and informed by over fifty years of research among the Gwembe-Tonga begun in 1956 by Elizabeth Colson and Thayer Scudder (Scudder and Colson 2002; Cliggett 2002). The sample population in the current study (discussed in this paper) originates from the relocated 1957 population: some household heads in the current study were either children or young adults at the time of relocation, or are direct descendants of those who were relocated.

Field site

In 1979, the Zambian government announced on the radio the de-restriction of six "previously uninhabited" wildlife management areas, and their opening for human settlement. Any Zambian wanting more land was free to settle in any of the newly-opened areas, and many of the displaced farmers from the Gwembe Valley saw this as an opportunity to improve their living conditions through increased agricultural landholdings. Since that time, a number of migrants have settled in an area known as "Chikanta," part of the Bbilili Springs game management area bordering Kafue National Park. Upon arrival, the migrants encountered difficult conditions, including dense Miombo woodland requiring clearing for farming, spotty and unevenly distributed water resources and a plethora of wild animals.

Today, the Gwembe-Tonga farmers have achieved some success in carving out large agricultural fields from the woodlands although they still face other environmental challenges. Most households grow cotton and maize for local and national sale, and maize and other crops for home consumption and many still gather food from the surrounding landscape. In most years, migrant farmers can grow enough to feed their families, and often to share with relatives back home in the valley; many produce surplus for sale even in lean, drought years. At the same time, there is talk of hunger, and most migrants say they experience food shortages, especially during the annual hunger season.

In addition to food, migrants also face challenges in regards to health e.g., they experience a host of devastating problems, including malaria, HIV/AIDS, diarrhoea, "whooping cough," and eye infections. While migrants have extensive knowledge of local health remedies and use them intensively and extensively, they have extremely circumscribed access to biomedical health care resources. Although a health clinic was built in 2004-2006 as a result of a recent development project, as of this writing, the clinic is only partially staffed and carries only a small supply of basic medicines.

Sample and methods

The field site consists of a number of adjacent villages with an approximate population of 6600 people in 1100 households. Since 1994 Cliggett has carried out short periods of ethnographic research in the field site, and in 2001 began an intensive focus on this field site, with the equivalent of two years of field work conducted between 2001 and 2007. Crooks has carried out three seasons of fieldwork, totalling approximately seven months, since 2004. From 2004-2006 Cliggett and Crooks led three summer field schools for training graduate students in anthropological research methods (sponsored by the National Science Foundation). Field school students and a number of local research assistants assisted in data collection, both ethnographic and anthropometric. To date we have conducted anthropometric measurements (height, weight and arm circumference) according to procedures outlined in Lohman et al. (1988) in five primary schools and two preschools (430 school children; 222 boys and 208 girls), as well as in all the households in which we conduct intensive interviews (27 to-date). Crooks, Cliggett, student researchers and local research assistants conduct household interviews to gather information on migrant histories, livelihood strategies, diet and illness, and all involved in the project provide data via participant observation techniques.

One reviewer of this paper expressed concern that using "anthropometric techniques" was reminiscent of "colonial repression" or "racial stereotyping" – legitimate concerns from previous eras of social science. However, we argue that contemporary methods of health measurement are increasingly set in a "bio-cultural" framework emphasising the social context in which physical outcomes of growth and nutrition are found (Bogin et al., 2007; Schell 1986; Schell and Magnus 2006; Pike and Williams 2006). Indeed, we present our discussion of linking anthropometry with qualitative research specifically to encourage more qualitative researchers to consider the value of such complimentary methods.

Before moving on to findings, it is important to clarify issues of cultural sensitivity, rapport and trust in the context of anthropometric techniques. Collecting anthropometric measurements must be carried out with good knowledge of local cultural systems (for another example, see Fairhead et al. 2006). In Chikanta, fear of witchcraft, Satan Worship and trading / marketing in body parts required that before beginning data collection we met with all local leaders in public meetings, met with individual families and other "cultural brokers" in the community to explain our activities. Perhaps more importantly, after collecting measurements, we reported back to all communities and families with our findings, giving each family and local leader summary reports of the growth status of children. At the time of reporting our findings, and giving printed summaries, we gave a "lesson" to all adult family members, local leaders and school personnel, in how to read the charts and understand what these anthropometric findings mean. By returning the findings to the community, the local population had evidence which they could present to regional political leaders and development groups in an effort to argue for increased infrastructure and resources (such as more wells for clean water, school food programs, etc.). Additionally, reporting back to the community helped to allay fears that the anthropometric techniques we use were in the service of malicious or supernatural powers.

Summary of findings

Preliminary findings document a few important outcomes of migration to the farming frontier. First, the anthropometric data from the 2004 field season school measuring days indicates that migrant boys and girls have different nutritional and growth patterns (reported in Crooks et al., paper submitted to Ecology of Food and Nutrition, forthcoming). The data show that while all boys and girls in the sample population are growing less well than World Health Organization references, girls in the sample population are doing slightly better than boys. And while the sample migrant children are not doing as well as the global reference children, comparing the recent data with earlier data from the sending community (Gillett and Tobias, 2002; Gillett-Netting, 2007; Gillett-Netting and Perry, 2005) suggests that, on average, children in the migrant population are doing better than their counterparts (and indeed their families) from the early 1990s in the sending communities. It is important to recognise that our sample is independent from earlier samples (snapshots in time rather than a panel comparison), but never-the-less indicative of improved status of a closely linked population (see Crooks et al., forthcoming for the detailed discussion of findings from earlier studies in comparison to the current sample). Key in these results is the ability to see change, through empirical data collection and analysis, in nutritional status between sending communities and migrant communities, and over time.

As a complimentary finding to the community level data and the data documenting differences between sending and migrant communities, we have documented the range (i.e., disparity) of well-being in the community by also collecting data at the household level. Findings to date drawing from the household level data indicate that some households are doing better than others in promoting their children's nutritional status. Combining life history data from the longitudinal project started in the 1950s, and our ethnographic interview data (that captures livelihood decisions and change, along with knowledge about good farming) with the anthropometric data, we can link variability in nutritional well being with particularities of household dynamics (for a full summary of these preliminary findings, see Crooks et al 2007).

Some of the most salient findings in this particular analysis point to the importance of post-marital residence patterns as an influence on child well-being (newlyweds co-residing with husbands' parents for the first few years of marriage); engagement with entrepreneurial activities correlates positively to households with good nutritional status; and well nourished children are more frequently found in households with articulated knowledge of "what makes a good farmer", a characteristic that goes beyond simple statements of "early preparation" and "cattle and plows." In this analysis, we have concretely linked nutritional well being at the household level with household socio-economic decision making and social practice in order to argue that those characteristics have very real outcomes in child health and well-being.

Conclusion

The findings generated from this collaborative, multi-method research agenda demonstrate the persuasive power of linking in depth qualitative research with more empirically founded research methods such as anthropometry. Either method can, and often does, stand alone, but the linkage of these methodologies clearly has a sum greater than the parts. During an era when universities, funders and development programs increasingly encourage "interdisciplinary" study of important issues, seeing how some researchers have incorporated complementary methods offers an example of ways to answer the challenge of "interdisciplinarity" and multi-method studies.

Using anthropometric methods to assess child nutrition and well being adds strength to more qualitative studies that seek to identify costs and benefits of migration. Studies that capture income variability, mortality, political and legal factors, changes in identity and attachment offer important insights into migration. However, studies that give attention to nutrition, health and well being, produce an important dimension to our understanding of the migration experience. For qualitative scholars with concerns about the power dynamics or repressive potential of using anthropometric measurements for assessing well being, it is important to see examples of linking these complimentary methods in new ways that emphasise the social and cultural context of "well-being."

With such studies, we can answer questions such as, what are the subtleties that influence why some migrant households fare better than others? What factors influence why children within one migrant household have better nutrition than others? And how, at a very basic level, do migrants fare in providing a nutritional foundation for children (at the least) in their homes? – a foundation that determines the long term outcomes of the migrant experience.

If we see voluntary migration as a choice to change, and possibly improve, household well being, looking at the nutritional status of migrant children offers one clear indicator of well being. Ultimately, healthy children equal potentially greater possibilities for economic, political and social benefits in subsequent generations.

References

Bogin, B., 1999, *Patterns of Human Growth*, Second Edition. Cambridge: Cambridge University Press.

Bogin, B., M.I.V. Silva, L. Rios, 2007, Life history trade-offs in human growth: Adaptation or pathology? *American Journal of Human Biology 19(5):631-642.*

Boas, F., 1912, *Changes in the bodily form of descendants of immigrants.* New York: Columbia University Press.

Brown, D. E., 1981, General stress in anthropological fieldwork. *American Anthropologist* 83:74-92.

Cliggett, L., 2000, Social components of migration: Experiences from Southern Province, Zambia. *Human Organization*, 59, 125-135.

Cliggett, L., 2002, Multigenerations and multidisciplines: Inheriting fifty years of Gwembe-Tonga Research. In Kemper and Peterson-Royce (Eds.), *Chronicling Cultures.* Walnut Creek: AltaMira Press, pp. 239-251.

Cliggett, L, E. Colson, R. Hay, T. Scudder, J. Unruh 2007, Chronic Uncertainty and Momentary Opportunity: A half century of adaptation among Zambia's Gwembe-Tonga. Special Issue, Eds Jane Guyer and Eric Lambin. *Human Ecology.* 35(1):19-31.

Cohen, JH, 2001, Transnational Migration in Rural Oaxaca, Mexico: Dependency, Development and the Household. *American Anthropologist* 103(4):954-967.

Colson, E, 1960, *Social Organization of the Gwembe-Tonga.* Manchester: Manchester University Press.

Colson, E, 1971, Social *Consequences of Resettlement.* Manchester: Manchester University Press.

Crooks, DL, L Cliggett; R Gillett-Netting, (forthcoming) Migration Following Resettlement of the Gwembe-Tonga of Zambia: The Consequences for Children's Growth. *Ecology of Food and Nutrition*; paper submitted and accepted for publication.

Crooks, DL, L. Cliggett, S. Cole, 2007, Child growth as a measure of livelihood security: The case of the Gwembe-Tonga. *American Journal of Human Biology 19:669-675).*

Fairhead, J., M. Leach, M. Small, 2006, Where techno-science meets poverty: Medical research and the economy of blood in The Gambia, West Africa. *Social Science and Medicine* 63:1109-1120.

Gillett-Netting, R, 2007, Effects of resettlement on the growth and physical status of Gwembe Valley Tonga Children: A biocultural analysis. In C. S. Lancaster and K. P. Vickery (Eds.): *The Tonga-Speaking Peoples of Central Africa.* Lanham, MD: University Press of America, Pp. 258-279.

Gillett-Netting, R, A Perry, 2005, Gender and nutritional status at the household level among Gwembe Valley Tonga children, 0-10 years. *American Journal of Human Biology*, 17, 372-375.

Gillett, R, PV Tobias, 2002, Human growth in Southern Zambia: A first study of Tonga children predating the Kariba Dam (1957-1958). *American Journal of Human Biology,* 14, 50-60.

Kanaiupuni, SM, KM. Donato, 1999, "Migradollars and Mortality: The Effects of Migration on Child Mortality." *Demography,* 36(3): 339-53.

Lohman, TG., AF. Roche, R. Martorell, 1988, *Anthropometric Standardization Reference Manual.* Champaign, IL: Human Kinetics Books.

Massey, DS, J. Arango, G. Hugo, A, Kouaouci, A Pellegrino, E Taylor, 1998, *Worlds in Motion..* Oxford: Oxford University Press.

Pearson JD, James GD, Brown DE, 1993, Stress and changing lifestyles in the pacific: Physiological stress responses of Samoans in rural and urban settings. *American Journal of Human Biology* 5:49-60.

Pike, I.L., S. R. Williams, 2006, Incorporating psychosocial health into biocultural models: Preliminary findings from Turkana women of Kenya. *American Journal of Human Biology* 18(6):729-740.

Schell, L.M., 1986, Community health assessment through physical anthropology: Auxological epidemiology. *Human Organization45(4):321-327.*

Schell, L.M. and P.D. Magnus, 2007, Is there an elephant in the room? Addressing rival approaches to the interpretation of growth perturbations and small size. *American Journal of Human Biology 19(5):606-614.*

Scudder, T., 1962, *The Ecology of the Gwembe-Tonga.* Manchester: Manchester University Press.

Scudder, T., E. Colson, 2002, Long-term research in Gwembe Valley, Zambia. In Robert V. Kemper and Anya Peterson Royce (Eds.), *Chronicling Cultures.* Walnut Creek: AltaMira Press, Pp. 197-238.

Trager, L, (Ed), 2005, *Migration and Economy.* Walnut Creek, CA. Altamira Press.

CHAPTER 5

VISUAL METHODS IN RESEARCHING MIGRANT CHILDREN'S EXPERIENCES OF BELONGING

Marta Moskal

Abstract

This chapter examines drawings and mental maps made by children (used alongside with conventional interviewing techniques) as method of investigating migrant children sense of belonging. Children's visual methods have gained renewed interest as many social scientists search for methods that align with the current conceptualisation of children as social agents and cultural producers. Drawing upon a qualitative study of Migration and the Integration of Polish families and children in Scotland, I analyse children's presence and participation in processes of transnational migration, giving some empirical example of how visual methods can be evaluated as a research strategy.

Children as social agents

In this chapter, I refer to the recent scholarship of human geography, social anthropology, sociology of childhood and community development that treats children as active participants in their own socialization (Aitken 2001; Barker and Weller 2003; Hart 1999; James et al. 1998; James and Prout 1997; Johnson et al. 1998; Mitchell 2006; Orellana et al. 2001; Prout 2000; Thorne 1987; Zelizer 1985; White, 2002) and explain how this approach extends upon visual research methods (with the focus on drawings). In the past, researchers regarded children as "adults in training" and their voices were not legitimated as meaningful for understanding social and cultural phenomena. Children, (especially children of minorities and immigrants) were rarely asked for their ideas or perspectives, as adults often assume that they "know better." Consequently, the words and expressions of children were rarely given much weight. This trend has slowly begun to change, as many social scientists begin to view minors, as not simply the reproducers of culture, but as "cultural agents and social actors in their own right" (Mitchell 2006:60). As children become viable participants of social research, there increasingly comes a need to develop research methods relative to the developmental level of children. For children to be able to participate in research, it might be necessary to develop different non-adult centred methods[1]. This has created the need to rethink the current research methods involved in studying adults (Mitchell 2006).

There is much diversity amongst children, and many, though not all, child-centred methodologies could equally be used with adults. Punch (2002) argues that where the differences do exist these are produced by the way adults conceptualise children and children's disempowered position in society rather than from some fundamental difference between adults and children. In some ways, it might be a more useful way to think about rights based approach, rather than child-centred research which might be based on assumptions about the nature of children and childhood. This would look for methods that reflect the way they experience and communicate with their worlds, ultimately reflecting the method of communication the participant is most comfortable with (Cousins and Milner 2007). Boyden (2003) suggests a need for "age-appropriate" methods that "empower children" and lead to "valid child-led data". There is a need to ask children certain kinds of questions and not others. Child-centred methodologies are not focused solely on what may be meaningful to a child participant, but what is meaningful to larger contexts of children's lives.

Conducting research with children – drawing, mapping and interviewing

I consider drawings and mental maps as an artefact as well as an intermediate technique which facilitates the process of the children's engagement with the research. Visual methods present several advantages as participatory methods for engaging children in research. Therefore, they are being used creatively in diverse social and cultural contexts to elucidate children's perspectives on health and illness (Geissler 1998), social change (Katz 1986; Stokrocki 1994), tourism (Gamradt 1995), identity (Walsh 2003; Cowan 1999), identity and consumption (Croghan, et al. 2008), time (Christenson and James 2000), place and mobility (Orellana 1999) and poverty (Sime 2008). One of the main reasons that drawings have attracted such attention for work with children is that they are widely regarded as "child-centred". Mitchell (2006) argues that visual methods are said to be "child-centred" in the sense that drawing and other visual methods may be familiar, even enjoyable to the child. Drawing is something many children do, without complex technology, at school and in play, thus its child-friendly status is valid. When a drawing is familiar to the child, it can be particularly "effective in bringing out the complexities of their experience" (Nieuwenhuys 1996:55). Drawing is regarded as appropriate for the cognitive

[1] Among the challenges discussed by various researchers, the issue of adult–child power imbalances looms particularly large. The relative powerlessness of children in comparison to the adults in their lives necessitates particular attention to how access to children is negotiated through parents and teachers, ensuring that children's participation is voluntary and their consent is informed in a meaningful way (Alderson 1995; Barker and Weller 2003; Orellana 1999; Sime 2008).

and communicative skills associated with being a child. Through drawing, it has been suggested, "even non-literate children [have] an opportunity to portray life as it really is or has been for them" (Gordon 1998:68).

Creating artefacts (drawings) can also be a way for researchers to give voice to, and work toward reciprocity, with under-represented subjects such as migrant children (Grover 2004). The value of visual methods as a catalyst for more conventional interviewing techniques was reflected by Punch (2001) in her study of children in southern Bolivia. She describes visual methods (drawings, photographs) as one strategy in her ethnographic work which was most useful in the initial exploratory stages of the research for the investigation of broad themes and for seeking children's definitions of the important aspects of their lives. The textual methods were used to examine those issues that children had raised in more detail, and the home visits were useful to provide a broader perspective of their social worlds. Similar to Punch research Croghan, Griffin, Hunter and Phoenix (2008) study on young consumers in two UK cities found that the visual images (photographs) allows participants to introduce new and possibly contentious topics in ways that are not possible in a purely verbal exchange. The presence of the visual image provided a platform from which interviewees could expand and introduce some sensitive issues.

To summarise these methodological considerations, researchers in diverse disciplines have sought research methods that may be particularly well-suited to working with, rather than 'on' children. In this regard, visual methods like drawing or mental maps have attracted particular interest as a means of understanding children's worlds. Enabling children's perspectives through drawing can make their knowledge and concerns visible to adults and can be the basis for involving children in identifying and solving issues that concern them. In my research among migrant children in Scotland, drawing is a strategy to collect the research material itself and to facilitate narrative interviews, especially with the younger children. In this article, I try to evaluate these drawing activities, as a 'child-centred', useful and informative research.

Children and Transnational Migration – research context

The paper examines the experiences of families and children of recent Polish migrants in Scotland. It is based on a project which has involved narrative interviews with 65 members of immigrants' families, including 41children (27 at primary school, 14 at secondary school). The study involved children (between the ages of 5 and 17). The research material was collected through individual and small group interviews as well as through the drawings and mental maps used as a research method. The study examines the family and childhood experiences of migration and settlement in the contexts of EU enlargement and transnationalism[2].

Labour migration from Poland to Scotland is a process that involves new transnational practices and relationships. The primary characteristic of the transnational family is having members spread out across nation states but still maintaining a sense of collective welfare and unity. While growing numbers of studies show that concern for family reunification and the well-being of family members represents one of the major reasons for mobility, increasing numbers of families are separated by the decision to move and become 'transnational' (Bryceson and Vorela, 2002).

Transnational family patterns also characterise new arrivals from Poland who have settled and work in Scotland. Numbering over fifty thousand, the majority of these new arrivals were married men or women who supported their families in Poland with the expectation of either returning to them or bringing them over to settle in Scotland. Although many ultimately wished to return home with their immediate and extended family, family reunification in the UK invariably provide bridges into daily life that, in conjunction with children's own integration, consolidated patterns of belonging and embedded settlement (Moskal 2007)[3].

Analysing migrant children's visual maps and drawings

In order to do so to map the varied childhood experience and organisation and meaning of immigrant childhood, I asked children to draw maps of places where they spend time: Children drew maps from memory that helped delineate their spatial awareness, the locations of their activities, as well as a sense of belonging to the particular place. Participants sometimes had difficulty constructing their maps, and this was based on a lack of spatial concepts among the children. Perspective, symbolization and other standard map qualities were very rarely observed. However, some of the children demonstrated the use of national symbols, namely the Polish and Scottish flags by the 13 and 6 years old boys (Fig. 1 and 2). The mental maps produced images that were very diverse in terms of numbers of elements included, and perspective take. They immediately highlighted a breadth of individuality

---

[2] Without firm roots in their country of origin, children often come to identify with their new homeland in ways that parents may not. At the same time, children play an important role in linking nations, and keeping parents connected to their homelands. This is especially true when the immediate family is split, with some children left behind. Even when all the children of a family live in the UK, families may maintain ties with the home country because they want their children to know and value their roots; or the children themselves may ask for this connection. In helping to develop and maintain multiple connections to their places of origin and destination, children may effectively change the contexts for their own development and identity formation.

[3] The data indicating the number and characteristics of migrant's families in Scotland are hard to find. There is however evidence of an increasing population of Polish children in schools throughout Scotland. According to the annual Scottish Government pupil census in publicly funded schools in Scotland there were 4677 Polish children in Scottish schools (according to the main home language survey in 2008 (Pupils in Scotland 2009)) and Polish was the most common main home language after English.

amongst the participating children. In particular the variation in leisure

Figure 1. A mental map by Adrian, 13 years old: Handball ground, bicycle, school, home, friends, Poland, family

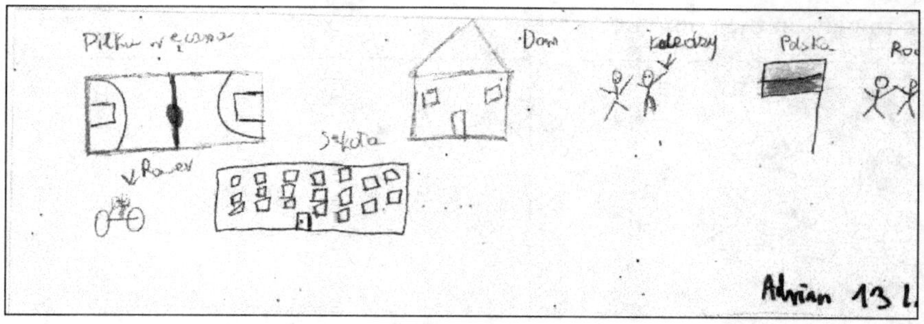

Figure 2. A tree of attachment by *Kacper*, 6 years old

spaces was apparent. For example, the some participants drew only a single element map with the home (Fig. 3) or cinema (Fig. 4) as the only places to spend time in. There are some very basic and schematic maps with a single line and blocks like Tomek's map (Fig. 5) with his home, school, playground and shop (represented by the empty rectangular shapes) connected by the lines. Tomek (14 years old) came to Scotland seven months prior to the interview

Figure 3. A mental map by Jakub, 9 years old: My home, and two sentences at the bottom: 'I don't like school'; 'I like to play on the computer'

Figure 4. A mental map by Maciek 11years old: 'Cinema World/ Wanted'

Figure 5. A tree of attachment by Tomasz, 15 years old

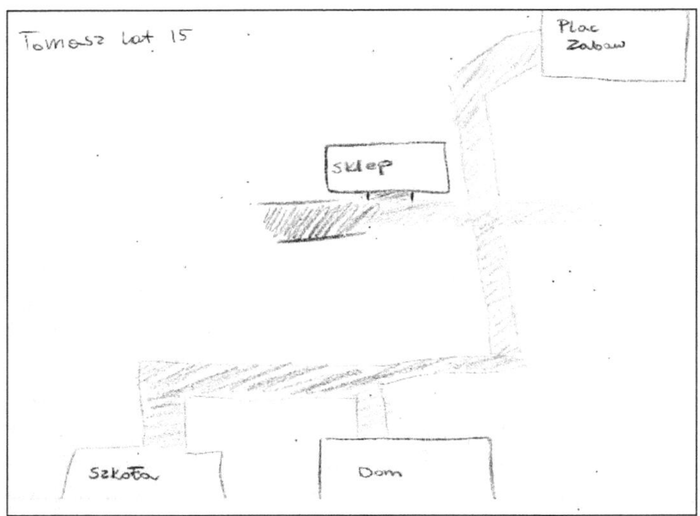

with his 2 older brothers (twins 19 years old) and dad following his mum who came a few months earlier. His older sister lived in Poland. At the moment of interview he did not feel well settled in the city he lived: 'I have no Scottish friends, because of my English language is not good enough'- he said. 'I know, they play a lot of football because I use to see them on the football ground'. My [few Polish] friends, stay at home and do nothing, they are slightly lazy [...]. They don't like to explore new places either or they know already some places. I don't know'.

Figure 6. A tree of attachment by Weronika, 7 years old:

Home and mum

In a second technique, children were again given blank sheets of paper and asked to create the drawings of the tree with the roots and to draw or write by the roots the things and/ or the persons there are attached to. The creation of a more than one drawing was used as a way to allow children to express multiple ideas about themselves; however, some children chose to make only one drawing or were tired after the first drawing. This format also recognised the researchers' observation of short attention spans in the respondents. Younger children sometimes did not understand the idea of the thematic drawings or drew some of the elements like the tree with some significant things around them or asked for another sheet of paper to draw something quite different - whatever they would feel inspired to draw. For example, 7 years old Weronika drew her mum and big house next to the tree (Fig. 6), on the second peace of paper she drew only some houses. After the interview, it became clear that the family (divorced mother with 2 children) had a very unsettled post- migration period with the frequent changes of the living places, including the period of living in a caravan. It was by engaging in a creative manner with the children that the researcher could get an entry into data collection, and further simultaneously bring in more traditional interview techniques to bring out the children's voices, help the children to tell their stories, and ultimately enhance the researcher's ability to reliably interpret the data.

Figure 7. A mental map by Kasia, 9 years old: School in Edinburgh, Home in Poland, Garden in Poland, Playground in Poland

Figure 8. A mental map by Alicja, 9 years old: School, two houses: our home and home, zoo, shop and museum with the boat

The drawings clearly brought to my attention the children's ideas and concerns about their transnational experiences and practices. Four examples illustrate this. One is particularly striking: on Figure 7 is a personal map of 9 years old Kasia who sees her world as one street along which she put next to each other the buildings and places which belong to two different worlds (countries): school in Scotland, home in Poland, garden in Poland, playground in Poland. Second, the drawing of Alicja, 9 years old (Fig. 8) shows many elements where she spends her time, including two homes, 'our home' (which is in Poland as Alicja explained later during the interview) and home.

Figure 9. A tree of attachment by Rafal 11 years old: Family – mum (Scotland), dad, brother, grand mum, grand dad (Poland); animals; friends – Patryk, Patrycja (Poland), Richard, Sherry –Ann, Lindsay-Mackay, Den (Scotland), and two homes

The third interesting example is Rafal's tree of attachment (Fig. 9); "I placed under the tree all the important people: In Poland my father, brother and grand mum and grand dad and in Edinburgh my mum. I won't place any things because the people are more important that the things. There are also my friends there in Poland and in Scotland", explained Rafal, 11 years old during his interview. "And how do you keep in touch with these people from Poland?" I asked. "Through the computer and Skype: Also with my father and brother I communicate through Skype and with my grandparents through phone because they don't have Skype".

In a further part of the interview, I asked him: "Thinking about your home what do you imagine?"

R: About which home in here or in Poland?

M: Do you feel like you have two homes?

R: Yes, I am rich men (laugh).

M: Would you like to come back to Poland or to stay here in the future?

R: I know that I would like to finish a school here and university. And to Poland, I would like to come back for holidays but not to stay for the rest of my life… like in here very much, and I don't feel like going back to Poland, I don't know why, perhaps because of the school, I didn't like school in Poland'.

Later I have also remarked that Rafal placed two homes under his tree of attachment.

My forth example is interesting because the interview was conducted with an older girl (15 year old Monika) who under her tree of happiness made a very elaborated scheme (Fig. 10) - hierarchy of important things which include: Team in Poland, The best friend and the other friends in Poland, Friends in Edinburgh, Trainer in Poland, Team in Edinburgh, Friends from school, 'Football is very important form me' This is showing again the participate life within two worlds.

Strict visual analyses without the ability to engage with the child seem to be difficult when we try to correctly identify the images on the drawings and to identify the most important features. This is an important methodological issue, as visual data collection strategies can become so 'child-centred' that the researcher has difficulty with interpretation. Therefore, in this study, pictures were used to prompt more detailed oral information, keeping the images as the central reference point. I also ask the capable children (excluding those over eight years old) to sign the drawn objects.

In order to connect a drawing to the social life, intent and interests of its producer, the analysis of drawings should move reflexively between "the image and verbalization" (Harrison 2002:864). In work with children, embedding the analysis of an image within its producer's account of that image is especially relevant since it is often assumed that children need someone to speak for them. However, as with adults, children vary in their ability and inclination to talk about their visual productions. For example, Maciek, 11 years old wasn't very talkative, on the activity map drawing he drew a rectangular building with a sign 'Cinema World / Wanted' (Fig.4). Encouraged by his classmates participating in the same small-group interview he did not want to reveal anything more during the interview that he like to go to the cinema. We might try to say something about his isolation-after-migration and lack of other social and interpersonal engagements. However, the ways in which we interpret the drawings are a continual reminder of

Figure 10. A tree of attachment by Monika 15 years old: Family, Friends in Poland, Team in Poland, The best friend and the other friends in Poland, Friends in Edinburgh, Trainer in Poland, Team in Edinburgh, Friends from school, 'Football is very important for me'

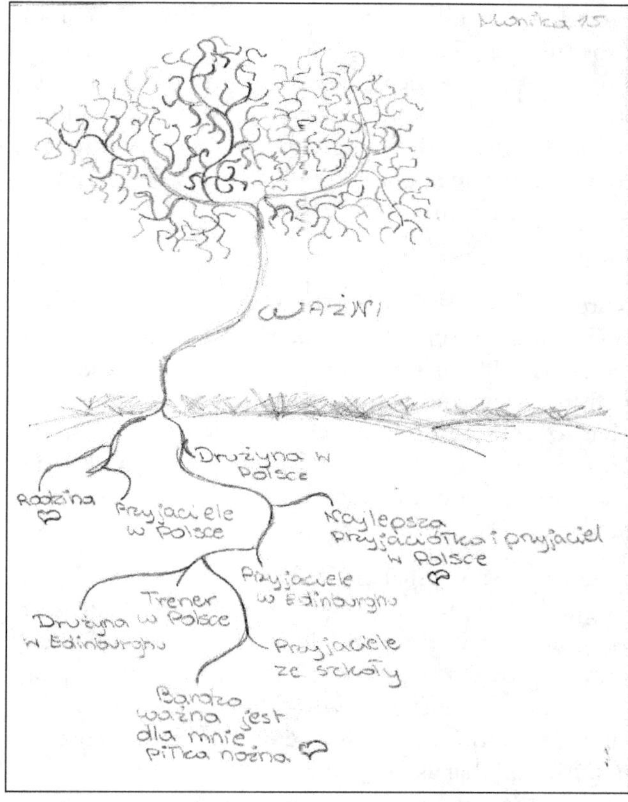

Myers critique of ethnographers becoming visual translators who tell the viewer "what they should see" and what the drawings mean (1995:60).

A drawing may sometimes express what a child cannot or does not wish to say aloud. For example, interviewing Jakub 9 years old wasn't very 'successful' either as he wasn't really interested to talk with me and he just waited for the moment I would free him and allow him to go out to pay football. Nevertheless, Jakub left me his drawing with a big house in the middle and a path leading to the house and two short sentences at the very bottom of the page:

"I don't like school", "I like to play on the computer" when I asked him to describe the picture and to read the sentences he said that he likes to spend time at home and he has a big family. However, he refused to read aloud the sentences he had written down.

My general experience was that children were generally willing to describe the elements of their drawings verbally, but rich narrative accountings were infrequent. There were few examples of the children who did not want to talk. This observation highlights more than children's differing communicative competence or the ethnographic fact that adults rarely ask for children's opinions in this community. Drawings are not a substitute for children's voices and the absence or muting or fragmentation of children's speak about their images means researchers need to be particularly cautious about over-interpreting their images. Therefore, I placed greater importance on using the maps and the drawings as 'catalysts for further oral discussion' to properly interpret the images. However, children are not used to interviews, so the structure of the interviews depended on particular child and its age- less structured interviews were conducted with younger children. Therefore, for individual interviews with young children, even children as young as 5 and 6 years olds the drawings were essential to provide a point of reference and to enable communication.

Concluding reflections

Two visual methods are used in the study: mapping of activity spaces and key features of the individual environment and thematic drawings. Visual methods were not used exclusively but were employed as a supplementary methods to the narrative interview and observation in the family or/and school context in order to maximise opportunities for researchers to understand the children's experiences. The combination of methods also allowed researchers to be more perceptive about the ways children expressed themselves with the visual methods.

The value of eliciting and analysing visual methods is now well established and widely used in ethnographic research among adults (Pink 2001; Prosser 1998), although surprising little of it examines drawing. As the following overview makes evident, a growing number of researchers are taking seriously Wagner's suggestion that "placing images in the foreground of our talk with children can increase opportunities for getting a clearer sense of what kids think" (1999:4). I found that asking children to draw a picture or a map related to the topic and then to tell a story to go with this is a good strategy to facilitate an interview. Particularly, a standard, lengthy series of questions and answers may not work as well for children as for adults.

My research in Scotland, provides evidence of the value of using drawing and mental maps accompanied by interviews as a research strategy among migrant children. Mitchell (2006) argues that interviews or focus groups in which children respond to questions posed by an adult researcher characterise the power imbalances while visual methods are said to offer a means of redressing or minimising that. However, drawing is not an inherently child-centred activity, but one in which relationships of power, authority, and difference also needs to be acknowledged and integrated into the analysis. In fact, often the drawings are received as a "natural form of expression" for children and an activity that "allows children to be children." As Christiansen and James have noted, "there is nothing particular or indeed peculiar to children that makes the use of any technique imperative" (2000:2).

References

Aitken, S. (2001). Geographies of Young People: The Morally Contested Spaces of Identity. London: Routledge.

Alderson, P. (1995). Listening to Children: Children, Ethics and Social Research. Barkingside: Barnardo's.

Barker, J. and Weller, S. (2003). "'Never Work with Children?' The Geography of Methodological Issues in Research with Children", Qualitative Research 3(2):207–227.

Basch, L., Glisk Schiller, N. Szanton Blanc, C. (1994). Nations Unbound: Transnational Projects, Postcolonial Predicaments and Deterritorialiazed Nation-states, Amsterdam: Gordon and Breach.

Boyden, J. (2003). "Children under Fire: Challenging Assumptions about Children's Resilience." Children, Youth and Environments, 13(1)

Bryceon, D. and Vuorela, U. (eds) (2002). Transnational Families. Oxford: Berg.

Christensen, P. and Allison J.eds. (2000). Research with Children: Perspectives and Practices, New York: Falmer Press.

Cowan, P. (1999). "Drawn" into the Community: Re-Considering the Artwork of Latino Adolescents". Visual Sociology 14:91–107.

Cousins, W. & Milner, S. (2007). "Small Voices: Children's Rights and Representation in Social Research". Journal of Social Work Education, 26 (5): 447 – 457

Croghan, R, Griffin, Ch., Hunter, J., Phoenix, A. (2008). "Young People's Constructions of Self: Notes on the Use and Analysis of the Photo-Elicitation Methods", *International Journal of Social Research Methodology*, 11(4): 345 – 356.

Fine, G. A., and K. L. Sandstrom (1988) Knowing Children: Participant Observation with Minors. Newbury Park, CA: Sage Publications.

Gamradt, J. (1995) "Jamaican Children's Representations of Tourism." Annals of Tourism Research 22(4):735–762.

Geissler, P. W. (1998). "Worms are our life, part II: Luo Children's Thoughts about Worms and Illness". Anthropology and Medicine 5(2):133–144.

Gordon, G. (1998). "How To: The Process" In Victoria Johnson, Edda Ivan-Smith, Gill Gordon, Pat Pridmore, and Patta Scott, (eds.), Stepping Forward: Children and Young People's Participation in the Development Process. Southampton Row: Intermediate Technology Publications.

Gottlieb, A. (2000). "Where Have all the Babies Gone? Toward an Anthropology of Infants (and their Caretakers)". Anthropological Quarterly 73(3):121–132.

Harrison, B. (2002). "Seeing Health and Illness Worlds—Using Visual Methodologies in a Sociology of Health and Illness: A Methodological Review." Sociology of Health and Illness 24(6):856–872.

Hart, R. (1997). Children's Participation: The Theory and Practice of Involving Young Citizens in Community Development and Environmental Care. London: Earthscan.

Johnson, V., Ivan-Smith, E., Gordon, G., Pridmore, P. and Patta S., (eds.) (1998). Stepping Forward: Children and Young People's Participation in the Development Process. Southampton Row: Intermediate Technology Publications.

James, A., Jenks, Ch. and Prout A. (1998) Theorizing Childhood. New York: Teachers College Press.

James, A. and A, Prout (eds.) (1997). Constructing and Reconstructing Childhood: Contemporary Issues in the Sociological Study of Childhood, 2nd edition, London/Philadelphia: Routledge Falmer Press

Katz, C. (1986). "Children and the Environment: Work, Play and Learning in Rural Sudan." Children's Environments Quarterly 3(4):43–51.

Levitt, P. and M. C. Waters (2002). "Introduction." In The Changing Face of Home. (ed.). P.

Levitt and M. C. Waters. New York: Russell Sage Foundation.

Levitt, P. and N. Glick Schiller (2004). Conceptudizing Simultaneity: A Transnational Social Field Perspective on Society, International Migration Review, 38(3): 1002-1040.

Myers, F. (1995). "Representing Culture: The Production of Discourse(s) for Aboriginal Acrylic Paintings." In The Traffic in Culture. George Marcus and Fred Myers, eds. 55–95. Berkeley: University of California Press.

Mitchell, L. M. (2006). "Child-centred? Thinking critically about children's drawings as a visual research method", Visual Anthropology Review 22 (1), 60–73

Moskal, M. (2007). "To which space do I belong? The Polish migrants sense of place and imagining citizenship." *'European multiculturalism as a challenge – policies, successes and failures'*, Political Geography Studies 1: 77-88.

Nieuwenhuys, O. (1996). Action Research with Street Children: A Role for Street Educators. Theme Issue, "Children's Participation," PLA Notes 25.

Orellana, M.F. et al. (2001). "Transnational Childhoods: The participation of children in processes of family migration." *Social Problems*, 48 (4): 573-592.

Orellana, M.F. (1999). "Space and place in an urban landscape: Learning from children's views of their social worlds." *Visual Sociology*, 14, 73-89.

Parreñas, R.S. (2005). Children of global migration: Transnational families and gendered woes. Stanford: Stanford University Press.

Pink, S. (2001) Doing Visual Ethnography: Images, Media and Representation in Research. London: Sage Publications.

Prosser, J. (ed.) (1998). Image-Based Research: A Sourcebook for Qualitative Researchers. New York: Routledge.

Prout, A. (2000). "Childhood Bodies: Construction, Agency, and Hybridity." In The Body, Childhood and Society. Alan Prout, ed. 1–18. Hampshire, England: MacMillan Press.

Punch, S. (2002). "Research with Children: The Same or Different from Research with Adults?" Childhood, 9 (3): 321-341.

Punch, S. (2001). "Multiple Methods and Research Relations with Young People in Rural Bolivia." In Limb, M. and Dwyer, C. (eds.) Qualitative Methodologies for Geographers, London: Arnold, 165-180.

Sime, D. (2008). "Ethical and methodological issues in engaging young people living in poverty with participatory research methods", Children's Geographies, 6(1), 63-78.

Smith, R. (2002). "Life Course, Generation, and Social Location as Factors Shaping Second-generation Transnational Life". In The Changing Face of Home. (ed.) P. Levitt and M. C. Waters. New York: Russell Sage Foundation.

Thorne, B. (1993). Gender Play: Girls and Boys in School. New Brunswick: Rutgers University Press

______. (1987). "Re-visioning Women and Social Change: Where Are the Children?" Gender and Society 1: 85-109

Wagner, J. (1999). "Visual Sociology and Seeing Kid's Worlds". Visual Sociology 14:3–6.

Walsh, A. (2003). Drawing on Identity: The Inkameep Day School. In Untold Stories of British Columbia. Paul Wood, ed. 61–70. Victoria, B.C.: The Humanities Centre, University of Victoria

White, S. (2002). Being, Becoming and Relationship; Conceptual Challenges of a Child Rights Approach in Development, Journal of International Development 14, 1095-1104.

Zelizer, V. (1985). Pricing the Priceless Child: the Changing Social Value of Children, New York: Basic Books.

Zhou, M. (1997). "'Parachute Kids' in Southern California: The Educational Experience Experience of Chinese Children in Transnational Families", Educational Policy, 12:682-704.

CHAPTER 6

GENDERED DIFFERENCES IN EMIGRATION AND MOBILITY PERSPECTIVES AMONG EUROPEAN RESEARCHERS WORKING ABROAD

Elisabeth Scheibelhofer

Abstract

This paper focuses on gendered mobilities of highly skilled researchers working abroad. It is based on an empirical qualitative study that explored the mobility aspirations of Austrian scientists who were working in the United States at the time they were interviewed. Supported by a case study, the paper demonstrates how a qualitative research strategy including graphic drawings sketched by the interviewed persons can help us gain a better understanding of the gendered importance of social relations for the future mobility aspirations of scientists working abroad.

Introduction

This paper focuses on the question of gendered mobilities of scientists crossing the international borders of developed countries. The considerations presented here are based on an empirical study including qualitative interviews with 21 Austrian scientists. The research explored the mobility aspirations of researchers who had been working in the USA on a medium-term or longer basis at the time they were interviewed. The analysis of the research project led to the elaboration of three ideal types of mobility: Migration, short-term research stays, and transnational modes of mobility[1]. In this contribution, the focus will be on gendered transnational mobility patterns of researchers as they came to the fore in this analysis. This issue will be discussed based on the case studies collected for this project.

As existing research indicates, transnational mobility aspirations with a focus on the impact of gender, in particular, have long been neglected (Dannecker 2005; Pessar and Mahler 2003). Based on the case study, this paper will discuss gendered forms of researchers' mobility in a transnational setting and the methodological questions they raise. The qualitative data generated in this study, including graphic drawings of the interview partners, allowed insights into the important role attached to social relations for future mobility aspirations. The gendered difference in caring for social relations, a

[1] See Scheibelhofer (2005) and (2008a) for a detailed report of the results of the study.

role that is still ascribed to women, may represent a key factor when looking at highly mobile women from Western Europe, as the present case study indicates.

The missing argument: Highly qualified women and mobility

The case that Eleonore Kofman (2000; 2004) makes in her contributions regarding gendered global migrations holds true for the issue developed in the present article. Kofman describes how the globalisation of migration has brought about increasingly diversified and stratified forms of migration. Such approaches as transnationalism (Basch et al. 1994; Levitt et al. 2003; Pries 2002) or alternative circuits of globalisation reflect the complex character of migration under present-day circumstances. Most of the scholarly attention so far has been focused on socio-economically disadvantaged female migrants working in private households or in the sex industry (Kofman 1999: 53).

However, the interest in highly skilled migration has been growing over the past fifteen years (Ackers 2004; Ackers 2005; ARGE MOMO 2000). These studies emphasise the importance of gender and of life-course dynamics to be taken into account for understanding the mobility and migration patterns of highly qualified workers (Kofman 2000; Raghuram 2002).

This study aims contributing to a better understanding of the gendered differences in future mobility plans of female researchers who are working abroad. This paper reflects in particular on the need to adopt a research methodology that is open to the everyday-life of the research participants in order to adequately analyse gendered differences. In theoretical terms, an approach is required that gives space to perceive the individual as embedded in social relations such as the workplace, the scientific community, family and friendship circles. To do so, a qualitative network approach seems the most promising way to conduct such research. A network approach also allows us to include all relevant interaction partners seen from the interviewees' perspective. The relevance of a network approach in migration studies is becoming increasingly evident by means of the empirical evidence produced during the last years. Thus, we now understand that classic concepts of migration are limited in scope, as they are frequently no longer able to reflect the multifaceted character of migration (Dahinden 2009, Haug 2000, Pries 2008).

The empirical example presented also shows that we cannot assume all relevant and decisive interaction partners to be located in the same physical area as our interview partners. Our methods thus need to reflect these social realities. In the presented empirical study, a triangulation of methods (qualitative interviews and graphic drawings sketched by the interview partners) proved to be helpful in this respect.

The empirical study

The case described in detail below is drawn from an empirical study carried out in 2002. In total, 21 scientists from Austria were interviewed who all found themselves in an early stage of their careers[2] when they went to the USA. Most of the interviewees were supported by an Austrian research grant. The sample was selected accordingly in an attempt to analyse gender differences. The data collection was done in the USA and the problem-centred interview (PCI) method was applied (Witzel 1982, 1996, 2000). Andreas Witzel designed this interviewing method along the lines of which an open, initial interview sequence is followed by a semi-structured topic guide that is flexibly used according to the interview situation. The interview method is based on the research strategy of Grounded Theory (Witzel 2000). It encompasses a short questionnaire (in order to collect data on social characteristics relevant to research) and a postscript (intended to complement the interview tape recordings, also cf. Scheibelhofer 2004). The analytical strategies of the PCI are various, yet a case-specific approach focussing on biographic stages is prevalent.

In the discussed research project, the interview is based on the method of the narrative interview developed by Fritz Schütze in order to carry out biographical studies (cf. Schütze 1983). This ensured that the interviewees would have as much freedom as possible to structure their answers[3]. Yet, the first interviews showed that it was difficult to gain insights, via classic open interviewing, into the various meaningful social relations the interviewees were part of. Thus, after these test interviews, we decided to introduce another phase after the PCI was completed: The informants were asked at that point to draw their most important interaction partners on a sheet of paper in the middle of which a circle already indicated the position of the interviewees themselves.[4] The interview partners were told that the distance from the circle in the middle should be an indication of the importance these individuals had for them at the very moment the conversation took place. Upon completing these drawings, they were prompted to explain who the persons included in the graphic drawing were and what kind of relationship the interviewees entertained with them.

Analysing the interview data subsequently, this additional method of graphic drawing proved useful in overcoming the problems encountered during the first wave of interviews: In the course of these interviews, either

[2] As Bazeley (2003) defines the concept of early career in research, the project focused on individuals who held a PhD (or doctorate in Austria) and were involved in research without holding a tenure-track position. Unlike Bazeley's early career status definition, the project did not focus on researchers who received their PhD only five years before.

[3] For a closer methodological reflection upon the combination of the narrative and the problem-centered interview, cf. Scheibelhofer (2008b).

[4] For a discussion of these drawings, cf. Scheibelhofer (2006); for a detailed description of the methods used, cf. Scheibelhofer (2003).

many people were named without describing the quality of the relationship, or the focus was on a limited number of people and the broader picture of a social network was lost. Also, the drawing led the interviewees to explain in detail the significance of their ties– in terms of academic matters as well as private relations (e.g. family relations, partnerships, friendships, etc).

The analyses of the collected interviews and drawings were informed by a constructivist Grounded Theory research strategy (Charmaz 2000), with a coding process leading to case studies of each interviewee and containing a chronological biography.[5] This biography was then broken down into different phases that were described in detail according to the specific circumstances of each biographic phase [6]. Consideration was also given to the interviewees' aspirations over time, their activities and evaluations as conveyed in the interviews (also cf. Witzel 1996 for this biographic model and Scheibelhofer 2004). Subsequently, the biographies were compared to one another and showed to differ in the following issues: the individuals' identity constructions, social networks, professional situations, plans for mobility, and living situations. The interviews also revealed that their initial plans to return after a one- or two-year stay changed as career and working opportunities subsequently took on new shapes for many of the interviewees.

Analysing the drawings and explanations provided by the interviewees, we were also able to focus on the mobility aspirations for the future. It turned out that mobility aspirations were closely linked to the scientists' social networks – be it the influence of career opportunities or be it considerations that are linked to their partnering (also cf. Ackers 2004 for dual career couples in research). Thus, especially by triangulating the PCI with graphic drawings, it became clear that individual social networks and future mobility aspirations were closely interlinked.

In relation to the above-mentioned issues, the empirical investigation identified three main forms of mobility. First, individuals on short-term research stays who were determined to return after a well-defined period abroad; second, those settling down in the USA and thus qualifying as classic work migrants; and finally, individuals with transnational lifestyles based on continuous physical and communicative mobility between Austria and the USA.

[5] The empirical work was based on a constructivist take on Grounded Theory. This implies that the principle of the comparative method within Grounded Theory (leading in this study to the description of three types of mobility) has guided the research process. Open coding was the main analytical work that gradually led to axial and selective coding within the coding process. In addition, the strategy of theoretical sampling was applied: Consequently, both men and women were interviewed, and different disciplines were selected such that varying circumstances for scientific work could be included into the study. Also, interviewees in varying private situations (children, married, in a relation) were specifically explored.

[6] This was carried out according to the scheme proposed by Andreas Witzel in his analytic work (Witzel 1996): For each identified phase in a biography, the aspirations for this phase, the realizations and evaluations are reconstructed.

In the next section, one case is selected and analysed in-depth. The results of this analysis for the transnational mobility type are presented in order to clarify highly qualified women's patterns of gendered transnational mobility for future debates.

The case study of Vera Jungwirth

Vera Jungwirth[7] is a 36-year-old political scientist who had been living in New York City for ten years when the interview was carried out. After completing her M.A. in Austria, she obtained an Austrian grant to study at a university in New York. Two years later, she received her diploma and her New York M.A. advisor encouraged her to apply for a PhD fellowship at that university. She won this fellowship, began her PhD studies and went into instructing undergraduates. At the same time, she was part of an Austrian-based research team carrying out independent research projects for Austrian funding institutions. At the time of the interview, Mrs Jungwirth taught at two universities in New York and at one university in Austria. Additionally, shortly before the interview took place, she won a prize for her research in Austria, thus stabilising her financial situation for another two years.

The close and diverse connections with peers, both on a professional and a personal level, were specific for this case when contrasting Vera Jungwirth's social relations with those of other interviewees. Her most important interaction partners were described as being her husband, with whom she lives in New York City, and her family living in a small provincial town in Austria. She has a very close friend, an Austrian woman who is also a political scientist living in New York and in Austria. They often cooperate in research projects or coach one another when involved in research teams with others. She pointed out that many other people she meets are also constantly on the move between their places of origin and New York. These contacts were explained to be convenient, as she can consult with her acquaintances about various difficulties arising from their common transnational lifestyle. As she has annual teaching assignments in Austria and spends part of the summer holidays there, Vera Jungwirth still rents her Viennese apartment that she shares with a roommate.

In the course of the interview, Mrs Jungwirth reflected upon her own position as a scholar and saw herself as a translator between the American and German-speaking scientific communities. She defined her contribution as transmitting research agendas from one community to the other. Her activities and orientations were described as highly self-determined. Her work and social networking have resulted in social relations with important scholars in her field of research. While discussing the insecurities of her

[7] All names, dates and specifics of the fieldwork presented here have been altered in order to make the data anonymous.

present situation as a researcher, Mrs. Jungwirth was at the same time forging strategies of how to cope with the exigencies of the field and the circumstances she has to work in. Making use of resources (contacts, information, teaching possibilities and research funds) both in Europe and in the USA is crucial for her engagements.

Nevertheless, her economic and working situation at the time of the interview suggested uncertainty regarding her future plans. It was clear to her that she would not gain a tenure-track position in New York without prior research stays at other institutions in the USA. At any rate, she had decided that she would live nowhere else than New York City, or another intellectually and culturally important – highly competitive – city in the USA. For private reasons, going back to work in Austria was not an option, as her American husband did not speak German and would thus be unlikely to find adequate employment in Austria.

Another aspect impairing Vera Jungwirth's status was that, in view of future aspirations and mobility, she was aware that she would immediately move back home to the Austrian periphery should her aged parents ever need continual care and help. As a single child, she made it clear in the interview that there was no other solution to this problem that she saw would come up at some point in time. She mentioned that in general, she avoids thinking about these insecurities, as she could not figure out how her professional and private life, with her husband being in the USA, might develop after leaving for Austria to take care of her parents. In the course of other interviews, such gender-specific norms and views about caring for one's parents or small children were only reproduced by female scientists. The issue of children and their education, on the other hand, was also brought up by male scientists who already were fathers.

Conclusions

It has become clear that the issue of how mobility is gendered is rarely considered with respect to highly qualified individuals from Western Europe who move across borders. Highlighting the biographic embeddedness of migration and mobility aspirations, is useful in this respect. The empirical project based on the strategy of Grounded Theory presented here demonstrates that the borderlines between short-term mobility, circular mobility, transnational lifestyles and migration are fluctuating phenomena. Interpreting the interview data and the graphic drawings result in a reconstruction of shifts between these forms of mobility. Such shifts can only be adequately understood as biographic events that are embedded in a specific social and gendered context. If intervening circumstances (such as offers of employment or finding a partner of a different nationality), the choices of mobility might be viewed in a different light and thus lead to changing mobility perspectives. In Mrs. Jungwirth`s case, the opportunity to teach and do research in more than one place – together with her close, private social relations with her family in Austria, her social relations and her husband in the USA – have guided her to forge a transnational mode of living that involves diverse insecurities but also a high degree of choice.

In order to perceive and capture such creative and fragile social realities, methodologies are to be adapted that allow a certain openness vis-à-vis the research field. As discussed elsewhere (see Scheibelhofer 2005), the so-called brain drain debate is mostly based on hypothesis-testing empirical studies. As research has long failed to consider transnational working and living modes, these issues have not yet been thoroughly discussed. The reconstruction of individuals' self-perceptions and aspiration must therefore be taken into consideration in an attempt to explore forms of social organisation that have not yet been recognised in the scholarly discussion. The triangulation of methods has proved to be helpful. Combining PCI with interviewees' graphic drawings helped us to gain complex insights into the interconnections between interviewees' social relations and their future mobility aspirations. We have to consider these relationships as gender-specific, as demonstrated by the case of Vera Jungwirth.

This approach allows us to acknowledge in what ways gender gives shape to mobility and migration in social milieus initially not considered when reflecting on the theme of gendered mobilities. Clearly, young researchers who decide to leave Austria in order to work in the USA are in a structurally advantageous position as compared to other low-skilled migrants (cf. Kofman 2000; 2004 as discussed above). Future research needs to compare mobility experiences of female scientists and their male colleagues, applying a qualitative approach that takes biographic events and their social embeddedness into account. Against this background, we can assume that we will be confronted with gendered differences that produce social hierarchies in this field. The empirical research discussed here demonstrated that female scientists were far more burdened with issues of child care, partner relations and caring for the elderly in their families than male scientists. However, male scientists had also to organise their family lives while living abroad. We therefore argue that physical presence to provide care work is still very likely to be expected from women – irrespective of their high qualifications and successful careers.

References

Ackers, L. (2004), Managing relationships in peripatetic careers: Scientific mobility in the European Union, *Women's Studies International Forum* 27, 189-201.

_____. (2005), Moving People and Knowledge: Scientific Mobility in the European Union, *International Migration* 43:5, 99-130.

ARGE MOMO (2000), *Räumliche Mobilität und Karrieremoblität von Wissenschaftlerinnen und Wissenschaftlern in Österreich.* Wien, Bundesministerium für Bildung, Wissenschaft und Kunst, Forschungsschwerpunkt "Politikrelevante Hochschulforschung: Frauen in Wissenschaft und Forschung".

Basch, L. et al. (1994), *Nations Unbound. Transnational Projects, Postcolonial Predicaments, and Deterritorialized Nation-States* (Amsterdam: Gordon & Breach Science Publishers).

Bazeley, P. (2003), Defining "early career" in research, *Higher Education* 45: 257-279.

Bozeman, B. and Corley, E. (2004), Scientists' collaboration strategies: implications for scientific and technical human capital, *Research Policy* 33, 599-616.

Dahinden, J. (2009), Are we all transnationals now? Network transnationalism and transnational subjectivity: the differing impacts of globalization on the inhabitants of a small Swiss city, *Journal of Ethnic and Racial Studies*, 32 (8): 1365-1386.

Dannecker, P. (2005), Transnational Migration and the transformation of gender relations: The case of Bangladeshi labour migrants. *Current Sociology*, vol. 53(4), pp. 655-674.

Denzin, N. K. and Lincoln, Y.S. (eds.) (2000), *Handbook of Qualitative Research*, Thousand Oaks, Sage.

Ehrenreich, B. and Hochschild, A. (eds.) (2002), *Global Woman. Nannies, Maids and Sex Workers in the New Economy*. London, Grenta Books.

ETAN, (2000), *Science policies in the European Union: Promoting excellence through mainstreaming gender equality*, European Commission Report, Brussels.

Gill, B. (2005), 'Homeward Bound? The experience of return mobility for Italian scientists', *Innovation* 18:3, 319-341.

Haug, S. (2000), *Klassische und neuere Theorien der Migration. Arbeitspapiere Mannheimer Zentrum für Europäische Sozialforschung*, http://www.uni-mannheim.de/publications/wp/wp-30.pdf.

Kofman, E. (1999), The invisibility of skilled female migrants and gender relations in studies of skilled migration in Europe, *International Journal of Population Geography* 6:1, 45-59.

_____. (2000), The Invisibility of Skilled Female Migrants and Gender Relations in Studies of Skilled Migration in Europe, *International Journal of Population Geography* 6, 45-59.

_____. (2004), Gendered Global Migrations: Diversity and Stratification, *International Feminist Journal of Politics* 6:4, 643-665.

Levitt, P. et al. (2003), Perspectives on transnational migration. An Introduction, *International Migration Review* 37:3, 565-575.

Pessar, P.R. and Mahler, S.J. (2003), Transnational Migration: Bringing Gender In. *International Migration Review*. Vol. 37, nr. 3, pp. 812-846.

Pries, L. (2002), Transnationalisierung der sozialen Welt? *Berliner Journal für Soziologie* 12:2, 263-272.

_____. (2008), *Transnationalisierung der sozialen Welt. Sozialräume jenseits von Nationalgesellschaften.* Frankfurt/M., Suhrkamp.

Raghuram, P. (2004), The difference that skills make: Gender, Family migration strategies and regulated labour markets. *Journal of Ethnic and Migration Studies*, vol. 30, nr. 2, 303-321.

Regrets, M.C. (2003), *Impact of skilled migration on receiving countries.* SciDevNet: Policy Briefs.

Roth, K. (ed.) (2003), *Vom Wandergesellen zum „Green Card" -Spezialisten. Interkulturelle Aspekte der Arbeitsmigration im östlichen Europa*, Münster, Waxmann.

Scheibelhofer, E. (2004), Das Problemzentrierte Interview – Möglichkeiten und Grenzen eines Erhebungs- und Auswertungsinstruments, *Zeitschrift Sozialwissenschaften und Berufspraxis*, 27/1, 75-90.

_____. (2005), Mobilitätsperspektiven junger WissenschaftlerInnen im Ausland, *SWS-Rundschau*, 1,117-139.

_____. (2006), Migration, Mobilität und Beziehung im Raum: Netzwerkzeichnungen von InterviewpartnerInnen als interpretative Methode, in: Hollstein, B., Straus, F. (eds.), *Qualitative Netzwerkanalyse. Konzepte, Methoden, Anwendungen, Verlag für Sozialwissenschaften*, 311 – 332.

_____. (2008a), Gender Still Matters: Mobility Aspirations among European Scientists Working Abroad. In: Uteng, Tanu Priya and Cresswell, Tim (eds.), *Gendered Mobilities.* Aldershot, Ashgate, 115-128.

_____. (2008b), Combining narration-based interviews with topical interviews: Methodological reflections on research practices (2008), *International Journal of Social Research Methodology*, vol. 11, Issue 5, 403-416.

Schütze, F. (1983), Biographieforschung und narratives Interview, *Neue Praxis*, vol. 13, Issue 3, 283-293.

Stalford, H. (2005), 'Parenting, care and mobility in the EU. Issues facing migrant scientists', *Innovation* 18:3, 316-380.

Weyer, J. (ed.) (2000), *Soziale Netzwerke. Konzepte und Methoden der sozialwissenschaftlichen Netzwerkforschung.* München: Oldenbourg Verlag.

Witzel, A. (1982), *Verfahren der qualitativen Sozialforschung. Überblick und Alternativen.* Frankfurt am Main/New York: Campus Verlag.

_____. (1996), Auswertung problemzentrierter Interviews: Grundlagen und Erfahrungen, in: Strobl, R. (ed.), *Wahre Geschichten? Zu Theorie und Praxis qualitativer Interviews. Beiträge zum Workshop Paraphrasieren, Kodieren, Interpretieren.* Baden-Baden: Nomos Verlag, 49-76.

_____. (2000), The Problem-Centered Interview. In: *Forum qualitative Sozialforschung.* http://www.qualitative-research.net/index.php/fqs/article/view/1132.

CHAPTER 7

A PARTICIPATORY APPROACH TO RESEARCH WITH MIGRANT WORKING ADOLESCENTS

Rita Bertozzi

Abstract

Child-centred approaches focus on the children's perspective and on partic-ipation. Participatory action research can be a fruitful methodology for in-vestigating delicate topics such as child labour in migrant communities. This article presents a peer research project conducted in Rome (Italy) which actively involved a group of foreign working young people over two years and employed a variety of methodologies. Research methods will be illustrated and critically discussed, with a particular focus on the benefits for the mi-grant youths involved and ethical questions arising from this type of re-search. A brief summary of the main findings will also be provided.

The increasing attention towards children's and adolescents' rights and the involvement of minors in issues directly concerning them have led to a gradual methodological shift from research carried out 'on' children to research carried out 'with' children, and most recently, research carried out 'by' children (Brownlie et al. 2006; Wilkinson 2000; Laws and Mann 2004; Liebel 2008; Kellett 2005). There are now many international studies on child-centred research that present empirical results and explore ethical and methodological issues (Laws and Mann 2004; Wilkinson 2000; Jones 2004; Kirby 2004; Boyden and Ennew 1997; The Concerned for Working Children 2002 and 2006; Liebel 2008; Kellett 2005; Brownlie et al. 2006; Bennett and Roberts 2004; Alderson and Morrow 2004).

In this article, I will present a participatory research project on working migrant young people in Rome.

Ethnic minorities are often included in the category of vulnerable persons, and they are often prevented from actively participating in research due to a variety of problems (Steel 2001). The same holds true for working children and adolescents who, especially in some cases, run the risk of social exclusion.

The topic of working migrant minors is an intricate one due, on the one hand, to their relative invisibility and, on the other, to their vulnerability. The picture is further complicated by the need to take a number of cultural, economic, social and legal variables into consideration, given that migration projects, models of inclusion, different representations of childhood and inter-generational relationships can all affect decisions about work (Bertozzi 2007). During the nineties, research on child labour in Italy focused exclusively on Italian minors. Migrant minors were overlooked, due to the difficulty of exploring the most marginalized jobs in which they were involved and entering the tightly knit immigrant communities (Istat 2002).

This paper presents a study on migrant young people using participatory research. Participatory research approaches arose out of efforts in East Africa in the 1970s as an alternative social science research methodology (Clark 2004). They include participatory action research, community research, participatory learning and action, peer research, and participatory rural appraisal (Laws 2004; Hart 2006). The key features of participatory research include methodological eclecticism and a different relationship between researchers, their subjects and topics of inquiry, all of which requires the active involvement of community members in the presentation, analysis and interpretation of their own reality (Clark 2004).

The participatory approach may be a promising methodology for investigating migrant children's labour and social life. Enabling working migrant young people to be researchers themselves means for them, firstly, to claim the right to express their opinion and participate in the life of their community, and secondly, to claim the right to influence their public image and the decisions and policies concerning them, thereby avoiding and eliminating situations of invisibility.

However, one should also be aware of the possible limitations of participatory research approaches. A common concern is that these approaches may not always meet the standards of scientific research[1]. At the same time, there is the risk that the research outcomes may not be utilized by the participants in order to promote social change. A considerable amount of time, energy, and other resources are required if participants are to become part of such a project in an appropriate and ethically respectful way. Finally, especially when delicate issues are at stake, young people do not necessarily wish to be interviewed by their peers. Thus, the choice of this approach should be carefully weighed against other possibilities (Laws and Mann 2004).

1. A Peer Research Project with migrant working adolescents

The peer research project presented here was part of a larger research project on migrant children's work in Rome, developed by Save the Children

[1] More specifically, participatory approaches may produce results with relatively low internal reliability, as peer researchers may collect data in a variety of ways in order to respond to questions that 'academic' researchers might not have included in a standardised research project. However, data thus collected have a very high ecological validity as they are grounded on the participants' views and provide deep insights on the phenomena under investigation.

Italy in collaboration with the Research Centre of CGIL, one of the most important Italian trade unions, in 2007 and 2008. The project included other more conventional methodologies such as surveys. The aim of this peer research project was to analyze migrant youth's work, its meanings and characteristics. We investigated the work of children under the age of fifteen (whose work would be considered illegal according to the International Labour Organization Convention n.138) and the experience of youths aged 16 to 18. The focus of the research was on the working activities and the illegal economic activities that young people defined as work[2].

The unique feature of this two-year research project was the pivotal role played by the young people themselves, which informed the entire research process and contributed to its definition, revision and ongoing re-adjustment.

In peer research, young people are considered part of the research team, so that investigators share with the participants their age, present and past experiences, life contexts and cultural heritage. Peer researchers may take on a variety of roles, such as supporting adults in making decisions about research agendas, approaches and methodologies, collecting data themselves, or being involved in data analysis and report writing (Laws 2004; Kirby 2004).

In peer research, participation and action are intertwined. Participation is a fundamental concept in this approach, which aims to involve research subjects and to promote a "democratization of the processes leading to the construction of social knowledge" (Cannarella et al. 2007: 170). Action, on the other hand, may be one by-product of the research or may be intimately connected to it, but it is not a necessary condition. In other words, peer research is always participatory research (although the nature and degree of participation may vary)[3], which may, in turn, become action research when it aims not just at knowing reality but also at solving problems and promoting good practices.

From participatory peer research to participatory peer action research

Table 1 summarizes the main elements of the peer research carried out in 2007 and 2008 in Rome.

The research had two main goals:

- understanding the characteristics of the minors' jobs and the forms of exploitation of child labour in Rome, focusing primarily on migrant youths and, in the second year, also on young Italians at risk of social exclusion;

---

[2] In accordance with the official position of Save the Children, *Position Paper on child work* (www.savethechildren.it).

[3] The two variables of participation and action are to be separately analyzed for both researchers and participants.

- enabling these youths to speak with their own voice, in order to understand their perspectives on the phenomenon and to promote their training and participation as active participants, rather than treating them as passive research subjects. This also implied advocating for and with the young people involved in the project.

Table 1 – Main features of peer research 'with' and 'by' migrant young people

	1st year	2nd year
Goals	Gaining knowledge on: - Characteristics and meanings of migrant youth's jobs	Gaining knowledge on: - Characteristics and meanings of migrant youth's jobs - Forms of exploitation of child labour Experimentation of a micro-observatory Devising possible practical interventions
Methods	1.Individual semi-structured interviews 2.Photographs	1.Individual and group semi-structured interviews 2.Internet 3.Analysis of job offers on newspapers and websites 4. Save the Children front desk
Research products	1.Final peer researchers' report 2.Final adults' report	1.Joint participatory report 2.Peer-to-peer information materials 3.Employers' information material 4.Audio-recording of 10 interviews

During the first year, only in a few cases did young researchers spontaneously make their peers aware of their rights on the workplace. In the second year, adult facilitators and peer researchers took a more action-oriented approach, establishing a micro-observatory connected with street-units and planning strategies for intervention. This implied more involvement and greater commitment on the part of peer researchers and a more extensive collaboration with other peer groups.

Methods and Stages of the peer research project

A number of ethical issues arise in connection with children's participation in research (Laws and Mann 2004; Wilkinson 2000; Alderson and Morrow 2004; Camacho 2007). In our case, these included telling the participants explicitly about the purposes of the research, the costs and benefits of their involvement, issues surrounding confidentiality, the recruitment of researchers and related compensation, the use of flexible methods, respect of the migration projects, and their possible involvement in dissemination and advocacy activities.

From the very beginning, we chose to acknowledge the educational value of the activity (in terms of skills acquisition) with a financial reward for the time spent on the research. An advertisement was published in order to locate the six young participants who were awarded scholarships for the two years. After being fully informed about the research project, each youth was asked for his or her personal consent to participate in the project, as well as the consent of his or her parents or legal guardians.

For each of the two years, the research group consisted of 6 peer researchers aged 15 to 18, each of whom had work or work-like experiences as a minor. There were 3 girls and 9 boys. They came from Ecuador, Romania, Afghanistan, Morocco, Moldavia, India, the Republic of Guinea, or were a gypsy who came from Bosnia or Romania. Participants were contacted among the most represented ethnic minorities in Rome at the time of the study. Another criterion for inclusion in the research group was a good command of Italian. Some of the young people lived with their families; others lived in hosting communities because they were unaccompanied minors, while still some others lived in 'gypsy camps'.[4]

Two peer tutors and three facilitators from Save the Children supervised the young researchers and were in charge of institutional relations. The participants interviewed were migrant working young people from 8 to 18 years old.

The research group discussed the aims of the research and the field of inquiry, starting from the members' personal experiences, and decided to use a variety of methods. During an initial brainstorming session, the facilitators invited the peer researchers to reflect on the reasons that had led the young people to work. Discussion was stimulated through the use of photographs depicting working minors, which opened up the debate on the concept of work, its conditions and varieties. The group also collected and discussed newspaper articles in order to gain a better understanding of minors' work in Italy and, more specifically, in Rome.

A training course took place during each of the two years, focusing on research methods. A jurist and a media educator informed the researchers on workers' rights and precautions for the use of new technologies.

After this initial training, the peer researchers selected the research tools and, together with the adult facilitators, worked out how they would apply them. The main research method was the semi-structured interview. These were adapted by peer researchers to different contexts and situations, in an attempt to facilitate contact with the interviewees, to make them feel comfortable, and to respect their point of view and their rights. For example, in the "gypsy camp," the peer researchers decided not to make any recordings. Some interviews were conducted while walking, such that

[4] Social policies towards immigrant families vary greatly across local and regional contexts, and they also tend to change rapidly over time. General reviews can be found in Donati (2009), Zanfrini (2007), Ambrosini (2005).

researchers had to write down their interviewees' responses afterwards

Interviews were carried out in the youths' mother tongues and in Italian, both face to face and at the Save the Children front desk. The interviewers also used some of the stimuli developed in the preparatory phase, such as photographs or newspaper articles, to elicit their respondents' experiences, opinions and attitudes. Anonymity and confidentiality were guaranteed, although some youth had already met each other before. Anonymity and confidentiality were also maintained in the subsequent phases of interview transcription and analysis. The young researchers started the interviews in their local areas, working initially with their friends and people from the same country of origin.

Over the two years of the project, 105 young people from 18 different countries were interviewed and 120 working experiences were analyzed. At the end of each year, the peer researchers analyzed all of the interviews and discussed what they felt they had learned from their respondents, suggesting possible strategies for intervention.

The peer researchers proposed additional information sources, such as Internet social networks. These networks were used only to disseminate information on minors' rights and to promote discussion among youths who knew each other and who were informed of the research project's aims. In no case were the social networks used to collect data without participants' informed consent. Another important resource suggested by the young researchers were job offers in newspapers.

The front desk of the Save the Children was another important source for gathering information and enhancing participation. It was a well-equipped meeting place for young people, connected with street units and street workers that facilitated contact with many working migrant youths for research purposes.

Peer researchers contributed significantly to writing the research reports, with adults and peers as their target readers. The convention between the two project partners (Save the Children *Italy* and Ires-Cgil) included the publication of a book reporting the project outcomes (Ires Cgil and Save the Children Italia 2007). The youths wrote their own report in the first year[5]. Some of them asked for help with Italian grammar, although they were all encouraged to draw on their own expressive means. Writing the report allowed them to reflect upon their own experience as research participants, to acknowledge the project's potentials and limitations, and, in so doing, contributed to raising their self-esteem and valuing their work. During the second year, researchers and adults drafted a joint participatory report. Video recordings and information files on youth rights in the workplace were

[5] Cfr. *Ragazzi ricercatori. Una ricerca partecipata sul lavoro dei minori migranti*, 2007, www.savethechildren.it.

written for young people and employers and were later translated into four languages. Research materials were disseminated through press conferences in which the young people directly participated, and through publications.

In addition to monitoring during the process, peer researchers evaluated the work done at the end of each research cycle by means of a questionnaire. The facilitators also produced a final report on the process and its possible effects. Save the Children Italy included the proposals made by the young migrants among its advocacy initiatives.

Main research findings

The research revealed that migrant youths are employed in a wide range of jobs, sometimes for a significant number of hours, the majority in the "non-conventional" labour market (table 2).[6]

Among these activities, we included every job that the minors defined as work. For example, petty theft or begging were included as work activities, and young people were interviewed about them, because, as some peer researchers told us, the youth involved had considered them as jobs. This was one of the positive outcomes of this approach. In fact, we were able to compare the formal definitions of work activities (as stated by the law) with the experiences of working youths and, in so doing, adopted a broad category of 'child work'. Then, in the data analysis stage, the peer researchers and facilitators initiated a discussion about what we could define as working activities and in what ways they could be distinguished from illegal activities or informal money-making activities. In this way, the peer researchers and participants could understand the discrepancy between law and reality as well as the benefits of holding a regular job.

Some young people managed to combine school and work activities, although the majority of them did not attend school. They had little knowledge of their rights and obligations, as prescribed by the Italian educational system. Many young people who had arrived in Italy at the age of 14 or 15 gained illegal access to the job market without first completing their compulsory education.

These youths also had little knowledge of the rights and conditions under which a person from 16 to 18 years old is allowed to work in Italy. Their main concern was to earn money, and exploitation was usually perceived only in connection with the remuneration. Despite this lack of awareness, however, there were several situations of exploitation, due to long working hours, demanding duties, and the absence of a work contract or security. Building, farming jobs and prostitution were the more exploitative working situations described. Youths who were unaware of their rights, who were poorly protected and had a relatively low quality of life emerged as those

[6] A full presentation of the research findings can be found in Bertozzi (2007 and 2009).

more vulnerable and more open to exploitation.

Several discussions were conducted on this topic with the research group in collaboration with the jurist. This topic stimulated some critical observations by the peer researchers during group interviews, as a result of their new-found awareness. For these reasons, among the final products, peer researchers decided to produce peer-to-peer materials on the rights of working young people, as stated in Italian law, as well as an information kit for employers.

Table 2 – Jobs of respondent aged 8-18 years old that were analysed within the research[7]

Job types	Number of minors
Catering *(cook, pizza maker ,confectioner, waiter, barman, dishwasher)*	32
Building *(bricklayer, hodman, painter)*	11
Home care	4
Services *(hairdresser, decorator, Internet point attendant, librarian, cultural mediator, porter, filling station attendant, parker, car-washer, cleaning staff, herbalist, bathing attendant)*	28
Crafts *(mechanic, tailor, satellite-dish maintenance worker)*	6
Arts *(photographer, actor, lap-dancer)*	4
Trade *(greengrocer, market seller, fishmonger)*	3
Farming	4
Street seller	2
Begging	8
Illegal activities	10
Prostitution	2
Illegal parker	6
Total	120

Benefits and challenges

The inclusion of peer researchers promoted equal relations with young

[7] Some of the young people had more than one working experience as a minor. During the second year of the research, each experience was analyzed as a different case; therefore, 61 working experiences were collected, although there were only 42 participants in the study.

people and the choice of the most effective methods for understanding their issues and concerns. Peer interviewers, who shared similar experiences and languages, were able to access invisible and irregular working situations, which were otherwise inaccessible to Italian adults. Being a peer further enabled trust and openness in young people, particularly in some delicate situations, as with stigmatized social groups. The young researchers' point of view also provided additional insights into the interpretation of the influence of cultural variables and of changes related to migration. Peer action-research also allowed for more effective and targeted actions of the groups of interest.

The main benefits of this participatory approach can be seen in peer researchers' empowerment. The peer researchers developed a greater awareness of work-related matters and their own conception of rights changed. This led some of the researchers to look for non-exploitative jobs. Others became more aware of their rights in negotiations with their employers. Some even initiated discussions with their peers about work and related issues. The experience, thus, enhanced their conscious self-confidence, through a continual exchange with adults involved in the project and in the actions which followed.

As one girl remarked: *"All of this gave us the opportunity to read the society in which we live in a different way and to gain knowledge for our own future" (Tatiana, 17 years old).*

Young people's involvement in the research also raised particular ethical concerns.

A fundamental concern was that of informed consent, understood as the expression of free choice to participate in the research. Consent is usually asked of minors, parents or legal guardians. This leads to a series of issues: Is parents' consent necessary for young people? Where there are differences, should we take into consideration the youths' consent, or do we bide by the adults' consent (Alderson and Morrow 2004)? How can participation, protection, and informed consent be solicited at the same time, when participants live in irregular situations or when they come from families whose cultural models deny children significant decision-making power? The involvement of the peers made it easier to obtain consent based on trust, but it was important to ensure that such consent was actually informed and that there was no exploitation. Peer mediation mitigates the power and cultural imbalance of the relationship where consent is asked, and it can help lessen mistrust in youths and adults. Parents' (or legal guardians') consent was asked for the peer researchers involved in the project. More often than not, however, immigrant parents are in a position of lesser power when negotiating in the host society. Efforts were thus made to ensure that parents understood the informed consent form by simplifying its language and, through cultural mediation, explaining to them the goals and methods of the research project. The peer researchers themselves were responsible for gaining informed consent from the participants they interviewed.

Another dilemma which we faced was in making sure that participation in the research did not pose risks for the young people and, at the same time, that the protection of the youths did not inhibit or limit their participation. For this reason, great care was taken in handling possibly irregular or illegal situations, in order not to expose the researchers to risks and dangers, even when this meant losing the opportunity to further explore emerging topics. Anonymity was guaranteed in interviews with prostitute minors, and the young researchers limited themselves to sensitizing their peers in order not to breach the agreement of confidentiality that had been established in the contact phase. Save the Children has a number of street education projects in Rome that also involve prostitute minors.

Another controversial issue that arose was whether young people should be remunerated for their work. In our case, we chose to award scholarships to emphasize the experience's formative qualities. This incentive motivated the participation of immigrant youths as they were all responsible for supporting themselves or their families.

The trust that peer researchers gained from their interviewees raised the issue of how information that is confidentially elicited should be utilized. All of the data were read together with peer researchers in order to exclude from publication the most sensitive personal information, while at the same time preserving an overall picture of the phenomena being observed.

Research carried out by migrant young people serves as a way of expressing their participation, and the participation "of minors involves the development of their rights, the encouragement of their action in society, and the expression of their needs and interests" (Ruggero 2007). In the context of a multi-method approach to a phenomenon as complex as migrant children's labour, peer research provides a qualitative focus grounded in young people's point of view.

References

Alderson, P. and Morrow, V. (2004). *Ethics, social research and consulting with children and young people.* Barnardos: Barkingside.

Ambrosini, M. (2005). *Sociologia delle migrazioni.* Bologna: Il Mulino.

Bennet, F. and Roberts, M. (2004). *From input to influence. Participatory approaches to research and inquiry into poverty.* Joseph Rowntree Foundation.

Bertozzi, R. (2007). "La ricerca partecipata di Save the Children con i minori migranti", in Ires and Save the Children Italia *Minori al lavoro. Il caso dei minori migranti.* Roma: Ediesse.

_____. (2009). "Research with and by Migrant Children in Rome", in J. Fiedler and C. Posch (eds) *Yes, they can! Children researching their lives*, Germany: Hofmann, Schorndorf.

Boyden, J. and Ennew, J. (1997). *Children in Focus. A Manual for Participatory Research with Children.* Sweden: Save the Children Sweden.

Brownlie, J. et al. (2006). *Children as researchers.* June: Scottish Executive Social Research.

Camacho, A.Z. (2007). "Ethical and Methodological Concerns related to Relevant Child

Participation in Research on Children in Migration", Varsavia, 20-21 Marzo 2007.
Cannarella, M. et al. (2007). *Hermanitos. Vita e politica della strada tra i giovani latinos in Italia.* Ombre Corte.
Clark, J. (2004). "Participatory research with children and young people: philosophy, possibilities and perils", *Action Research Expeditions*, 4 (11): 1-18.
Donati, P. (eds) (2009). *Famiglia, migrazioni e società interculturali: quali regole di convivenza civile?.* Milano: Franco Angeli.
Hart, R. (2006). "Guide to participatory research", in H. van Beers et al. (eds) *Beyond Article 12. Essential Readings in children's participation*. Bangkok: Knowing Children.
Ires CGIL and Save the Children Italia (2007). *Minori al lavoro. Il caso dei minori migranti.* Roma: Ediesse.
Istat (2002). *Bambini, lavori e lavoretti. Verso un sistema informativo sul lavoro minorile. Primi risultati.* Roma.
Jones, A. (2004). "Involving Children and Young People as Researchers", in S. Fraser et al. (eds) *Doing Research with Children and Young People*, Milton Keynes: The Open University/Sage.
Kellett, M. (2005). *How to Develop Children as Researchers.* Sage Publications.
Kirby, P. (2004). *A Guide to Actively Involving Young People in Research: For researchers, research commissioners, and managers.* INVOLVE.
Laws, S. (2004). "Involving Children in Primary Research", in S. Laws and G. Mann (2004). *So You Want to Involve Children in Research?.* Sweden: Save the Children Sweden.
Laws, S. and Mann, G. (2004). *So You Want to Involve Children in Research?.* Sweden: Save the Children Sweden.
Liebel, M. (2008). *Child-led research with working children*, Conference organized by the International Childhood and Youth Research Network, 28-29 May, Cyprus.
Ruggero, R. (2007). "Diritti e bambini", *Rassegna bibliografica,* 1: 5-21, Istituto degli Innocenti.
Steel, R. (2001). *Involving Marginalized and Vulnerable People in Research: A Consultation Document.* INVOLVE.
The Concerned for Working Children (2002). *Children and their research. A process document.* Bangalore.
_____. (2006). *Taking a Right Turn. Children lead the way in research.* Bangalore.
Wilkinson, J. (2000). *Children and Participation: Research, Monitoring and Evaluation with Children and Young People.* London: Save the Children UK.
Zanfrini, L. (2007). *Sociologia delle migrazioni.* Bari: Laterza.

CHAPTER 8

POTENTIAL OF QUALITATIVE NETWORK ANALYSIS IN MIGRATION STUDIES - REFLECTIONS BASED ON AN EMPIRICAL ANALYSIS OF YOUNG RESEARCHERS' MOBILITY ASPIRATIONS

Elisabeth Scheibelhofer

Abstract

Based on the example of an empirical research study, the paper examines the strengths and limitations of a qualitative network approach to migration and mobility. The method of graphic drawings produced by the respondents within an interview setting was applied. With this method, we argue to be able to ana-lyse migrants' specific social embeddedness and its influence on future mobility aspirations. Likewise, connections between the migratory biography and the in-dividuals' various social relations are investigated.

Introduction

Based on an empirical project exploring mobility aspirations among young researchers, this article discusses the usefulness and limitations of a network approach in qualitative migration studies. Existing migration research clearly points to the usefulness of a network approach for many research ques-tions. Network approaches in migration research seem appropriate because classic concepts of migration are limited in scope due to their shortcomings to reflect the actual character of migration (Dahinden, 2009; Pries, 2008). In particular, this holds true with respect to gendered differences in such mo-bilities (Ackers, 2004 and 2005; Ackers and Stalford, 2007; Kofman, 2000 and 2004; Raghuram, 2002).

Studies on migration and mobility presently point out that forms of integration or modes of incorporation cannot be explained with such theoretical tools of classic migration research as assimilation theories (Glick Schiller, 2007; Wimmer, 2007). This theoretical shortcoming becomes most obvious within the empirical evidence provided by transnational migration studies. Transmigration research has shown that the nation-state is no longer necessarily the vessel in which all meaningful and socially decisive social relations are to be found (Faist, 2005). Rather, many migrants are embedded in social relations that cut across nation-state borders while being firmly established in specific localities. Empirical migration research thus needs to take the multiplicity of current social relations and their effects on social action into account. Network analyses seem to be a fruitful venue that recently has started to be explored within qualitative migration research (Hollstein, 2006; Scott, 2000; Wasserman and Faust, 1994). Both qualitative and quantitative network analyses cover a wide array of migration issues. Yet what has been criticized especially with regard to quantitative approaches using social network analyses is that many studies remain limited to the topic of economic resource access. With a qualitative network approach, we can also understand the noneconomic implications of migrants' specific social embeddedness and their shaping of meaning within these relations. As Gold (2005: 36) explains, networks also give form to the goals and norms of in-dividuals, while defining commendable and condemned behaviour. The empirical project referred to in this paper introduces qualitative network analysis in a very specific manner. We were particularly interested in the qual-ities of the given social relationships. Here, ego-centred personal networks have been applied in order to analyze the relationship between private and working relations, as well as mobility aspirations. Thus, qualitative problem-centred interviews (Witzel, 2000; Scheibelhofer, 2004) have been combined with graphic drawings produced by the respondents.

In this study, 21 scientists from Austria were interviewed who all found themselves in an early career position when they were selected as interview partners. At the time they had gone to the USA, most of them were supported by an Austrian research grant. As the working conditions vary considerably with the disciplines, the sample of the study encompassed both social and life sciences. Also, gender differences were to be expected as based on the results of feminist studies in this research field (Ackers, 2007; Arge Momo, 2000). The data collection was done in three different areas, all located on the East Coast (Boston, New York City and Washington, D.C. area). We applied the method of problem-centred interviews (PCIs) as established by Witzel (2000). In the PCIs, an open, initial interview sequence was followed by a semi-structured topic guide flexibly used according to the interview situation .

The first interviews showed that it was difficult to gain insights, via classic open interviewing, into the various meaningful social relations the interviewees were part of . Thus, we decided to introduce another phase after the test PCI was completed. The informants were asked at that point to draw their most important interaction partners on a sheet of paper. In the middle of the sheet, a circle indicated the interviewees' own position . The interview partners were told that the distance from the circle in the middle should indicate the importance these individuals had for them at the very moment the conversation took place. Upon completing these drawings, they were prompted to explain who the persons included in the graphic drawing were and what kind of relationships the interviewees entertained with them.

Analysing the interview data subsequently, this additional meth-od of data collection proved to assist in overcoming the problems encoun-tered during the first interviews. In the course of our interviews, many peo-ple were named without describing the quality of the relationships. Alterna-tively, the focus at times was on a limited number of people such that the broader picture of a social network might have been lost. In addition, the drawings led the interviewees to explain in detail the significance the previ-ously indicated persons had for them. This applied to scientific matters as well as private relations, such as family relations, partnerships and friend-ships. Thus, the interviewees' complex social relations with their most im-portant interaction partners were studied based on these drawings. With this methodological perspective, the gendered influence and intertwining of private and work relations came to the fore. At this point of the analysis, consideration was to be given to the well-established critique of feminist theory highlighting the problematic differentiation between a "public" and a "private" sphere. Respective research has emphasized that such a dichotomization cannot withstand theoretical reflection, as the very definition of "private" and "public" (or "work relations", as they are called here) cannot be maintained (Benhabib, 1992; Gerodetti and Bieri, 2006; Landes, 1998). As to the project at hand, we were aware of this problematic issue and see the concepts of "private relations" and "work relations" as societal con-structs that should be seen critically. However, they should also be perceived and thus analysed as instrumental within the empirical world.

The theoretical considerations guiding the study were also informed by the shortcomings of previous investigations of the mobility of researchers and other highly skilled persons. Studies with such a focus have been quite well established since the 1960s. They have been based on the assumption that highly skilled scientific migration represents a unidirectional flow of individuals and their knowledge. This led to the assumption that migrants' countries of origin are losing "human capital", while their countries of settlement are increasing their share of highly skilled workforce (see Lowell, 2003; Meyer and Brown, 1999). Sociologically more convincing, another approach is that a human capital perspective would capture only one part of an individual's relevant body of knowledge (Regets, 2003), as monetary values are measured but learning processes are ignored. Yet learning is a complex and time-consuming socio-cognitive process. Complementary aspects of codified knowledge and tacit knowledge (see Polanyi, 1962) are brought to the fore against the background of these assumptions. Additionally, these aspects are reinforced by a heightened sensibility towards the processes of knowledge production (see Gibbons et al., 1994). Therefore, knowledge (and especially its tacit part) is seen as socially and spatially embedded in specific interactions. It can only be mediated within social processes em-bedded in social networks. Cognitive networks of individuals and institu-tions forming a scientific community are pivotal, as specialization is based on local conditions for research. Along with other network theorists, Powell and Smith-Doerr (1994) emphasize the close interrelationship between individual competencies and the units to which a person is connected (Callon, 1986; Callon and Latour, 1981). This perception of knowledge also leads to the assumption that the mobility of highly qualified persons such as scientists might be studied more fully in terms of circulatory models (e.g., see the investigations carried out by Kaplan, 1998; Kaplan et al., 1999; Mahroum, 1999; Meyer, 1996; Meyer and Brown, 1999). Based on existing empirical studies and her own research, Louise Ackers states that "flows may not be uni-directional, homogenous, or permanent and may be mitigated by certain 'compensatory' mechanisms" (see Ackers, 2005: 99).

The debate shows that we are in need of a theoretical framework allowing us to study the meaning of individuals' social embeddedness in social networks and its implications for diverse modes of migration and mobility. Such a framework would help us understand the migratory and mobility patterns of highly qualified people such as the researchers we studied. Also, we have seen that both professional contacts and individual situations, including correspondent social relations, are decisive for geographic mobility. In terms of physical space, we cannot assume that all relevant interaction partners are located in the same place as our interview partners.

Based on this body of knowledge provided by other empirical research, we came to the conclusion that we needed to approach our research project from a very specific angle. Particular attention would be given to embeddedness in social environments, especially in terms of social networks. Turning to the results of the discussed study, atypical forms of migration and mobility, such as circulatory movements, were decisive for some case studies . In this report, one specific case is discussed in an attempt to give a clearer insight into the implications of such a transnational lifestyle and its embeddedness in diverse social networks.

The case study of Vera Jungwirth: "Two centers of vital interest, two fiscal domiciles, and two tax consultants"

Vera Jungwirth is a 36-year-old political scientist who had been living in New York City for ten years when the interview was carried out. After completing her M.A. in Austria, she obtained an Austrian grant to study at a university in New York. Two years later she received her diploma and her New York M.A. Her advisor encouraged her to apply for a PhD fellowship at that university. She obtained the fellowship, began her PhD studies and went into instructing undergraduates. At the same time, she was part of an Austrian-based research team carrying out independent research projects for Austrian funding institutions. Vera Jungwirth had known most of the members of this research group since her student days in Vienna. Additionally, she cooperated with two scientist friends who – like herself – lived partly in Austria, partly in New York City. At the time of the interview, Mrs. Jungwirth lectured at two universities in New York and at one university in Austria. Additionally, shortly before the interview took place, she had won a prize for her research in Austria, thus stabilizing her financial situation for another two years. After this period, she planned to allocate research funds in the USA, whilst up to that moment, her research funds mainly came from Austrian or European funding sources. During the interview, she was also asked to produce a graphic drawing including her most important interaction partners at that time (Figure 1). To do so, she was provided with a white sheet of paper and two pencils: One coloured green to indicate private relations and another coloured yellow to indicate work relations. The interviewee herself decided to use both colours for several individuals indicated in the drawing.

This drawing is quite complex as compared to others done by our interview partners. After completing her drawing, Mrs. Jungwirth informed me that her husband ("E") should move closer to the center compared to the other persons indicated on the sheet of paper. I then asked her to tell me in detail the meaning of the relationships she entertains with these various persons. Mrs. Jungwirth reacted by telling me the following: As most im-portant interaction partners, she described her husband with whom she lives in New York City and her family living in a small province town in Austria (no. 6). After graduating from a high school in that town, Mrs. Jungwirth moved to Vienna which is one day's travel distance from her parents' home in order to study. She also named a very close friend, a woman from Austria who is also a political scientist living in New York and in Austria ("F" in the graphic drawing above). They often cooperate in re-search projects or coach one another when involved in research teams with others.

Vera Jungwirth described that another two female researchers who also move back and forth between Austria and the USA are very close friends (no. 3 in the drawing). Thus, Mrs. Jungwirth is part of a social network in which many participants are used to continuously move between two places. She pointed out that many other people she meets are also constantly on the move between their places of origin and New York. These contacts were stated as being convenient as she can consult with them about various difficulties arising from their common transnational life style. She pointed out that organizational matters are tremendous once you have employment contracts in two countries. As she has annual teaching assignments in Austria and spends part of the summer holidays there, Vera Jungwirth still rents her Viennese apartment that she shares with a roommate.

Figure 1: Schematic display of an interviewee's graphic drawing (Vera Jungwirth)

E. Husband USA

F. Friend (f) USA/A

1. Professor (f) USA

2. Social scientist (f) A

3. Social Scientists (f) USA/A

4. Befriended scientists A

5. Friends USA

6. Family A/province

7. Friends A/province

8. Colleagues USA

9. Mentor USA

10. Professors USA

Her work and social networking have resulted in many and well-established relations she entertains with important scholars in her research field (no. 1, 9 and 10 in Figure 1). While discussing the insecurities of her present situation as a researcher, Mrs. Jungwirth was at the same time forging strategies of how to cope with the exigencies of the field and her working conditions. Making use of resources (contacts, information, teaching possibilities and research funds) both in Europe and in the USA is crucial for her engagements. Also, the content of her work is characterized by transnational aspects: She perceives her academic work as translating scientific ideas from one side of the Atlantic to the other.

Nevertheless, her economic and working situation at the time of the interview implied precarious plans for the future. It was clear to her that she would not gain a tenure-track position in New York without prior research stays at other institutions in the USA. At any rate, she was decided about living nowhere else than New York City, or another intellectually and culturally important city in the USA. For private reasons, going back to work in Austria was not an option as her husband, an American, did not speak German and thus would barely find adequate employment in Austria. One possibility the couple had discussed before in a long-term perspective was to go to London or perhaps Berlin so that both would have chances to find professional positions in their respective fields. Bearing in mind a cou-ple's rather than an individual's mobility options, Vera Jungwirth was able to reduce the pressure to find an adequate academic position in New York City. However, she felt this position to be highly competitive such that it would leave few realistic chances to make her living as a researcher in the long run. At the moment of the interview, Mrs. Jungwirth still felt she pre-ferred to concentrate on her project that would finance her life for another two more years and take further mobility decisions later on.

Another aspect impairing Vera Jungwirth's mobility aspirations for the future was that she was aware that she would immediately move back home to rural Austria should her aged parents ever need continual care and help. A single child, she made it clear in the interview that there was no other solution to this problem that she saw coming up sooner or later. She mentioned that in general, she avoids thinking about these insecurities, as she could not imagine how her professional and private life, with her husband being in the USA, would develop after leaving for Austria at one time. During other interviews, such gender-specific norms and views about caring for one's parents or small children proved typical for female scientists. While the issue of children and their education was also brought up by male scien-tists who already were fathers, caring for the elderly was of no bearing to them in our interviews.

Conclusions

A look at the impact of social networks on migration and mobility within the discussed project shows to what extent the meaning these highly mobile individuals attach to specific social relations shapes their future mobility aspirations. It is the embeddedness of an individual within these diverse and heterogeneous fields of social relations that we want to understand when studying migration and mobility. Such embeddedness in social relations might also be gendered in some ways, as the case of Vera Jungwirth suggests: Her mobility aspirations depend upon the health state of her aged parents who live in the Austrian periphery. If they would need her assistance, she would be ready to interrupt her work immediately and also to leave the U.S. without her husband. Comparing this case study with other cases analysed in our empirical project, such caring responsibilities have not been brought up by male interviewees. Further research should thus not only investigate the gendered reasons and circumstances for staying "back home" initially (cf. Ackers, 2005), but also for returning.

Summing up, the openness of a qualitative approach and method in this project has proved to be useful in acquiring insights into the individual life worlds of these highly mobile persons. The method presented here allows the interviewees to make their own relevance systems visible by describing the social relations and their specific character in manifold ways. In the discussed project, methodological triangulation was helpful in addressing these issues. Prompting interviewees at the end of PCIs to generate graphic drawings is seen as an appropriate way to collect abundant qualitative data on mobile individuals' heterogeneous social relations. Based on the drawings, the interviewees could reflect upon the various persons they had indicated before without losing track of other actors during the interview. Also, this form of visualizing social relations prompted interviewees to narrate aspects of their migration and mobility decisions that they had not mentioned in the preceding phases of the PCI. Yet the research project discussed here represents only a snapshot in the migration and mobility histories within such social networks. Thus, further research on the impact of social rela-tions maintained by highly mobile persons such as young researchers should be based on empirical data that additionally embraces a longitudinal perspective.

References

Ackers, L. (2004). Managing relationships in peripatetic careers: Scientific mobility in the European Union. Women's Studies International Forum 27: 189-201.

Ackers, L. (2005). Moving People and Knowledge: Scientific Mobility in the European Union. International Migration 43(5): 99-130.

Ackers, L. and Stalford, H. (2007). Managing Multiple Life-Courses: The Influence of Children on Migration Processes in the European Union., in: Clarke, K., Maltby, T. und Kennett, P (eds.), Social Policy Review 19: Analysis and Debate in Social Policy. Bristol, Policy Press.

ARGE MOMO (2000). Räumliche Mobilität und Karrieremobilität von Wissenschaftlerinnen und Wissenschaftlern in Österreich. Wien, Bundesministerium für Bildung, Wissenschaft und Kunst, Forschungsschwerpunkt "Politikrelevante Hochschulforschung: Frauen in Wissenschaft und Forschung".

Bazeley, P. (2003). Defining "early career" in research. Higher Education 45: 257-279.

Benhabib, S. (1992). Gender, Community and Postmodernism in Contemporary Ethics. Polity Press.

Callon M. (1986). The Sociology of the Actor-Network: The Case of the Electric Vehi-cle. In: Callon et al. (eds.), Mapping the Dynamics of Science and Technology. Sociology of Science in the Real World. London: The Macmillan Press ltd, S. 19-34.

Callon M., Latour B. (1981). Unscrewing the Big Leviathan: How Actors Macro-Structure Reality and How Sociologists Help Them to Do So. In: Knorr-Cetina K., Cicourel A. V. (Ed.), Advances in Social Theory and Methodology. Toward an Inte-gration of Micro- and Macro-Sociology. Boston: Routledge, S. 277-303.

Dahinden, J. (2009). Are we all transnationals now? Network transnationalism and transnational subjectivity: the differing impacts of globalization on the inhabit-ants of a small Swiss city. Ethnic and Racial Studies 32 (8): 1365-86.

Faist, T. (2005). Social Space, in: Ritzer, George (Ed.), Encyclopedia of social theory. Thousand Oaks, Sage: 760-763.

Gerodetti, N. and Bieri, S. (2006). (Female hetero)Sexualities in transition: train stations as gateways. Feminist Theory, 7: 69-87.

Gibbons M. et al. (1994). The new production of knowledge. The dynamics of science and research in contemporary societies, Sage.

Glick Schiller, N. (2007). Beyond the Nation-State and Its Units of Analysis: Towards a New Research Agenda for Migration Studies. Essentials of Migration Theory. Transnationalisation and Development(s): Towards a North-South Perspective, Bielefeld, COMCAD.

Gold, S. (2005). Migrant Networks: A Summary and Critique of Relational Approaches to Inter-national Migration. In: Romero, M. and Margolis E. (eds.): The Blackwell Companion to Social Inequalities, Blackwell, pp. 257-285.

Haug, S. (2000). Klassische und neuere Theorien der Migration. Arbeitspapiere Mannheimer Zentrum für Europäische Sozialforschung, http://www.uni-mannheim.de/publications/wp/wp-30.pdf.

Hollstein, B. (2006). Qualitative Methoden und Netzwerkanalyse - ein Widerspruch?, in: Hollstein, Betina und Straus, Florian (eds.), Qualitative Netzwerkanalyse. Konzepte, Methoden, Anwendungen. Wiesbaden, VS Verlag: 11-36.

Johnson, J.M., Regets, M.C. (1998). International Mobility of Scientists and Engineers to the United States – Brain Drain or Brain Circulation? (National Science Foundation). http://www.nsf.gov/sbe/srs/issuebrf/sib983.htm.

Kaplan D. (1998). Migration of the Professional, Semi-Professional and Technical Occupations in South Africa: Past Patterns, Current Trends and Policy. In: Charum J. et al. (eds.), International Scientific Migrations Today, ORSTOM-COLCIENCIAS, CD-ROM, Paris-Bogota 1998.

Kaplan D. et al. (1999). Brain Drain: New Data, New Options. In: http: sansa.nrf.ac.za/tradmon.pdf

Kofman, E. (2000). The Invisibility of Skilled Female Migrants and Gender Relations in Studies of Skilled Migration in Europe. International Journal of Population Ge-ography 6: 45-59.

Kofman, E. (2004). Gendered Global Migrations: Diversity and Stratification. Interna-tional Feminist Journal of Politics, 6 (4): 643-665.

Landes, J. B. (ed.) (1998). Feminism, the Public and the Private, New York: Oxford University Press, 1998.

Lowell, L. B. (2003). The need for policies that meet the needs of all. SciDevNet: Policy Briefs, http://www.scidev.net/en/policy-briefs/the-need-for-policies-that-meet-the-needs-of-all.html.

Mahroum, S. (1999). Highly Skilled Globetrotters: The International Migration of Human Capi-tal. In: Proceedings of the OECD Workshop on Science and Technology Labour Markets, DSTI/STP/TIP(99)2/FINAL, S. 168-185.

Meyer, J.-B. (1996). Fuite des cerveaux: comment mobiliser les compétences expatriés. In: Fiches Scientifiques de IRD, fiche 27.

Meyer, J.-B. und Brown, M. (1999). Scientific Diasporas: A New Approach to the Brain Drain. Management of Social Transformations - MOST Discussion Paper (published by Unesco) No. 41.

Polanyi, M. (1962). Personal knowledge: Towards a post-critical philosophy, New York.

Powell, W. W., and Smith-Doerr, L. (1994). Networks and Economic Life, in: The Handbook of Economic Sociology, Princeton University Press/ Russell Sage Foundation, Princeton New York.

Pries, L. (2008). Transnationalisierung der sozialen Welt. Sozialräume jenseits von Nationalgesell-schaften. Frankfurt/M., Suhrkamp.

Raghuram, P. (2004). The difference that skills make: Gender, Family migration strategies and regulated labour markets. Journal of Ethnic and Migration Studies, 30 (2): 303-321.

Scheibelhofer, E. (2004). Das Problemzentrierte Interview - Möglichkeiten und Grenzen eines Erhebungs- und Auswertungsinstruments. Zeitschrift Sozialwissenschaften und Berufspraxis, 27(1): 75-90.

Scheibelhofer, E. (2005). Mobilitätsperspektiven junger WissenschaftlerInnen im Ausland. SWS Rundschau, 45 (1): 117-139.

Scheibelhofer, E. (2006). Migration, Mobilität und Beziehung im Raum: Netzwerkzeichnungen von InterviewpartnerInnen als interpretative Methode, in: Hollstein, Betina und Straus, Florian (eds.), Qualitative Netzwerkanalyse. Konzepte, Methoden, An¬wendungen, VS Verlag für Sozialwissenschaften: 311-332.

Scheibelhofer, E. (2010). Gendered differences in emigration and mobility perspectives among European researchers working abroad, Migration Letters, 7 (1): 33-41.

Scott, J. (2000). Social network analysis. London, Sage.

Strauss, A. L. and Corbin, J. (1998). Basics of qualitative research: techniques and procedures for developing grounded theory. Thousand Oaks, Sage.

Wasserman, S. and Faust, K. (1994). Social network analysis. Cambridge, Cambridge University Press.

Wimmer, A. (2007). How (not) to think about ethnicity in immigrant societies. Toward a boundary-making perspective. ESRC Working Papers Series WP no. 44.

Witzel, A. (2000). The Problem-Centered Interview, in: Forum Qualitative Sozialforschung/ Forum: Qualitative Social Research 1(1), http: http://www.qualitative-research.net/index.php/fqs/article/view/1132/2522 (last retrieved 31st January 2011).

CHAPTER 9

OVERCOMING CHALLENGES OF INTERNATIONAL MIGRATION RESEARCH: A CASE STUDY APPROACH IN SOUTHERN MEXICO

Julie Boyles

Abstract

An ethnographic case study approach to understanding women's actions and reactions to husbands' emigration -or potential emigration- offers a distinct set of challenges to a U.S.-based researcher. International migration research in a foreign context likely offers challenges in language, culture, lifestyle, as well as potential gender norm impediments. A mixed methods approach contributed to successfully overcoming barriers through an array of research methods, strategies, and tactics, as well as practicing flexibility in data gathering methods. Even this researcher's influence on the research was minimized and alleviated, to a degree, through ascertaining common ground with many of the women. Research with the women of San Juan Guelavía, Oaxaca, Mexico offered numerous and constant challenges, each overcome with ensuing rewards.

Introduction

Emigration from Oaxaca, Mexico is dominated by males (C. Hernandez, Oaxaca State Population Council, personal communication, February 20, 2008; Lowell, Pederzini, & Passel, 2008; Cohen, 2004 & 2008). As many as four males emigrate from Oaxaca for every one female (C. Hernandez; Cohen, 2004). Of Mexico's 31 states and one federal district, the state of Oaxaca ranks third with the lowest ratio of males to females—91.4 males for every 100 females ("México Hoy," 2007: 48). Therefore, male migration impacts a substantial number of Oaxacan women who remain in their rural or semi-rural sending communities.

The majority of migration literature deals with one of four specific topical themes: the lives of migrants in receiving communities (Hellman, 2008; Hirsch, 2003); the debate if remittances foster development *or* dependency (Cohen, 2001, 2004); social networks of migrants and how those social networks serve, abet, dissuade, or challenge migrants (Kanaiaupuni, 2000; Massey & España, 1987); and gendered migration studies of women in a United States context (Hirsch, 2003; Hondagneu-Sotelo, 1994; Parrado, Flippen, & McQuiston, 2005; Pessar, 2005). Considerably less emphasis has been placed on migration research that strives to understand women's challenges within the *sending* community when faced with a husband's emigration, much less, a husband's potential emigration. In general, the literature has often disregarded or omitted the impact on family members who remain behind. Several researchers have addressed the subject of stay-behind or left-behind women (Ahern Bryan and Baca, 1985; Hellman, 2008; Hondagneu-Sotelo, 1994; Stephen, 2007); none, however, have focused on stay-behind or left-behind women as central to their research.[1] Instead, most researchers and writers use the context of the life of stay-behind women as definition and character or background to a related, but separate, migration theme. This gap in migration literature and the high ratio of women left- or remaining-behind led to my decision for dissertation fieldwork in Oaxaca, Mexico. Migration research that incorporated women's lives in relation to male migration, or potential migration, was rewarding, but the myriad of challenges that a semi-rural Oaxacan context presented could not have been adequately anticipated.

An inductive, mixed-method, case study methodology allowed for a type of "bottom up" approach. Research questions were posed within a theoretical framework but with latitude for additional findings to emerge. Empirical details—comments gleaned through casual conversation or open-ended interviews, observations within a humble home or along a dirt path, or opinions or passionate statements gathered from surveys—evolved and emerged from within the context of the case study approach. San Juan Guelavía Health Center data and documents, posted signs in shops along the street, interviews and engaging conversations while wandering through the streets, and attendance at local events all offered valued pieces to the larger picture. Converging lines of inquiry—a process of triangulation—were the most appropriate for this mixed methods, case study approach since neither quantitative nor qualitative data alone could offer a sufficiently-rich picture.

The converging lines of inquiry derived from a variety of empirical sources must be considered within the context of participants' point of view—the "meanings social actors attribute to their social experiences" (Hamel, Dufour, & Fortin, 1993: 31). The meanings that social actors derive and develop from their own experiences and social surroundings establish the direct knowledge and inference that social actors have of their own personal experiences and that of their social community. Their reality is relayed, parleyed, communicated, and conferred through inflicting meaning upon their experiences.

"Social actors" are capable of attributing meaning to the environment from which they come" (Hamel et al., 1993; Bryman, 2004). Empirical details

[1] The only possible exception here is "Migration and La Mujer Fuerte" by Ahern, Bryan, and Bacca, which dates back to 1985.

must be considered within the locale—particularly relevant for a semi-rural setting geographically located near a metropolitan area. While not isolated but not attached or included, semi-rural locations offer unique characteristics. San Juan Guelavía, situated 28 kilometers from the city of Oaxaca, offered research participants that are protective and insular yet fairly informed and resourceful. They have options and opportunities for work. They have, to some extent, educational options for their children. Yet most citizens of Guelavía are also burdened with limits of financial resources and time availabiity to access those resources in nearby larger cities. The case study places value on the meanings that "social actors" (participants) place on their *own* experiences within their *own* geographical context. With the framework developed from the broader associated literature and the larger research context incorporating personal experiences of visiting and living in Mexico, an inductive research approach was undertaken and a context for migration research was sought in the state of Oaxaca, Mexico. A semi-rural locale, San Juan Guelavía, Oaxaca, offered the criteria necessary for this study.

Mixed methods approach to overcoming challenges of migration research design

A mixed-method approach using a case study design was most appropriate and well suited to the inquiry of this research. A survey instrument of every eighth "home" in the community of San Juan Guelavía, Oaxaca gathered demographic data. The quantitative data gathered through surveys were supplemented by open-ended, qualitative responses. Survey questions about husbands' migration status, remittances (or lack thereof), savings, and women's belief of men's future emigration plans, for example, were followed with open-ended questions inquiring as to why women responded as they did and why women thought what they thought. The quantitative data allowed correlations by one of three age categories, by husbands' migration status, and by women's role in decision making, to name just a few. The qualitative responses provided the richness, depth, and complexity of women's lives only communicated and told through women's own responses rather than through simplistic numerical data.

As an example of the richness of enhancing quantitative data with qualitative responses, women with absent husbands where asked if they received remittances and the average amount of those remittances. This data proved valuable. However, asking a follow up question provided insight into women's opinions, thoughts, and ideas. If women did not receive remittances from their U.S.-based husbands, the qualitative follow-up questions inquired as to why they believe they were not receiving or had not previously received remittances. It was this follow-up qualitative question that revealed women's suspicions of their husbands—as well as of Guelavían men, in general—of having relationships. Of the men currently in the United States, many wives and partners believed those relationships negated remittances coming back to their home to, in theory, sustain their family.

A second example of the benefit of a mixed methods approach is an array of questions asked of women with "anchored" husbands.[2] Women with anchored husbands were asked if they thought their family would be economically advantaged if their husbands were to emigrate. The quantitative data showed that women *did not* think their family would be better off. Women's qualitative responses as to *why* revealed that women often chose to dismiss the "economic" aspect of the question and, instead, communicated their prioritization of family unity as well as the value that women place on having the husband and father in the home over the likely economic benefits.

The strategy of using a survey that combined quantitative data responses with open-ended questions offered the sought-after rich data of women's realities in regard to husbands' emigration. Additionally, the observations; the casual conversations in stores, homes, and in the streets; the participation in festivals and events; the interviews with school personnel and town leaders and the eavesdropping on conversations in buses and taxis offered insight into women's challenges with male migration that simply could not have been gained or understood without a mixed methods approach.

Challenges of migration research in a foreign context

Challenges of the researcher on the research

Access, acceptance, and approval in a rural community in southern Mexico for the purposes of research is long and arduous, a process likely amplified for a light-skinned, middle-aged, middle-class, highly-educated, single, female citizen of the United States with adequate, but not perfect, Spanish. I point out these particular characteristics because most of them are in contrast to the majority of San Juan Guelavían women—mostly dark-skinned, indigenous, of lower socioeconomic class, occasionally un- and often under-educated, and married with Spanish, possibly Zapotec, as their primary language of communication of the home and the community. Living alone and traveling by myself further differentiated and distanced me from the vast majority of the community's women. There were numerous occasions that I was asked, with surprise, if I came to Guelavía and the Mexico alone. The valued common ground, however, for connection between many Mexican women and myself was motherhood. Mexican women in any town or the city can relate to motherhood and, from that common ground, many connections were made with communication then flowing more easily, openly, and with enhanced trust.

Luckily, and somewhat strategically, San Juan Guelavía was not a

[2] "Anchored" husbands is my own term for husbands that have not left Guelavía for purposes of emigration, primarily to the United States.

researcher-weary community. I was, on a few occasions, confused with the only other researcher that anyone could recall that had done academic research in the community a few years earlier. When I chose to clarify my own identity, it offered me a chance to illustrate the migration-related research that I was doing and my dogged persistence and interest in understanding how it impacted women in Guelavía.

Challenges of the context

San Juan Guelavía offered explicit, sought-after characteristics for this research project: an average level of male migration (according to INEGI statistics);[3] a high percentage of women who remain in the community when husbands emigrate; and, perceived openness and willingness by women to communicate and share their reality, their opinions, and their perceptions with an outsider. Additionally, adequate access to resources—geographically located near education and work opportunities—was important in that residents would, theoretically, have options and opportunities not possible in most rural communities of Oaxaca. This semi-rural setting, however, also proved to have a negative facet unknown to me when my research began. Numerous women communicated their concerns for their daughters in regard to the negative influences perceived that the city of Oaxaca offered: drinking, drugs, gangs, and promiscuity. This yin and yang of a semi-rural setting proved interesting.

As mentioned by Bryman (2004), "Cases [settings] are often chosen not because they are extreme or unusual in some way but because they will provide a suitable context for certain research questions to be answered" (51). This accurately portrays the validity in choosing San Juan Guelavía. Guelavía offers no outstanding characteristics or traits that would appear to make it unique in Oaxaca's semi-rural context. It is not a thriving weaving community like Teotitlán del Valle, just 11 kilometers across the highway. It is not a craftperson's enclave, like San Martin Tilcajete or Arrazola in the central Oaxaca valley. Nor is it one of the hundreds, likely thousands, of more rural communities populated with elderly residents and a few stay-behind women and children due to very high levels of male emigration to the United States. During the first several visits, Guelavía appeared to match its "high" rating in marginality (fourth of five levels of severity)[4]—not nearly as poor as many rural communities but with poverty as an obvious, noticeable issue. It appeared not to have an excessive migration flow and offered a small array of work-related activities. And, Guelavía is a farming community, like numerous rural and semi-rural Oaxacan communities.

---

[3] INEGI, the *Instituto Nacional de Estadísticas Geografía e Informática* (National Institute of Geographic and Informative Statistics; INEGI), is Mexico's government census agency. INEGI statistics show San Juan Guelavía as a community with an "average" level of migration based on a five-level scale. See http://www.inegi.org.mx.

[4] Based on INEGI data. See http://www.inegi.org.mx.

The public transportation challenges of logistical access to a semi-rural pueblo for my research proved minimal. It was a 45- to 60-minute route, length determined by the perpetual protests throughout the city of Oaxaca, from my humble residence in the city. The advantages of public transportation proved rich. The conversations overheard in the bus, the chats with *collectivo* drivers, and the everyday discussions among those waiting for or exiting public transit became parts of my overall understanding of the life in Guelavía.

While some researchers note the importance of "hanging around" as an essential component of access (Bryman, 2004), I was aware early on of the crucial nature of "being seen." Being seen—and eventually becoming known, first from afar, then from closer in—proved vital for anyone from outside of the community, but indispensable for a white, non-Zapotec, mid-level female Spanish speaker traveling alone and from the United States. The couple months spent wandering, discovering, and being seen proved valuable in a number of ways. I was already somewhat "known" by the time I approached the Guelavía Health Center staff asking for access to their research. I was also well received when I put out the word through Health Center staff that I was looking for responsible research assistants to whom I would pay a small stipend. I was also already known when I approached the *presidente municipal* (similar to a mayor or county commissioner in the United States) for "permission" to conduct research in "his" town.[5] Being seen wandering the town, purchasing items in the small, local *mercado*, and talking with anyone willing to chat proved instrumental in the smooth transition to the more focused, intentful, and systematic portions of the research.

Respecting the traditions, culture, and history of the town should always be an element adhered to and respected by both researchers and tourists. One of the challenges of the culture and respect is the role that gender plays in Mexican society, in general, but in a rural or semi-rural town in southern Mexico especially. Of Oaxaca's 570 *municipios* (similar to a county in the United States), 418 adhere to "*usos y costumbres*" (uses and customs), a semi-autonomous form of local government. "Usos y costumbres" is a governmental system used to elect municipal authorities and prohibit the intervention of electoral political parties (Vázquez García, 2011). Of the 418 *municipios*—each with its own head known as *presidente(a) municipal* (municipal president) —just 18 were headed by women, just 4 percent (31).

The *usos y costumbres* system had, in part, been responsible for a municipal government replete with males in Guelavía with one female in the traditional, typical role as secretary.[6] As in most rural and semi-rural Oaxacan

[5] Noted in quotation marks as his own recurring reference to "his" town.

[6] For a rich and extensive discussion of the correlations between the "usos y costumbres" system of governance, gender, and women's roles, see *Usos y Costumbres y Ciudadanía Femenina: Hablan las Presidentas Municipales de Oaxaca, 1996-2010*, by Vázquez García, primarily chapters 2 and 5.

communities, women participated in the health and education committees of the town, but women are very rarely elected or appointed to any position considered as having power. To conduct research in a Oaxacan *pueblo*, soliciting the permission of the *presidente municipal* in a Oaxacan town is not required, but *is* advised. It shows respect for the power structure and culture of the community. In my case, it also offered affirmation that I had "permission" to conduct research in Guelavía. The widespread challenges of maneuvering through the maze of male administrators to gain access to the *presidente municipal* (after three visits just for this specific purpose) was worth the effort as it exhibited respect for his position and the community of which he was the head. In the initial visit, the *presidente municipal* stridently portrayed Guelavía as a progressive, gender-equal, open-minded community despite any mention on my part of any related topic.[7] In contrast, numerous residents—including the director of a local social community center, a high school teacher, and several venders in the local mercado—spoke of Guelavía as being *more conservative and less gender inclusive* than surrounding pueblos. This contrast in verbiage proved interesting.

I eventually obtained a signed "permission" letter—something not required by my university's institutional review board nor by the Guelavía municipio—that was used during the survey collection process. The letter was presented during the initial introduction to each survey participant.[8] Simultaneously, it was emphasized that all data were confidential and would *not* be shared with anyone from the municipal government nor anyone else. Only one of 72 women that were approached for survey gathering chose not to participate. It is likely that the permission letter played a positive part in that.

Challenges of the survey instrument

During the initial months of visits and being seen in Guelavía, I developed a survey instrument to better understand the women who had experienced a husband or partner's emigration, their views and opinions on male migration, and an array of related topics such as remittances and return migration. The survey generated socio-demographic data, quantitative data of migration, and responses to numerous open-ended questions about women's work, children's education, and women's views and opinions on a wide variety of migration-related topics.

From a language, culture, and ethical perspective, the challenges of the

---

[7] The *presidente municipal* communicated various examples of how Guelavía was different and more progressive than nearby communities. With noticeable pride, he expounded on the fact that many women had run for local political office in Guelavía (which I later found to be untrue). He seemed to communicate stories that he wanted me to hear and views that he wanted me to espouse of Guelavía rather than the likely reality of the town of which he was the head. I understood this response as related to my being female, from U.S. culture, a researcher, and an outsider. Similar examples are noted in Cohen 1999.

[8] The letter was kept in a plastic cover, a sign to most Mexicans of its sense of importance (as suggested by several Oaxacans with whom I consulted throughout my research).

survey instrument were numerous. The survey required grammatically correct Mexican Spanish, but possibly even more importantly, it required wording and phrasing that was familiar and quickly comprehensible by the general female population of Guelavía. Two months was devoted to enhancing, editing, and perfecting the survey instrument to meet these objectives. Three Oaxacans—all from rural or semi-rural towns where Spanish tends to be slightly different than in the city—were continuously consulted on the nuances of each question. While piloting the survey instrument, I noted how quickly women responded to questions taking very little time to contemplate or reflect or to admit that they may not have understood the question. Extensive time was devoted to appropriate wording that quickly and accurately would convey the intent of the question.

Two examples demonstrate the attention required in formulating appropriate questions that would produce the intended data leading to validity in the survey instrument. First, it would be inadequate and would generate inaccurate results to simply inquire if a woman "worked" or even "worked outside of the home." "Working outside of the home" would omit many women that combine domesticity with income-producing activities *within* the home: making (and selling) tortillas; preparing (and selling) tamales, or raising (and selling) *guajolotes* (wild turkeys). Simply inquiring if a woman "worked" would also yield inaccurate or unclear data due to misconstruing domestic work done in the home and for the family and income-producing work. Inquiring if a woman "worked" could also be interpreted as salaried or wage labor and omit women who generate their own income through self-employment. In order to elicit accurate responses in a straight-forward manner, the direct: "*¿Trabaja por dinero*?" (Do you work for money?) was used. This intentionally eliminated domestic, non-paid work within the home, field or crop work for family consumption, and work done for other family members without remuneration. "*¿Qué tipo de trabajo hace para ganar dinero?*" (What type of work do you do to earn money?) was the question that followed in order to emphasize that, in this context, "work" was associated with "income." Women's income-generating activities were important for correlation with husbands' migration status.

A second example of extensive editing that contributed to generating quality data was a question about husbands that had emigrated and were not living in the home or husbands that had previously emigrated, returned, and were, once again, living in the home. After asking women of their husbands' migration status, a follow-up question about remittances was ultimately phrased as, "*Usted recibe remesas/dinero de su esposo quien vive en los EEUU*?" (Do you receive remittances/money from your spouse who lives in the United States [modified for husbands who *had* lived in the United States and had returned]). Due to the sensitive nature of questions involving money (with judgment and social issues wrapped within the framework of migration and remittances), the question was verbally prefaced with informal language: "We understand that issues of migration are sensitive and private, but it would help us to know ...". Additionally, at this point in the survey, confidentiality was reiterated. Appropriate and accurate wording was important so, in this case, "*remesas o dinero*" (remittances or money) was used to ensure that women who were not familiar the more formal "*remesas*" would still clearly, and quickly, understand the question.[9] The carefully constructed wording proved valuable as *every* woman answered the sensitive questions pertaining to migration and remittances without hesitancy. Heightened attention and consideration for questions and topics that may invoke anxiety, hesitation, or confusion require extensive piloting and flexibility in order to yield quality, anticipated responses. Appropriate wording, verbal prefacing, and additional language for potentially unfamiliar terms proved invaluable, especially in relation to the challenges of migration research in an international context.

Challenges of survey data gathering

San Juan Guelavía is an indigenous Zapotec community with the majority of residents speaking both Zapotec and Spanish.[10] A key local informant strongly suggested that two questions regarding indigenous identity, ancestry, and/or language be deleted from the survey. The woman emphatically articulated—abruptly and unmistakably—that *Guelavía is an indigenous community* and that the two questions were unnecessary, "*somos Zapotecos*" (we *are* Zapotec). After further inquiry with several other Guelavians as well as other Oaxacans, the two questions were deleted from the survey instrument.[11]

A primary research assistant and two secondary assistants—`all with at least minimal Zapotec, at least 18 years of age, and high school graduates—were used for survey data gathering, with my primary research assistant also participating in interviews and transcription. The value of using a research assistant in migration research with sensitive topics proved vital. Choosing my valued primary research assistant to assist in conquering the challenges of research in Guelavía proved to be one of my best decisions during my fieldwork. She knew the majority of families in Guelavía, she knew how many small homes existed behind one large *portón* (garage-type door), and she knew which homes were abandoned and which had occupants that may simply be away for the day. Her knowledge of every nook, cranny, alley, and path that

[9] "Envios" was also verbally communicated as a third descriptor if women hesitated or if they appeared to be unclear of the question. "Envios" is a commonly-used term referring to "something sent," but most often understood as money sent from the United States.

[10] According to Health Center data, 66 percent of Guelavíans speak both Spanish and Zapotec, 30 percent speak only Spanish, and just 4 percent of residents speak only Zapotec.

[11] For discussion of what it means to be "indigenous" and the challenges surrounding indigenous identity, see Trine Lunde's (2009) dissertation, "Escaping Poverty: Perceptions from Twelve Indigenous Communities in Southern Mexico." In the case of male emigration and women's experiences, opinions, actions, and reactions for this fieldwork, the designation of "indigenous" was of little importance due to the centralized study of all women of Guelavía.

contained another family home—some of which would have gone unnoticed to an outside researcher without an inside assistant—proved vital to the integrity of the survey data that was gathered in a systematic every-eighth-home manner. Of equal value, she also offered insight to the traditions and culture of the town that an outsider could not possibly know and would never be privy to. She was a young woman with a studious manner, a good reputation in the town, and was a respected member of the community, all of which became obvious during the first few surveys as she was warmly welcomed into *every* home without hesitancy. My research assistant was literally my entry into the lives of women in Guelavía.

The challenges of survey data gathering ensued by approaching every eighth home—from the town center outward—and requesting to speak with the "woman of the home."[12] Greetings were quickly exchanged followed by a brief introduction of myself and my work. Since most women had not previously encountered a U.S.-based researcher and were often perplexed as to my interest in their small community, it was important to elucidate my reasons for choosing Guelavía. This introduction was followed with three components: 1) a visual and verbal description of the *presidente municipal's* letter; 2) a visual and verbal description of the Human Subjects Review Board letter from Portland State University with a copy given to each woman; and 3) a brief verbal discourse on confidentiality with assurance that responses would not be shared with any government administrator and that research assistants were required to keep all information confidential. After agreeing to be surveyed, the research assistant smoothly segued into the initial socio-demographic questions. All survey questions were communicated verbally due to the challenges of illiteracy and, more so, semi-literacy. Women's self-reported data was hand-written by the research assistant.

Since this was a survey instrument and larger research project focused exclusively on *women's* views, opinions, data, and discussion, the challenge of securing confidential, private responses was vital. Some husbands were not working and were present in the home at the time of survey gathering. The challenge of women's responses being overheard by husbands present in the home or yard was overcome early in the survey gathering process by having my research assistant and me entering the home together with each taking a different role. The research assistant asked the survey questions and recorded data. I had the unencumbered flexibility to ask for clarification or elaboration, to observe the women's manner, posture, or multi-tasking capabilities, and to note the home's setting and accoutrements. In regard to potentially interfering husbands, I was able to keep men at bay by playing the role of a naïve, U.S. visitor curious about plants, animals, or construction

[12] Many homes or compounds in rural and semi-rural Oaxaca include more than one residence or living environment. When our knock was answered, our brief introduction included a request to speak with the "woman of the home" determined by the person or persons answering the door. This occurred naturally and appeared to need no additional explanation.

materials located on the other side of the yard or at the back of the house. This collaborative approach proved successful in that all surveys were conducted privately, fully out of listening range of any male of the home.

The early questions of the survey were primarily demographic; the middle portion of the survey included questions of a more sensitive nature. Informal discussions with several Oaxacans from small towns with experience of family migration informed my decision to politely and gracefully exit the survey data-gathering interview prior to the more sensitive questions regarding husbands' migration, remittances, and the possible abandonment by men who had emigrated and never communicated, remitted, or returned to the community or to their homes. These topics were best asked from fellow Mexicans, in this case, from my research assistant. My primary research assistant conducted the majority of survey interviews and her trustworthy nature, her manner, her apparent objectivity, and her reiterated role as a research assistant with the responsibility of confidentiality proved to overcome the challenges that these sensitive questions evoked. The recommendation by several trusted Oaxacans that women's responses would likely be more honest, more complete, and offer more comfort to women if asked by a fellow Mexicana (without the presence of a researcher who they perceived as quite different from themselves) proved successful. We encountered no perceived resistance or disapproval during the discussion of these sensitive topics.

Challenges of semi-structured interviews

Shortly after data survey gathering concluded, a snowball sample was developed for open-ended interviews. A representative sample of women with absent, returned, and anchored husbands was sought.[13] Challenges continued through the series of six interviews, three individual and three two-person interviews.

Social research that involves "real people" brings with it everyday challenges and real life struggles of women, and by default, for the researcher. One woman with an anchored husband that I had chosen for an interview became unavailable due to her husband's recent death. Her husband had fallen in a well the previous weekend at the end of a three-day wedding. Inebriated the last time anyone had seen him and then missing for two days, her husband's body was discovered in the well that, unfortunately, was located next to the outdoor bathroom of the wedding party's home. This tragedy proved to be the most dramatic and sorrowful of the experiences of my fieldwork, but numerous less intense events and challenges also filled my fieldwork.

After selecting six women for four interviews for the first day—two

[13] Three women were interviewed who had not been survey participants. Survey data were gathered on the three women as background information but not included in survey findings.

individual and two two-person interviews—the challenges of time constraints and/or differences in time priorities and commitments for Guelavían women became evident. One woman reported to my primary research assistant that she had arrived 30 minutes early to say that she would not be attending and was upset that I arrived only 15 minutes early. An early arrival was, in my experiences in Guelavía, unheard of. The interview was reset for the following day, but the participant did not show up the following day nor any day thereafter. Four of the remaining five women *never* arrived on that first day even though my research assistant had visited their homes two times with reminders. Only one woman arrived for an interview on the first scheduled day, one-and-one-half hours late. Interviews proceeded at a slow pace over the next few weeks. With Guelavían women often handling a myriad of responsibilities and my research as considerably more important to me than to them, the lack of promptness or even attendance was understandable.

After several weeks, three individual and three two-person extensive interviews were conducted. Each open-ended interview began with a set of questions but with allowance for related topics as well as expansion on topics of greatest interest, passion, or opinion. All interviews were recorded as agreed upon by participants with no hesitancy or trepidation witnessed. They were subsequently transcribed. The recorded interviews proved valuable in contributing much more than notes could convey. The recordings offered details, additional stories, interactions among participants in the two-person interviews, clarifications, phrases, and even verbalized emotion and inflection. One of the most notable examples was a two-woman interview that included extensive dialog back-and-forth between the two women and included strong emotions of anger, sadness, and irritation peppered with bouts of laughter with a lot of crying. The women comforted one another at the times of most intense emotions as they could clearly empathize with one another's experiences and situations. The challenges of interview schedules were outweighed by the depth, richness, sincerity, and complexity of women's discussions in the individual interviews but also between the two women in the two-person interviews.

Conclusions

The ethnographic, mixed methods approach of this case study of women and male migration in San Juan Guelavía offered numerous challenges: the researcher's distinct differences from the participants, the researcher's impact and influence on the research, the culture of the semi-rural Oaxacan context, the language and terminology, and the sensitive nature of many of the migration-related topics. The quantitative data, 71 surveys of every eighth home in the community, formed the essential basis of understanding who women are and about their lives pertaining to their husbands' migration status. The qualitative data—open-ended survey responses, semi-structured interviews, numerous causal conversations and informal interviews, and many months of participation and observation in the town—enriched the results and findings of women's experiences, opinions, and perceptions of men's emigration. The challenges were vast in this ethnographic-based empirical study in vast part due to the challenges of working in an international environment with "social actors" quite different from myself, but therein lies the reward. The challenges and blockages instituted by a range of actors within any research project—often including the researcher herself—were conquered in striving to understand and accurately interpret Guelavían women's opinions, thoughts, ideas, passions, and experiences. The social actors that play the central role in an international context of migration research lay out a minefield of challenges including gender issues, cultural construct differences, language challenges, and meaning interpretation, all overcome, conquered, and valued through determination, compassion, empathy, fortitude, and sensitivity.

References

Ahern, S., Bryan, D., & Baca, R. (1985). Migration and La Mujer Fuerte. *Migration Today, 13*, 14-20.

Bryman, A. (2004). *Social Research Methods*, Second edition. New York: Oxford University Press.

Cohen, J. H. (1999). *Cooperation and Community*. Austin, Texas: University of Texas Press.

Cohen, J. H. (2001). Transnational Migration in Rural Oaxaca, Mexico: Dependency, Development, and the Household. *American Anthropologist, 103*(4), 954-967.

Cohen, J. H. (2004). *The Culture of Migration in Southern Mexico*. Austin, Texas: University of Texas Press.

Cohen, J. H., Rodriguez, L., & Fox, M. (2008). Gender and migration in the Central Valleys of Oaxaca. *International Migration, 46*(1), 79-100.

Hamel, J., Dufour, S., & Fortin, D. (1993). *Study Methods*. Newbury Park, California: Sage Publications, Inc.

Hellman, J. A. (2008). *The World of Mexican Migrants: The Rock and the Hard Place*. New York: New Press.

Hirsch, J. S. (2003). *A Courtship After Marriage: Sexuality and Love in Mexican Transnational Families*. Berkeley: University of California Press.

Hondagneu-Sotelo, P. (1994). *Gendered Transitions: Mexican Experiences of Immigration*. Berkeley, Calif.: University of California Press.

Instituto Nacional de Estadísticas Geografía e Informática. (2007). *México Hoy*. Retrieved from http://www.inegi.org.mx/prod_serv/contenidos/espanol/bvinegi/productos/integracion/pais/mexhoy/2007/MexicoHoy_2007.pdf

Kanaiaupuni, S. M. (2000). Reframing the Migration Question: An Analysis of Men, Women, and Gender in Mexico. *Social Forces, 78*(4), 1311-1347.

Lowell, B. L., Pederzini, C., & Passel, J. (2008). Demography of Mexico-U.S. Migration. In A. E. Latapí & S. F. Martin (Eds.). Mexico-U.S. Migration Management: A Binational Approach. Lanham, MD: Lexington Books.

Massey, D. S., & España, F. G. (1987). The Social Process of International Migration. *Science, 237*, 733-738.

Parrado, E. A., Flippen, C. A., & McQuiston, C. (2005). Migration and Relationship Power among Mexican Women. *Demography*, 42(2), 347-372.

Pessar, P. R. (2005). Women, Gender, and International Migration Across and Beyond the Americas: Inequalities and Limited Empowerment. *Expert Group Meeting on International*

Migration and Development in Latin America and the Caribbean.
Stephen, L. (2007). *Transborder Lives: Indigenous Oaxacans in Mexico, California, and Oregon.* Durham and London: Duke University Press.
Vázquez García, V. (2011). *Usos y Costumbres y Ciudadanía Femenina: Hablan las Presidentas Municipales de Oaxaca, 1996-2010.* Distrito Federal, Mexico: INMUJERES-CONACYT.

CHAPTER 10

DEALING WITH DILEMMAS OF DIFFERENCE - ETHICAL AND PSYCHOLOGICAL CONSIDERATIONS OF "OTHERING" AND "PEER DIALOGUES" IN THE RESEARCH ENCOUNTER

Angela Kühner and Phil C. Langer

Abstract

In this paper we review two qualitative interview studies, in which dilemmas of difference played a decisive role. With regard to the first study, which fo-cused on the influence of migration backgrounds in student's perception of Holocaust Education in Germany, we discuss several research decisions that were made to avoid methodological othering. Concerning a study on HIV risk behavior of gay and bisexual men, psychological challenges of a participa-tory approach that involved peer interviewers are outlined. We ar-gue that strategies of recognition of the "other" - seen as a reflexive agent - have to be developed systematically as an ethical precondition of socially responsible research.

Introduction

In research that deals with experiences of difference (such as race, class, gender or social stigma) a qualitative approach is usually considered as the adequate methodological choice. However, any such research either runs the risk of reproducing the very differences it is interested in by its own research design (Badawia et al. 2003) or of fearfully avoiding othering and essentialist ascriptions and thus underestimating both experiences of "being different" and of "being seen as different". This phenomenon is commonly acknowledged as "dilemma of difference" and several of these dilemmas have so far been critically addressed in the context of a politics of recognition (Benhabib 1996, Taylor 1994) or intercultural pedagogy (Kiesel 1996). As for any dilemma, there cannot be a best research practice that may claim to solve it. The only way to do justice to this dilemma seems to be "reflexivity" – a research attitude rather than a methodological tool, which seems increasingly appreciated in qualitative methodology (Guillemin & Gillam 2004; Mruck & Breuer 2003; Breuer et al. 2002; Finlay 2002; Macbeth 2001). Researchers claiming reflexivity try to be as transparent as possible about how they are part of the process of knowledge production, which is then seen as a joint production of meaning (instead of a one-way self-revelation; see Atkinson and Silverman 1997).

But reflexivity should not be seen as a virtue or ability of researchers only. Members of socially marginalized groups that share experiences of discrimination and living with stigma often may even be more aware than others of how knowledge production and power are entangled. Being subjected to discriminating and symbolically excluding discourses in society, they implicitly know that research meant to learn more about them influences and may (even unintentionally) fuel these discourses. As research subjects they are not just informants, but develop their own interpretation of the research project that may include the intention to cautiously choose, which information they are willing to provide. Yet, the power to control the signifiè is limited. In this perspective statements made by the interviewee can be interpreted as sometimes conscious, often subconscious, communicative reactions to something the interviewer has conveyed or to the wider public discourse that one tries to affirm or resist. Although most qualitative researchers would agree with the argument that interaction dynamics play a decisive role in co-constructing meaning in the interview situation, the far-reaching ethical implications of this perspective often remain underestimated.

What consequences do these considerations have for developing and conducting research projects? In our paper, we want to revisit two previous research projects in which the awareness of stigma, difference, and powerful public discourses played an important role. Both projects were conducted in an interpretative paradigm with strong (self-) reflexive claims. By re-examining the methodological and ethical challenges of dealing with "difference" in these projects we aim at showing the benefits but also the limits of our approaches. We hope that this can contribute to a deeper understanding of the vicissitudes of researching difference and stigma in general.

"We want to talk to you because you are different": Collective memories in an immigrant society

The first study aimed at exploring current challenges in teaching National Socialism and the Holocaust in Germany. One of the central research questions was, whether "globalized classrooms" make a difference in teaching this sensitive subject. The study was designed by an interdisciplinary working group of social psychologists, sociologists, and historians based at the Psychology Department at Munich University. In contrast to observation studies we focused on subjective, retrospective interpretations of how teaching is experienced and remembered both by students and teachers. Thus, semi-structured interviews were carried out with 48 students and 12 teachers in 14 secondary schools of different types in different metropolitan areas, smaller cities and towns as well as rural areas. In this following we will discuss how the supposed "otherness" of interviewed immigrant students was addressed throughout the study by critically reflecting on certain methodological decisions.

First stage: Questioning the research questions

The problem of othering was visible from the very beginning. Our research team was charged with the realization of the study by the "Task Force on International Co-Operation on Holocaust Education, Remembrance and Research", a regular working group of the European Union that was founded after the Stockholm Conference about the future of Holocaust memory in 2001. The group's interest in the study reflected an increasing concern of the representatives about how to teach about National Socialism and the Holocaust in multicultural contexts. They referred to dramatic narratives of teachers who feared to address the topic because of "Arab students", especially male Muslim adolescents who were said to be reluctant against the topic. These reports reminded us of a typical anti-Islamic stereotype in which "the Muslims" are discursively constructed as endangering "our" western progressive achievements – such as "our" elaborated ways of dealing with "our" difficult past(s). The underlying hypothesis of the study that immigrant students were compromising Holocaust Education turned out to be one of the main challenges of the study. There was a strong seduction of actively looking for Muslim male students, finding out and showing what they "really" think and feel.

If we look back and evaluate this first stage of our research we see a group of researchers unified by a self-identification as "sensitive Germans" with a strong commitment towards the topic of Holocaust memory. This commitment and the need to prove our sensitivity to each other - and perhaps also to the implicit international audience - prevented us from investing more time in actively examining the research questions and the interpretations that were presented. We were of course aware of the danger of simply reproducing social phenomena, thus it soon became clear, that we would not simply ask immigrant students or Muslim students. But we did not take the time to really question the hypotheses we were confronted with and to exchange our interpretations of them. From a psychological standpoint, focusing on heterogeneity "outside" led to hide the differences "inside" the research team. Retrospectively it is remarkable how much we talked about examining differences and at the same time seemed to have forgotten all the other differences in gender, sexual orientation, generation and even migration backgrounds present in the research team and the respective differences in priorities and perspectives. The main lesson to be learned from this is that we should have invested more time to critically asses the research question as a first stage of research itself.

Second Stage: Explorative investigations

When we started collecting data, we decided that we should emphasize the explorative character of the study. Thus we did not specifically look for immigrant students at this stage but to remain "open" and describe whatever phenomena would turn up. Interviewers went to school classes, presented the idea of the study and the students themselves could decide, if they wanted to be interviewed.

So our strategy at this point was to try to remain as open as possible, although the idea of an "innocent" researcher or a naïve object of investigation is of course a chimera, as pointed out above. Interestingly, at this stage of collecting data, immigrant students were underrepresented, especially the male Muslim adolescents. We understood this as an active choice and as a possible effect of the stereotyping they may have been feared. This interpretation was implicitly supported by the data analysis: There were many stereotypes about "Turks", some of them brought forward in a dramatically stigmatizing manner, for example in a teacher's statement saying "I don´t know if Turks do think at all". By doing closer analysis we realized, that the statements about what others think or do not think, did not only refer to immigrants or Turks, but to all kind of "others", like "other classes" who were said to have behaved stupidly at a memorial site. Many of them could be reconstructed as projective tendencies. Thus we interpreted that reporting about the thoughts and behavior of others seems to have an important psychological function in this field.

Third Stage: Looking for Immigration Experiences

In another stage of collecting data, we decided to address "immigration" more directly, but still avoid "othering" in the process of investigation. In the same manner as before, interviewers were sent to special classes for immigrant students. In these so-called "integration classes" the students had come to Germany two or three years ago, between the age of ten and fourteen. They were able to compare German memory culture to memory cultures they had been confronted with in their countries of birth. Methodological othering was thus avoided by choosing students who could actively compare experiences in different contexts: "Well", as one student calmly stated, "in Russia they emphasized that we were the good ones and here in Germany they are talking about the suffering of German civilians."

Lessons learned

Looking back, our design, firstly, helped us to reconstruct the function of "othering" in the context of dealing with emotionally difficult collective memories. The integration classes turned out to be a good compromise, which enabled us to address a possible effect of immigration without falling into the traps of methodological othering. As illustrated above, these students did indeed spontaneously compare their different experiences with collective memories. Thus they could really talk about differences and were not just ascribed some otherness. Yet, as a research team we avoided a direct confrontation with the hotter ethical question of how to deal with the strong stereotype of the "ignorant or aggressive Muslim". We pretended to be more open than we were. In a way we fell back behind our own awareness that both, the researcher and the subject of research, at least intuitively know that such research is enmeshed in political discourse and may later feed public debate. Retrospectively, we think most of the immigrant students understood that we were interested in immigrants´ perspectives. Here again, the important point is: We did not ask them - and thus, we do not really know. In the conclusions we will consequently propose to integrate such questions in the research process.

Secondly, the problems we faced can also be seen as typical on research about "migration and memory" (see Kuehner in press). In this context, one interesting path in avoiding essentialism is to replace the idea of researching qualities or practices of certain persons (e.g. by seeing memory as a property) by the idea of researching spaces or places. In this sense one would be interested in interviewees who can tell something about social practices at certain places rather than in exploring how they are like as "different persons". From this perspective our approach was an attempt to choose a place where "multicultural memories" may be relevant – yet this shift of perspective, again, could and should be made more explicitly.

"I want to talk to you because I am the same": Sexual risk behaviour of HIV-positive gay men

Against the background of rising HIV diagnoses in Germany since 2001, the study "Positive Desire" aimed at examining the psychosocial dynamics of sexual risk behaviour among gay men (Langer 2009). The special interest in this group reflects the significance of homosexual ways of transmission in the current epidemic. For this purpose it was envisaged to conduct in-depth interviews with HIV-positive gay men to identify the reasons for HIV-related risk behaviour.

Peer dialogues

The field of HIV/AIDS is commonly seen as highly sensitive, as it is still determined by issues of personal shame and guilt as well as social stigma and discrimination. Any research that asks about "reasons" for behaving risky in terms of HIV transmission – especially with regard to gay men that were stigmatized targets of public discourse from the very beginning of the epidemic – runs the risk of re-stigmatization (Tomso 2009). The study was therefore designed in the tradition of community-based participatory research to responsibly deal with these challenges: The team consisted of HIV-positive and homosexual researchers of different disciplines, community organizations were involved in the design of the study and the process of research. Furthermore, the interviewees were accosted by an HIV-positive gay "peer" as interviewer, using an active interview approach (Holstein & Gubrium 2004) that includes a personal openness of the interviewer about his own story with HIV/AIDS.

The peer approach worked out better than expected. The number of responses to the study notification in community magazines, web forums, and HIV centres exceeded the interview resources by far. Referring to Grounded Theory (Strauss & Corbin 1998), 58 interviews were finally carried out from November 2006 to July 2007. The sample implied a wide range of participants aged 19-72 years, with different socio-economic backgrounds. 17.2% of the interviewees had migration experience.

Beyond its effects on the field access this approach implicated a far-reaching confidence and openness towards the peer interviewer who was perceived to share the same life experiences of being gay and HIV-infected. After the interview some participants reported to have told things e.g. about the infection situation and traumatic life events they had intended not to tell when they first decided to participate in the study. In this respect the reflection of the research process indicates at the importance of the topic of "the limit". Insofar as HIV can be understood as a transgression of limits (of the bodily integrity, of a safer sex norm, of individual responsibility for health), in the interview it seemed to be important for these interviewees to have the power to fix at least the limits of communication about it. The peer approach, however, suspended their intention, so they crossed the line of personal story they had drawn for themselves.

Interestingly, the peer situation in the interview produced the opposite effect in the study as well. The perception of the (desired) "other" as the (desirable) "same" led to affirmative in-group talks in some of the interviews in which established community discourses marked the limit of communication so that "one's own story" could only be told within this given frame. The reference to (assumed) same experiences of being a HIV-positive gay man by the interviewee as well as the interviewer covered up other differences of class, ethnicity, and age. In these interviews narrations dealing with experiences of stigmatization, discrimination, and violence due to migration backgrounds were difficult to develop as soon as a common ground of sexual life experiences was co-founded in the interview. This observation is of particular interest in the context of current intersectionality debates because the interpretation process called attention to the health vulnerability dynamics driven by these multiple experiences.

Methodological decisions

Hence, the peer approach not only presented great opportunities for the research encounter but also posed great challenges for the research process.

How should we deal with the sensitive data that was originally shared in an intimate situation with the HIV-positive positioned peer? What does it mean for the selection of appropriate interpretation methods? Where shall we stop the participation in this participatory approach? Did we not exploit the fantasies of being peers? To what extent is it possible or desirable to reproduce "difference" in this phantasmatic situation of "sameness"?

Three main decisions were made in order to meet with the implications of the peer approach. Firstly, from the very beginning of the interview process a psychological team-supervision was chosen to critically reflect upon the interaction dynamics driven by the peer encounter. It helped to understand the appearance of in-group talks that seemed to be strange to the topic, but nevertheless shed light on sexual decision-making processes. That, secondly, led to an adjustment of methods used for the interpretation. It was necessary to shift the focus of analysis from narrated past experiences of risk behaviour to current interaction dynamics in the interviews which was reflected in the importance of discourse analysis of occurring peer dialogues and their function for the interview. Finally, by appointing a scientific board that included community organizations and people living with HIV/AIDS a way of representative participation has been tried to achieve. In this sense the board used to act for the interests of the participants and critically control the ethical implications of the research.

Lessons learned

Reviewing this HIV study we understand peer interviewing as a powerful way to do research in sensitive fields. However, we would argue that participation should not be stopped or delegated at a certain point as we did after the interviewing. If one takes the participatory approach serious, an integration of the interviewees in the entire research process is constitutive. A (self) positioning of peer interviewers as "the same" (and thus as representatives of "the other") does not solve the dilemma of difference. Instead we would like to follow Frisina's (2006) discussion of the backtalk focus group as a method for a participatory interpretation of data and add the suggestion to involve interested interviewees even in the presentation of the results of a study. In this sense the peer dialogues that were established in the interviews can be continued in the publication as form of a dialogic writing in which the dilemma of difference between the "same" and the "other" appears as a peer co-construction of meaning.

The implications of the peer approach for the interaction dynamics and the production of data should not be seen as biases, but as research resources, wherever a reflexive analysis of the data and knowledge production in the study can methodologically be linked to the research interest. The argument is based on the assumption that in the interaction dynamics the issue at stake is displayed (Jensen & Welzer 2003). The described peer approach of course requires a far-reaching and sometimes painful reflection of one's own position as an highly involved actor in the interviews, an awareness of the "otherness" of the interviewed peer, and a handing-over of interpretation power to the "other" that we address as the "same" (see also Ganga & Scott 2006).

Towards a recognition of the researched subject as reflexive agent

The studies reviewed in this paper showed that there is no simple answer to the questions of how to deal with the dilemmas of difference that are decisive in research dealing with discourses of "otherness". In the first study a more diverse research team may have made it possible to address heterogeneity "inside" the team earlier and may have contributed to a different, more power-sensitive design and to include female heterosexual interviewers in the HIV study could have broken-up the in-group discourses. Both decisions, however, would have had new and different methodological implications to be taken into account.

In qualitative research a strong desire to bridge the gap of difference seems to be inscribed. Therefore it is noteworthy that the methodological construction of differences is constitutive for any knowledge production. Dilemmas of difference thus have to be addressed from the very beginning of a research project to prevent, psychologically speaking, the temptations of a non-reflected identification with the "other" on the one hand or of projective othering on the other. This implies to create an atmosphere of careful reflection from the first research team meetings. If one follows Devereux (1967) any research in the humanities is associated with fear of what one might find out - and could therefore start with an exchange of different fears inside the research team.

Yet, as already said above, the researchers are not the only ones who are able to reflect. Indeed it is imperative to take the researched subject of desire serious as a reflexive agent that is (more or less consciously) aware of possible social and political consequences or instrumentalizations of research. To put this into practice the interviewee has to be addressed much more explicitly as someone who does not only give information (or even authentic self-revelations), but as someone who has his or her own thoughts and interpretations about the research process. This can be done on two levels. Firstly, we propose to systematically use and enlarge what some qualitative interviewers already do - to ask the interviewee throughout her or his perception of the interview and research encounter: Was it "like expected", how was the researcher perceived, does the interviewee fear he or she has said something that will be misunderstood or over-interpreted, what recommendations would he or she give for further interviews? Secondly, we propose to devote one passage of the research encounter to talk about the project on a meta-level. In the HIV study a common discussion with the interviewee about the chances and pitfalls of such a study in general would have been fruitful. In the study on Holocaust Education we could have asked the pupils in the integration classes about their assumptions, why we came to their class and their thoughts about the project.

In the end, this text on dilemmas of difference has to finish with pointing out just another dilemma. By presenting these problems in the context of "methodological issues in migration research" we presume that they are of special relevance in the field of migration. On the one hand considering the outlined discourses, which construct the immigrant as the prototypical "other", we are right to do so. On the other hand this argument can also be misleading and may even be just another, more refined, way of "othering", especially if it suggests that this problem is an additional methodological challenge in migration research.

Yet, we think that the two studies presented here do not only point at additional methodological challenges of research around difference and stigma. Rather these projects forced us to become more sensitive about problems, tensions – or perhaps dilemmas – inherent in the paradigm of subject-related qualitative research. Any interviewee should be recognized as "the other" without being othered. This means that we should always treat the researched subject as someone who can reflect and perhaps has reflected about all these implications too - we may not be the only ones who have read "our" Foucault.

Acknowledgments

It would not have been possible to carry out the studies without the participation and commitment of our interviewees. We owe them a great debt of gratitude! Furthermore, we would like to thank our colleagues in the Holocaust Education Study Group - Gudrun Brockhaus, Daphne Cisneros, Heiner Keupp, Holger Knothe, and Robert Sigel - and the Working Group HIV - Jochen Drewes, Sascha Hübner, and Cornelia Möser. The study „Holocaust Education" was funded by the Bavarian Ministry of Education and Culture and the German Ministry of Foreign Affairs. The study "Positive Desire" was carried out on behalf of the Federal Center of Health Education and the Cometence Network HIV/AIDS and was funded by the Association of Private Health Insurances and GlaxoSmith Kline.

References

Atkinson, P. and Silverman, D. (1997). "Kundera's Immortality: The Interview Society and the Invention of the Self ", *Qualitative Inquiry*, 3(3): 304-325.

Badawia, T., Hamburger, F. and Hummrich, M. (2003). *Wider die Ethnisierung einer Generation. Beiträge zur qualitativen Migrationsforschung.* Frankfurt am Main: IKO-Verlag für Interkulturelle Kommunikation.

Benhabib, S. (1996). *Democracy and Difference*. Princeton: Princeton University Press.

Breuer, F., Mruck, K., and Roth, W.-M. (2002). "Subjectivity and Reflexivity: An Introduction", *Forum: Qualitative Social Research*, 3(3). Retreived form http://nbn-resolving.de/urn:nbn:de:0114-fqs020393.

Devereux, Georges (1967). *From anxiety to method in the behavioral sciences.* The Hague & Paris: Mouton and Cie.

Finlay, L. (2002). "'Outing' the Researcher: The Provenance, Process, and Practice of Reflexivity", *Qualitative Health Research*, 12(4): 531-545.

Frisina, A. (2006). "Back-talk Focus Groups as a Follow-Up Tool in Qualitative Migration Research: The Missing Link?", *Forum: Qualitative Social Research*, 7(3). Retrieved from http://nbn-resolving.de/urn:nbn:de:0114-fqs060352.

Ganga, D. & Scott, S. (2006). "Cultural 'Insiders' and the Issue of Positionality in Qualitative Migration Research: Moving 'Across' and Moving 'Along' Researcher-Participant Divides",*Forum: Qualitative Social Research*, 7(3), Retreived from http://www.qualitative-research.net/index.php/fqs/article/view/134.

Guillemin, M. & Gillam, L. (2004). "Ethics, Reflexivity, and 'Ethically Important Moments' in Research", *Qualitative Inquiry*, 10(2): 261-280.

Holstein, J. A. and Gubrium, J. F. (2004). "The Active Interview", in D. Silverman (ed) *Qualitative Research: Theory, Method and Practice.* Thousand Oaks: Sage.

Jensen, O. and Welzer, H. (2003). "Ein Wort gibt das andere, oder: Selbstreflexivität als Methode", *Forum: Qualitative Social Research*, 4(2). Retrieved from http://www.qualitative-research.net/index.php/fqs/article/view/705/1528.

Kiesel, D. (1996). *Das Dilemma der Differenz. Zur Kritik des Kulturalismus in der interkulturellen Pädagogik.* Frankfurt am Main: Cooperative-Verlag.

Kuehner, A., Langer, P. C. and Sigel, R. (2008). "Ausgewählte Studienergebnisse im Überblick", *Einsichten und Perspektiven*, Special Issue 1: 76-82.

Kuehner, A. (2010, in press). "Die Anderen der Erinnerung. Methodische Überlegungen zur Forschung über „Holocaust Education" in der deutschen Einwanderungsgesellschaft", in E. Boesen & F. Lenz (eds) *Migration und Erinnerung.* Konzepte und Methoden der Forschung.

Langer, P. C. (2009). *Beschädigte Identität. Dynamiken des sexuellen Risikoverhaltens schwuler und bisexueller Männer.* Wiesbaden: VS Verlag für Sozialwissenschaften.

Langer, P. C., Cisneros, D. and Kuehner, A. (2008). "Aktuelle Herausforderungen der schulischen Vermittlung von Nationalsozialismus und Holocaust. Zu Hintergrund, Methodik und Durchfüh- rung der Studie", *Einsichten und Perspektiven*, Special Issue 1: 10-27.

Macbeth, D. (2001). "On 'Reflexivity' in Qualitative Research: Two Readings, and a Third", *Qualitative Inquiry*, 7(1): 35-68.

Mruck, K. & Breuer, F. (2003). "Subjectivity and Reflexivity", *Forum: Qualitative Social Research*, 4(2). Retrieved from http://nbn-resolving.de/urn:nbn:de:0114-fqs0302233.

Strauss, A., & Corbin, J. (1998). *Basics of Qualitative Research. Techniques and Procedures for Developing Grounded Theory.* Thousand Oaks: Sage.

Taylor, C. and Gutmann, A. (ed) (1994). *Multiculturalism and "The Politics of Recognition".* Princeton: Princeton University Press.

CHAPTER 11

FORCED MIGRATION AND PSYCHOSOCIAL HEALTH: MEANING-MAKING THROUGH AUTOBIOGRAPHICAL NARRATIVES IN THE UK

Maria Psoinos

Abstract

This paper explores how refugees in the UK perceive the relation between their experience of migration and their psychosocial health. Autobiograph-ical narrative interviews were carried out with fifteen refugees residing in the UK. The findings reveal a contrast between the negative stereotypes con-cerning refugees' psychosocial health and the participants' own percep-tions. Two of the three emerging narratives suggest a more balanced view of refugees' psychosocial health, since- in contrast to the stereotypes- most participants did not perceive this through the lens of 'vulnerability'. The third narrative revealed that a hostile social context can negatively shape refu-gees' perceptions of their psychosocial health. This runs counter to the ste-reotype of refugees as being exclusively responsible for their 'passiveness' and therefore for the problems they face.

Introduction

This paper explores how refugees in the UK perceive the relation between their experience of migration and their psychosocial health. This aim was triggered by the observation that the 'vulnerable' and 'passive' images are too often assigned to this group when discussing their psychosocial health.

The paper draws from fifteen autobiographical narrative interviews, as part of an original research study, which explored how highly educated refugees in the UK perceive the relation between their post-migration experiences and their psychosocial well-being (Psoinos, 2007). The term 'refugees' here refers to all persons who have been granted by the UK Border Agency either ILR status (Indefinite Leave to Remain) or Refugee status, (as defined in the UN Refugee Convention of 1951).

In the following pages, the paper outlines the main clinical approaches on refugees' psychosocial health, and the negative stereotypes which have emerged from this clinical discourse and have been exacerbated by the media. Then the use of the narrative approach is justified and the interview context is described. The main body of the paper shows –through excerpts from the autobiographical narratives- the participants' perceptions of the relation between their migration experience and their psychosocial health. It also explores whether the stereotypes of the 'vulnerable' and 'passive' refugee are present in the participants' emerging autobiographical narratives. The paper finally discusses how the social context refugees live in influenced the shaping of their perceptions.

How the clinical discourse and the media coverage have contributed to the negative images assigned to refugees in the UK

Traditional clinical approaches such as the 'severe mental illness model' focus on refugees who urgently need clinical help because of severe disorders, often existing prior to migration (Bhugra & Jones, 2001; Silove, 1999). The 'psychopathology approach', which is based on the 'trauma' tradition, pays more attention to the effects of forced migration or post-migration problems (Ingleby, 2005). Finally the 'stress and coping approach' views the migration and psychological health -relation as a series of stressful life changes which demand coping responses, in order for distress to be alleviated (Shuval, 2001).

Even though approaches such as 'stress and coping' meant to provide a less disorder-oriented outlook on this population's psychosocial health, they continue to cultivate a 'pathological' image. In the clinical literature refugees are consistently considered to be vulnerable, that is, prone to distress symptoms such as anxiety, depression, and withdrawal (Ahearn, 2000; McColl & Johnson, 2006).

In addition the 'pathology-prone' approach does not explore holistically refugees' psychosocial health because it is grounded in the assumptions of the primacy of the individual and of the necessity of treating isolated symptoms (Das-Munshi, 2005; Watters, 2001). Due to these assumptions refugees are approached as beings detached from their social environment whose psychological health outcomes can be simply elicited through a questionnaire or an interview (Das-Munshi, 2005).

The clinical discourse has contributed to the construction of specific negative images assigned to refugees, and these images have been reinforced by the media coverage and seem to have become *stereotypes* in Western societies, including the UK (Donnellan, 2002; Hanyes et al., 2004). Indeed in the UK the media frequently portray refugees as prone to serious psychological problems but also as a 'burden' in the local community because they will passively accept their situation and simply "live at taxpayers' expense" (Bailey, 2005; Buchanan et al., 2003). This image of the 'passive' refugee who suffers from distress a*nd* lack of motivation applies mainly to refugees who lost the socioeconomic status they held in their country (Stubbs, 2005).

The 'pathological focus' has received criticism (Bala, 2005; Eastmond, 2000; Summerfield, 2001) and there have been efforts to shift attention to refugees' psychological resources and coping skills (Fozdar & Torezani, 2008; Hunt, 2008; Papadopoulos, 2007). At the same time the 'individualistic focus' has also been criticised and there is growing recognition of the importance of taking into account the *social context* when doing research on refugees' psychosocial health (Halabi, 2005; Powles, 2004).

Why choosing the narrative approach

The narrative approach was chosen precisely after observing that most clinical approaches focus on treating individual symptoms while usually ignoring the social context in which refugees live.

Narratives are means through which people "make sense of an event or of several events that they may have had difficulty in describing so that it becomes true to them" (Parker, 2005: 82). This is why the narrative approach privileges *subjectivity* (Kohler-Riessman, 2001). Of course this conception of individuals as constructing the meaning of their own social psychological world connects them to the context in which they live. Meaning and stories do not just 'emerge from within' the individual but develop through specific interpersonal contexts (Crossley, 2000). The narrative approach also gives prominence to human *creativity* because each individual constructs a unique story based on his/her experiences and interpretations (Faircloth, 1999). This is especially true of difficult life transitions: "respondents narrativise particular experiences in their lives, often where there has been a breach between ideal and real, self and society" (Kohler-Riessman, 1993: 3).

Forced migration is undoubtedly one such difficult life transition, which is why life history and autobiographical narratives are suggested as valuable tools for research in refugee contexts (Mollica, 2001; Rechtman, 2000).

Interview context

Locating channels for meeting refugees required the assistance of gatekeepers thus two organizations were approached, one that assists refugees and another which gives advice and support to ethnic minorities. By undertaking volunteering work in the first organization and becoming a member of the second group it was possible to make contact with refugees residing in the UK.

The research topic was explained to four clients who were interested in participating and they were informed that everything they would say would be kept confidential and that the transcripts would be anonymous. Using the snowball technique, eleven more individuals were recruited. Fifteen narrative interviews were conducted with nine men and six women aged between 25 and 45 years old, had completed undergraduate and/or post-graduate education in their countries and held refugee or ILR status. The interviewees originated from Africa, Eastern Europe and the Middle East, were living in the UK for six years in average and spoke English fluently. Several participants were interviewed in a public place (i.e. coffee shop), one interview was conducted in the organization for ethnic minorities, while a few female interviewees invited the researcher to their houses and were interviewed there.

It is expected that personal characteristics and professional roles of the researcher and the participants strongly influence the interview process (Richards & Emslie, 2000). The researcher was female and a PhD candidate, identities which could have prompted the female interviewees (also highly educated) to construct narratives where 'activism' was rather pronounced. In addition, the fact that all participants and the researcher were non-British could have made them feel more comfortable to discuss their migration experiences and perhaps encouraged them to disclose dissatisfaction with life in the UK because of experienced discrimination (see third narrative story in the next pages). At the same time the fact that the researcher had volunteered in the refugee group which some participants attended, could have indirectly pressured them to praise such organizations. Most participants agreed to be audio-recorded and few expressed their wish not to be recorded in which case hand-written notes were taken. Each interview lasted approximately 1.5 hour.

Interview agenda

Each interview began by using the generative narrative question (Riemann & Schütze, 1987), which intends to stimulate the interviewee's main narrative. The generative research question must be formulated broadly, but at the same time specifically enough for the experiential domain to be taken up as a central theme. The generative question was phrased as follows:

I want to ask you to tell me the story of your migration and how much did things change in your life since you came to the UK. A good way to do this would be to start from the time you first started thinking of migrating and then talk about the things that happened in your life until today. You can take your time in doing this, and also give as many details as you want, because I am interested in everything that is important for you.

The main question was followed by the *narrative enquiries* where narrative sections, not exhaustively detailed before, were completed. For example, according to what they said about others who offered their help, the participants were prompted to elaborate on who helped and how. Finally there was the *balancing phase*, where there are questions aiming at theoretical accounts of what happened and at balancing the story (Schütze, 1983). During this phase the interviewees were asked to discuss their psychosocial health and in particular their present sense of life satisfaction.

Analytic procedure

After reading through the whole interview transcript in order to get the gist of significant themes the three main elements found in every autobiographical narrative, that is, *narrative tone*, *imagery* and *themes* (McAdams, 1993) were identified.

Narrative tone is conveyed in the content of the story and also the manner in which it is told. For example, the tone can be predominantly optimistic or pessimistic. As far as *imagery* is concerned: every autobiographical narrative contains and expresses a characteristic set of images. In order to understand a narrative one must explore the unique way in which the narrator employs images, symbols and metaphors to make sense of who s/he is but also to describe others. Finally the researcher has to look for the dominant *themes* in one's narrative. By focusing on these, one tries to understand what kind of message the narrator tries to convey.

In this study it was important to look at what (content) and how (form) it was said but also under which circumstances it was presented. Parker (2005) identifies certain ideas in narrative analysis that hold the key to the way a story may be heard and retold by a researcher: *temporality*, *event*, *context* and *format*. Temporality refers to the order of telling; context refers to the socio-cultural background against which a narrative is set and format is the manner in which a story is told.

McAdams' (1993) analytic approach takes into consideration most of the above key-ideas. The *tone* in his approach seems to correspond to the *format* Parker (2005) mentions, while *imagery* and *themes* seem to correspond to the *events*. Yet his approach belongs to the individually oriented versions of narrative research. This means that psychological processes are regarded as the source of the strategies people use to shape how they tell their stories. As this approach highlights the importance of exploring the self, it gives less prominence to the contextual basis of a narrative. However in the present study the focus was not on idiosyncratic stories, but on the stories of a distinctive group, in a particular place and time, who constantly interact with others, thus it was crucial to include the dimensions of temporality and context.

Since it was of particular interest to see whether the participants would defy the images of the 'vulnerable' and 'passive' refugee, the interpretation phase began by tracing this 'activism' in the different narratives. It was detected primarily in the solutions/resources they said they used for coping with their problems. When narrative tone, imagery and themes were noted for all sections, those narratives that focused on activation of resources and strong life satisfaction were separated and the first story, i.e. the story of *hope* emerged. The story of *survival* emerged after clustering those narratives that focused on activation of resources but a modest sense of life satisfaction.

Finally, the narratives that mentioned activation of resources but emphasised the *inability to cope* and a present sense of life dissatisfaction produced the story of *disappointment*. The boundaries between the three stories were at times blurred but the dimension of life satisfaction was a good way to distinguish between them because each group of participants appeared through their narratives as very satisfied, not entirely satisfied and unsatisfied respectively.

Presentation of the findings

The story of hope

Four interviewees (three men and one woman, originating from Africa) expressed the relation between their migration experience and their psychosocial health through a narrative of *hope*. This story was detected by noting the *pervasive tone* of narration these participants used: a persistent optimism could be traced in all of these narratives. The general message was that "things will be all right in the future".

In addition, the *imagery* was very positive either towards others (e.g. pointing out how helpful they were) or towards the narrator's self (e.g. portraying one's self as an optimist who does not give up and as happy with one's life).

The *themes* evolved around the problems they faced shortly before migrating to the U.K. (e.g. getting the family's consent) or after migrating (such as language difficulties, finding employment, making friends) and on the actions they took for overcoming these problems (e.g. becoming involved in a refugee group that helped them find work and build social networks). Turning to a support group often emerged as a main theme and others, especially in local organizations and ethnic communities, were presented as the *catalyst* leading to resolutions, while they presented their self as active and determined. Another theme concerned their life satisfaction, as they perceived their present life in the UK in many ways better than life in their country.

As far as form is concerned, the order of telling was rather linear: first the problem was described, then the decision taken for overcoming it was discussed, and the catalyst that helped to reach a solution, while in the end of the section there was sometimes an evaluation of that decision. Turning to the question of context, these participants seemed to be present-oriented but also referred to the future. In addition, they appeared to focus on the place/country they were in at the time of the interview, as there was small reference to their home country. In the extract below, where the narrator discussed key events of her life in the UK, some of these issues were clearly seen:

"The first thing was the language. The second thing that was difficult was the job.

Because I am a professional and I came here and going to work as a cleaner was no good...And the third thing was to have a new life… When I arrived here, I did not speak English at all so I needed to ask my family for many things. So I went to a refugee group and I found there some very good people. Everybody tried to help me. I started to speak a little English and somehow I was not so shy... I tried to make people understand me and I tried to speak by myself because it was no good when I was asking all the time my family... Now I don't miss my country at all. I have made here more friends and I have met people here more honest and kind to me than the people I had met in forty years…So it's all good " (female, accountant, African)

The story of survival

Seven interviewees (five women, two men, originating from Eastern Europe or the Middle East) made sense of the relation between their migration experience and their psychosocial health through a narrative of *survival.* Unlike the *optimistic tone*, noted in the stories of *hope,* a rather *ambivalent tone* could be traced in the narratives of this group. The general message was that "things are very hard while living in the UK" and that "one has to keep on trying to make it through".

The *imagery* used for others was positive (e.g. portraying other people as helpful) and negative (e.g. pointing out how they can be unfriendly and biased). The self-imagery was also positive (e.g. presenting one's self as active and persistent) and negative (e.g. unsatisfied with one's life).

The *themes* were similar to those mentioned in the story of *hope*, e.g. pre-migration issues such as getting the family's consent to migrate. The themes referred also to post-migration difficulties, such as finding employment, and building social networks and the solutions they found for addressing these. However in the story of *survival* the emphasis was on how difficulties *remained*, unlike the previous group, where the themes evolved around *resolutions.* Another theme concerned their psychosocial health: they were feeling satisfied with certain things, but discussed how they still had to strive to achieve more and be fully satisfied.

With regards to temporality, the order of telling seemed circular: first a problem was described, then the decision taken for resolving it was explained, along with an evaluation of that decision, and in the end the focus was on the persisting problem. In terms of context, the participants appeared to be oriented at the present time and place. The following extract, where the interviewee narrated her first experiences in the UK, illustrates some of the above:

"The reason why I came to the UK and not another country is that I had a friend here…I could not speak the language, so I needed her. The beginning was awful because I could not speak the language.. it was already very difficult to work…and being alien to

the culture, you know, it was very difficult. Later that friend left, she went back because her visa expired…Then I had some contact with a (local support) group. I don't want to say they were not helpful, but I have to be honest that I didn't quite understand what they were doing and I did not benefit a lot from them. When I started learning the language I knew what I was doing so I just tried to find out things myself. I don't think I found a lot of information from groups, I read all the leaflets and then found out my own way through the system. I tried to live with myself and I went to University and that helped me a lot, I had an aim I suppose… also now I can travel and that makes a difference" (female, graduate in social sciences, Middle Eastern)

The story of disappointment

Finally, four interviewees (all men, originating from the Middle East) made sense of the relation between their migration experience and their psychosocial health through a narrative of *disappointment*. A *pessimistic tone* could be traced in their stories and the emphasis was placed on difficulties that *remained*, but unlike the narratives of *survival* where people took action to improve their lives, the general message was that "the present is bad so there is no point in hoping for a better future".

The *imagery* was mainly negative (e.g. others in the community portrayed as unfriendly). The self-imagery was positive when they discussed pre-migration times (e.g. presenting one's self as strong and active), but primarily negative when they talked about post-migration experiences (e.g. presenting one's self as unmotivated).

As far as *themes* were concerned: as in the stories of *hope* and *survival* this group talked about problems that made them leave their country, and post-migration difficulties, such as finding housing and employment and meeting others in the community. However, what was different in the story of *disappointment* is that, while discussing these problems, the emphasis was put on that one should neither hope nor persistently try to resolve them. This is why these participants did not discuss any solutions for tackling their problems, but elaborated on additional complications (e.g. local agency not helping them with finding employment). Actually how others in the community discouraged them from addressing their problems, was an important theme in this story, as seen in the extract below. Another theme referred to their life dissatisfaction in the UK, a feeling that was reinforced when they were contemplating the positive aspects of life in their country.

With regards to temporality, the order of telling was static, as a problematic situation was discussed, along with the catalyst that predisposed them and then a negative evaluation of the situation followed. In terms of context, they were oriented at the present time and place, but also referred to the past:

"When I visited the Home Office that was a very important experience for me, you know, in terms of contact with the agencies. The experience was absolutely bad. They treat everyone, all the people who come to England as people who will exploit the system, like parasites. That's how I actually felt when I first went there to apply for asylum. Later we had just problems. For some time we were actually living in a room, the housing problem was very difficult to solve… In general I believe that culture is a very complex thing…I believe understanding or living in a different culture is a very difficult thing to do…This is the general and big problem for all foreigners, all immigrants, whatever you call it, it is just a very difficult thing for everybody" (male, graduate in political sciences, Middle Eastern)

The influence of the social context in shaping the participants' perceptions

From the above it is clear that most participants did not perceive their experiences and their psychosocial health necessarily through the 'pathology' focus. But narratives are not reducible to individual sense-making ways, so the *social context* which influenced differently the formulation of their perceptions should also be explored.

Refugees often meet their compatriots (Daley, 2009) as well as other refugees in the community-context, e.g. in local organisations (Green, 2005; Tomlinson & Egan, 2002). In this study there were two ways in which such interactions influenced the shaping of the participants' perceptions: all narrators of the story of *hope* and some of the story of *survival* acknowledged the help they received from local organizations and this seemed to shape positively their perceptions. These participants also discussed in a positive way the interactions with their compatriots in the UK.

But some of the participants who presented the story of *survival* and all narrators of the story *of disappointment* regarded local organizations in a critical way because they discouraged them with regards to their resettlement prospects. Moreover the third subgroup was confronted by suspicion not only from local agents but also from co-ethnics. This subgroup consisted of four Muslim men originating from the Middle East, a population which in the contemporary 'Islamophobic context' (Sheridan, 2006) is perceived as unwanted- even by compatriots who are all competing over limited resources- and is consistently marginalised (Weller et al., 2001). Negativity surrounds also refugees of other ethnic background, e.g. Africans and former-Yugoslavs, but it is expressed more as indifference (Gibney, 1999) and less as hostility. Then it is by far not a coincidence that these four participants constructed the most pessimistic narrative and perceived so negatively their psychosocial health (Laird et al. 2007). In some ways through their narrative of disappointment they emerged as 'passive' but, unlike what clinical approaches focusing on decontextualised symptoms support, this was not an intra-individual trait but an attitude they developed when attempts to restore their lives were thwarted.

Conclusions

This study challenges the negative stereotypes assigned to refugees but the possibility of a high proportion of them feeling vulnerable and passive - as often reported in clinical research- cannot be dismissed. Nevertheless the above findings highlight the importance of 'giving voice' to refugees in order for their own understandings to emerge and to gain insight into how their psychosocial health can be promoted.

The findings are significant both in terms of policy and practice: The practical implications are that clinicians and social carers can use the typology of *hope*, *survival* and *disappointment* for diagnostic and therapeutic purposes when working with refugees. The policy implications are that experts who design health and social care services for refugees but also for asylum seekers and other migrants, by consulting service-users more closely and eliciting their own understandings of their experiences and needs, can suggest appropriate interventions that may enhance these populations' well-being.

It should be noted that it is not possible to see whether the image of 'activism' is relevant to all refugees, since the study focused on a small sample. Moreover, the participants were atypical when compared to other refugees because they were highly educated and their balanced psychosocial profile could be partly attributed to their educational background. Future research should therefore explore to what extent the findings apply to other populations through a larger and diverse refugee sample.

References

Ahearn, F.L. (2000). "Psychosocial wellness: methodological approaches to the study of refugees", in F. L. Ahearn (Ed) *Psychosocial Wellness of Refugees: Issues in Qualitative and Quantitative Research, Studies in Forced Migration, Vol. 7,* New York: Berghahn Books.

Bailey, O. (2005). *Multiculturalism and alternative diasporic media: In search for visibility*. Paper presented at the conference "The future of multicultural Britain: Meeting across Boundaries", Roehampton University, London.

Bala, J. (2005). "Beyond the personal pain: Integrating social and political concerns in therapy with refugees", in D. Ingleby (Ed) *Forced Migration and Mental Health: Rethinking the Care of Refugees and Displaced Persons*, New York: Springer.

Bhugra, D. and Jones, P. (2001). "Migration and mental illness", *Advances in Psychiatric Treatment*, 7: 216-223.

Buchanan, S., Grillo, B. and Threadgold, T. (2003). *What's the story? Results from research into media coverage of refugees and asylum seekers in the U.K.* London: Article 19.

Crossley, M.L. (2000). *Introducing Narrative Psychology: Self, Trauma and the Construction of Meaning.* Buckingham: Open University Press.

Daley, C. (2009). "Exploring community connections: community cohesion and refugee integration at a local level", *Community Development Journal,* 44(2): 158-171.

Das-Munshi, J. (2005). "Post-traumatic stress disorder; or how to make yourself a traumatised body without organs", *Social Theory and Health*, 3: 16-38.

Donnellan, C. (2002). *The Refugee Crisis.* Cambridge: Independence.

Eastmond, M. (2000). "Refugees and health: Ethnographic approaches", in F. L. Ahearn (Ed)

Psychosocial Wellness of Refugees: Issues in Qualitative and Quantitative Research, Studies in Forced Migration, Vol. 7, New York: Berghahn Books.

Faircloth, C.A. (1999). "Revisiting thematisation in the narrative study of epilepsy", *Sociology of Health and Illness*, 21(2): 209-27.

Fozdar, F. and Torezani, S. (2008). "Discrimination and well-being: perceptions of refugees in Western Australia", *International Migration Review*, 42(1): 30-63.

Gibney, M. J. (1999). *Observations on the Kosovo crisis: popular and unpopular refugees*. Available on: www.asylumsupport.info/publications.htm.

Green, A. (2005). *Local Integration of Immigrants into the Labour Market: U.K. case study- The Case of Refugees in London*. London Development Agency.

Halabi, J.O. (2005). "Nursing research with refugee clients: A call for more qualitative approaches", *International Nursing Review*, 52: 270-275.

Hanyes, A., Devereux, E. and Breen, M. (2004). *A cosy consensus on deviant discourse: How the refugee and asylum seeker meta-narrative has endorsed an interpretive crisis in relation to the transnational politics of the world's displaced persons*, Working Paper WP 2004-03. University of Limerick, Department of Sociology Working Paper Series.

Hunt, L. (2008). "Women asylum seekers and refugees: Opportunities, constraints and the role of agency", *Social Policy and Society*, 7(3): 281-292.

Ingleby, D. (2005). *Forced Migration and Mental Health: Rethinking the Care of Migrants and Displaced Persons*. New York: Springer.

Kohler-Riessman, C. (1993). *Narrative analysis, Qualitative research methods series, Vol.30*. Newbury Park, CA: Sage.

_____. (2001). "Analysis of personal narratives", in J. F. Gubrium and J. A. Holstein (Eds) *Handbook of Interviewing*, London: Sage.

Laird, L.D., Amer, M.M., Barnett, E.D. & Barnes, L.L. (2007). "Muslim patients and health disparities in the U.K. and the U.S.", *Archives of Disease in Childhood*, 92: 922-926.

McAdams, D. (1993). *The Stories we Live by: Personal myths and the Making of the Self*. New York: Morrow.

_____. (1998). "The role of defense in the life story", *Journal of Personality*, 66(6): 1125-1146.

McColl, H., and Johnson, S. (2006). "Characteristics and needs of asylum seekers and refugees in contact with London community mental health teams: a descriptive investigation", *Social Psychiatry and Psychiatric Epidemiology*, 41(10): 789-95.

Mollica, R.F. (2001). "The trauma story: a phenomenological approach to the traumatic life experiences of refugee survivors", *Psychiatry*, 64(1): 60-63.

Papadopoulos, R.K. (2007). "Refugees, trauma and adversity-activated development", *European Journal of Psychotherapy and Counselling*, 9(3): 301-312.

Parker, I. (2005). *Qualitative psychology: Introducing Radical Research*. Buckingham: Open University Press.

Powles, J. (2004). *Life history and personal narrative: theoretical and methodological issues relevant to research and evaluation in refugee contexts*. Working Paper No. 106, Evaluation and Policy Analysis Unit: UNHCR, Geneva.

Psoinos, M. (2007). *The relation between post-migration experiences and psychosocial well-being: an exploratory study of the perceptions of highly educated refugees in the U.K.* Unpublished PhD thesis, Queens' College, University of Cambridge, Cambridge, U.K.

Rechtman, R. (2000). "Stories of trauma and idioms of distress: from cultural narratives to clinical assessment", *Transcultural Psychiatry*, 37: 403-15.

Richards, H. and Emslie, C. (2000). "The 'doctor' or the 'girl from the University'? Considering the influence of professional roles on qualitative interviewing", *Family Practice*, 17(1): 71-75.

Riemann, G. and F. Schutze. (1987). "Trajectory as a basic theoretical concept for analysing suffering and disorderly social processes", in D. Maines (Ed) *Social Organisation and Social Process- Essays in Honor of Anselm Strauss*, New York: Aldine de Gruyter.

Schütze, F. (1983). "Biographieforschung und narratives Interview", *Neue Praxis*, 3: 283-93.

Sheridan, L.P. (2006). "Islamophobia pre- and post-September 11th, 2001", *Journal of*

Interpersonal Violence, 21(3): 317-36.
Shuval, J.T. (2001). "Migration, health and stress", in W.C. Cockerham (Ed) *The Blackwell Companion to Medical Sociology*, Oxford: Blackwell.
Silove, D. (1999). "The psychosocial effects of torture, mass human rights violations and refugee traumas", *Journal of Nervous and Mental Disease*, 187: 200-207.
Stubbs, S. (2005). "The politics of migration", in T. Pilch (Ed) *Perspectives on Migration*, London: The Smith Institute.
Summerfield, D. (2001). "The invention of post-traumatic stress disorder and the social usefulness of a psychiatric category", *British Medical Journal,* 322: 95-98.
Tomlinson, F. and Egan, S. (2002) 'From marginalization to (dis)empowerment: Organizing training and employment services for refugees' *Human Relations*, 55(8): 1019-1043.
Watters, C. (2001). "Emerging paradigms in the mental health care of refugees", *Social Science and Medicine*, 52: 1709-1718.
Weller, P., Feldman, A. and Purdam, K. (2001). *Religious Discrimination in England and Wales.* Home Office Research Study 220. London: Home Office.

CHAPTER 12

MIGRATION, LIFE NARRATIVES, MEMORY AND SUBJECTIVITY: REFLECTIONS ON AN ARCHIVAL PROJECT ON IRISH MIGRATION

Breda Gray

Abstract

This article considers three theoretical approaches (late-modern, post-modern and femi-nist) to the apparent obsession with self-narration and memory in the early twenty-first century as they relate to an archival project on Irish migration. This archival project fo-cused on the life narratives of those who witnessed mass out-migration from 1950s Ire-land. The article reflects on the extent to which this project and the motivations of both the researchers and contributors reflect these theoretical accounts of the biographical turn.

Introduction

Life narratives, as Sally Alexander argues, tell us 'something of what has been forgotten in cultural memory' because they 'always describe or rehearse a history full of affective subjectivity' (1994: 234) They give us access to what Foucault calls 'subjectification': this includes evidence for the ways in which human beings 'turn themselves into subjects and actively initiate their own self-formation into meaning-giving selves' (1982: 208; Rabinow, 1984:12). In addition, they provide clues to the nature of remembering and how it 'binds individuals into subjectivities and collectivities' (Kuhn, 1997). However, in order to remember, it is necessary to locate memories within 'meaningful narrative sequences' (Connerton, 1989: 26). The flux of memories is brought into a meaningful framework through narrative, which also makes events 'memorable over time' and produces a 'shareable world' (Kearney, 2002:3; emphasis in original). Narrative is, therefore, central to memory, subjectivity and community. However, only some narratives are permissible or 'tellable' at specific moments in time (Plummer, 2001: 186). Nearly half a century after the decade of highest out-migration from Ireland in the twentieth century, I directed a life narrative project focusing on how those who stayed experienced the mass emigration of family members and friends and constructed themselves as staying subjects. The aim was to capture experiences of social change during and since this decade as these narratives reflect on the public and private ways in which migration was negotiated at the time and since. These narratives, it was hoped, would reveal the meanings that individuals attributed to the events of emigration/staying, thus producing 'both deep and dense understandings of processes and interactions' and enabling us to 'grasp movement through time...but also movement through life course...' (Smart, 2007: 42).

Over 400,000 people emigrated from the Republic of Ireland in the 1950s, about two-thirds of these going to Britain. This out-migration was shaped by and reinforced a social structure that preserved the interests of 'the possessing classes' (secure farming, business, bureaucratic and professional classes) (Lee, 1989). However, both emigrants and those who benefited from their departure contributed to the reproduction of particular class, gender and familial relations in Ireland. Questions of who stayed and who left, therefore, need to be considered both in relation to the structure of Irish society at the time and how this in turn structured private familial dynamics of migration. The *Breaking the Silence: Staying 'at home' in an emigrant society project* (based at the Irish Centre for Migration Studies, University College Cork) collected 78 audio and 12 textual life narratives between 2000 and 2002. The goal of the project was to document and archive individual experiences of staying in Ireland in the 1950s, while these experiences were still available in living memory. The aim was to record the ways in which individuals accounted for the process, experience and decision making regarding staying or emigrating in this decade and the subsequent implications for the lived life. The target population was people who stayed and who were in the 65-74 age bracket at the time of interview for the project. Some individuals who emigrated and returned were included because of their particular interest in questions of staying-put and in some cases because they identified themselves as the ones who stayed.

An interview guide was used, which began with each interviewee's time and place of birth, and then loosely directed them through their life course, focusing in detail on their negotiations of staying or emigrating and ending with questions relating to their circumstances at the time of the interview. Although this interview guide influenced the narrative, it was primarily used as a checklist to ensure that certain topics were covered, rather than as a rigidly administered interviewing tool. The interviews usually took place in the interviewee's home and digitally recorded interviews lasted for periods of between one and four hours, with longer interviews taking place over two meetings. The enthusiastic response from potential and actual contributors to this project points to the continuing significance of mid-twentieth-century decisions to emigrate or stay-put in structuring subjectivity in Ireland at the beginning of the twenty-first century.

Until recently, most social scientists collected material for the specific purposes of meeting their own research aims. In this archival project, the aim was to produce a university library-based oral archive and an internet based archive.[1] This involved the traditional archiving of the life narratives on CD-Rom with all accompanying documentation and materials for serious academic research purposes and an Internet archive of 50 life-narratives with appropriate copyright permission. While many researchers are now depositing their data in archives, there have been fewer efforts to make the information more accessible to the individuals and communities who have offered their time and thoughts so willingly. The potential audience for an internet-based archive will include family members, relatives, friends as well as unknown web-users. With this in mind, many contributors to the *Breaking the Silence* project requested that edits be made to the published version (the library archive holds the original recordings) and their requests were always followed. For further background to the project and to listen to those life narratives with written permission for publication on the internet see http://migration.ucc.ie/oralarchive/.

My aim in this article is not to discuss the findings from this research but rather to focus on the project of producing an archive of life narratives and what many see as a contemporary obsession with recording, archiving and memorialising. I ask whether this project is symptomatic of our cultural moment and what both my own motivation to set up the project and the enthusiasm of participants to take part can tell us about the memory and life narratives at this time. For example, the project could be seen as in keeping with an intensified interest in the practice of telling, listening to, but perhaps most significantly recording and archiving life narratives as useful modes of historical and experiential reconstruction in a time of rapid change (Perks and Thompson, 1998). As generational memories wane due to the 'speed of technological modernization' (Huyssen 1995, p. 3), the *Breaking the Silence* project could also be seen as creating what Nora (1994) calls *lieux de mémoire* or sites of memory by using digital sound recordings and new technological storage equipment and the Internet to establish an archive of life narratives.

Recent theoretical debates locate this renewal of interest in narrating the self and collective memory within specific theorisations of social change. My aim here is to address three approaches to the theorisation of life narrative and the self that speak to the project of archiving life narratives of migration and staying-put. The first of these is the view of sociologists such as Anthony Giddens (1990) and Ulrich Beck (1992), who regard 'biographical autonomy' as a central characteristic of the late modern self. The second is the argument posited by Andreas Huyssen (1995) and others that fragmented narratives of the self are produced by globalising technologies and postmodern consumer culture. Finally, I examine the assertion that contemporary concerns with memoir and testimony represent a kind of superficial feminised culture.

[1] The concept of an internet-based archive with an accessible interface was developed by the Director of the Irish Centre for Migration Studies, Piaras MacÉinrí.

Narrating the life and memorialising –symptoms of late modernity

If in modernity 'we are fated to be free' then, in Weberian terms, we become responsible for the consequences of our actions and our life-course has to 'be ordered by ourselves' (Lash and Friedman, 1992:5). Late modernity, identified with Western societies in the latter decades of the twentieth and first decade of the twenty-first century, is characterised by increased individualisation and a fragmentation of traditional categories of belonging. Individualisation, understood as the compulsion to create and manage one's own biography at a time when most aspects of life become options amongst numerous possibilities, is identified by some sociologists as a central feature of contemporary social change (see Bauman 2001 and Beck and Beck-Gernsheim, 2002). The individual is seen as gaining primacy over community with the effect that 'biographical autonomy' becomes the central attribute of the late modern subject. Thus, Giddens argues that the self is a reflexive project in-so-far-as 'we are not what we are but what we make of ourselves', and goes on to claim that because the individual is confronted by rapid social change, personal meaninglessness becomes a problem of late modernity, to which tradition and memory are posited as potential solutions (1991: 5 and 75).

According to this view, the individual is engaged in a constant process of self-monitoring and an integrated sense of self is produced through narrative. As Giddens explains: 'A reflexively ordered narrative of self-identity provides the means of giving coherence to the finite lifespan, given changing external circumstances' (1991: 76 and 215). Furthermore, the perceived decline in the significance of traditional categories of identity such as class, gender, nation and religion and the rules and models that kept these in place, are understood as progressively releasing the individual from external forms of authority which, the argument goes, are being replaced by the authority of the individual who is involved in an ongoing process of self-invention (Adkins, 2002). In the context of late modernity, then, 'the standard biography becomes a chosen biography' (ibid.; see also Beck 1994). As globalisation, consumer culture and individualisation became more characteristic of Irish society in the early 2000s, similar analyses were being applied to 'Celtic Tiger' Irish subjectivities (Coulter, 2003).

The life narratives collected as part of the *Breaking the Silence* project both challenge and support sociological characterisations of chosen biographies and the late-modern self. Some of the narratives of migrants and non-migrants supported what are seen as late-modern reflexively inhabited modes of Irish femininity and masculinity, but legacies of 'traditional' categories of gender and class are also evident in regulating available feminine and masculine selves through these narratives. The 'sedimented habituality' of cultural norms, which are often mediated by particular modes of gender relations, mean that the individual is never a totally free agent but is embedded in cultural history; a product of both continuity and change (Smart, 2007:26). As researcher, I was conscious of a proliferation of repertoires of the self in early twenty-first century Ireland, but I was also conscious that transgenerational family narratives of the life experiences that continued to limit or constrain biography choices. As Smart argues '[t]he repetition of certain stories is a way of "fixing" certain cultural understandings' and despite the speed of social change since the latter decades of the twentieth century, this archive of life narratives is a reminder of the power of memories 'laid down' in childhood and early adulthood and the shadows they cast on both the lived life and narratives of the self (Smart, 2007: 94-5).

Narrating the self and the 'presentism' of postmodern culture

Theorists of postmodernity posit the fragmented, dispersed self as its exemplary subject (Baudrillard, 1994). This is often linked to new modes of remembering. Huyssen argues that in a postmodern world, memory works in fragmentary and chaotic ways, rather than in the consistent mode of memory associated with nation-state modernity. In the Irish context, Roy Foster argues that the memory frame of the national liberation narrative is being replaced by the 'presentism' of memoir, heritage and commemoration culture, practices of remembering which, he argues, involve new modes of memory regulation, including the celebration of only certain forms of memoir and a selective approach to the past (Foster 2001; see also Gray 2002, 2003). The perceived presentism of public culture in early-twenty-first-century Ireland is also associated with the amnesia of televisual instant entertainment and the spread of a consumer culture saturated with images of 'how young Ireland shops, dines and plays' (Coulter 2003: 16 and 13). Indeed, many contributors articulated a wish to contribute to the archive because in their experience younger generations showed disinterest or impatience with the life stories of parents and grandparents. Many also noted that in the drive towards economic development and the dominance of consumer culture, stories of poverty and survival in the past evoked shame and discomfort.

In his discussion of stories and changing modalities of memory, Richard Kearney suggests that in the 'cyber world of the third millennium' we are encountering the end of the story, which is displaced by depthless simulation, chat shows, parody and pastiche (Kearney, 2002). This culture is seen as surrendering the individual to an eternal presentness marked by moments of transience and the instantaneous, so that notions of a unified self and narrativised self-identity have to be revised (Lury, 1998: 106). Kearney argues that a 'vulgarisation' of intimacy and privacy via television chat shows and radio phone-ins means that the human need 'to say something meaningful in a narratively structured way' is being continually undermined (Kearney, 2002:10).

At the same time, however, Kearney is optimistic that new technologies and fragmented modes of remembering, rather than heralding the end of the narrative, will produce new relationships between memory and narrative, and with them 'alternative possibilities of narration' (2002: 12). George Marcus implies a similar synergy between new technologies and autobiographical genres. He argues that in 'the electronic information age' individual autobiography and personal testimony have gained new significance because they communicate historical experiences in personalised and accessible ways. Collective representations, he argues, are 'most effectively filtered through personal representations' at a time when 'the long-term memory function of orality and story-telling' is being displaced (Marcus, 1992:312). So while postmodern theorists of memory and the self suggest fragmentation, inconsistency and presentism, theorists such as Kearney and Marcus see technologically mediated postmodern societies as holding the potential for new modes of memory, narration and the self to emerge.

By recording life narratives, archiving them for the use of future researchers and publishing those with required consent and copyright on the internet, the *Breaking the Silence* project offered an alternative to media 'sound-bite' culture and a means of overcoming the absence of an audience in the present. The archival project and the technologies of digital recording and archiving enable non-synchronous telling and listening, thus producing otherwise unavailable modes of remembering and telling the self to emerge.

Life narration and the 'post-feminist', feminised public sphere

The proliferation of memoirs and media programmes based on personal testimony is also identified with feminine modes of telling and with forms of feminist politics (Summerfield, 2000:106). For example, Nancy K. Miller draws attention to the 'ambiguous back and forth between lives and stories, between experience and history' that has been central to the development of feminism, but which has also, perhaps in less positive ways, fed into 'the evolution of confessional culture in the nineties more generally' (Miller, 2002: xiv). The project of making the private public has, she suggests, contributed to transformations in women's lives since the 1960s, though it is easily denigrated as part of what has developed into a 'climate of over-the-top self-revelation' at the turn of the century (2002:1). Miller argues that autobiography, memoir, confession and life-telling are all genres of our contemporary culture, but that we need to be able to distinguish between the different sites and practices of these genres and their disparate effects. In an attempt to recover some of the potential for what she calls the 'memoir boom', Miller suggests that this should not be understood 'as a proliferation of self-serving representations of individualistic memory but as an aid or a spur to keep cultural memory alive [...]. Indeed, the point of memoir [...] is to keep alive the notion that experience can take the form of art and that remembering is a guide to living' (Miller, 2002:14).

The proliferation of phone-in radio shows and genre of the 'miserable Irish childhood' memoirs since the 1990s has, on the one hand, contributed to reproducing an ephemeral confessional culture, while on the other hand, opening up important public questions, as for example, in the case of testimonies of child physical and sexual abuse in Catholic Church-run residential schools, other church contexts and in families. This archive, which was developed as an archive for future researchers, includes guided life narratives that address migration and staying in Ireland in the 1950s and the impact on the subsequent lived life. The use of new technologies to reach research and wider public audiences and the fieldnotes and archival materials that accompany the library archive reflect the reflexive turn in research methodology and bring together the researchers' drive to know and understand with personal lives as narrated in a specific time/space.

Conclusion

The scholarly codes that shaped the conception and conduct of this project locate it outside of the contemporary confessional genres. Nonetheless, it is important to acknowledge that the telling may have been publicly and privately legitimated by a culture saturated by testimonies and narratives of the self. The enthusiasm on the part of the narrators for recorded self narration may not have been so true of 1950s Ireland, or at least the act of narration would be framed differently. However, the project can be seen as simultaneously reinforcing the 'biographical autonomy' that Giddens identifies with late modernity and producing an accessible mode of memory in response to the amnesiac culture discussed by Huyssen. Perhaps most importantly, the project offers the opportunity to scrutinise the presentation and uses of memory and self-narration in early twenty-first-century Ireland.

A sound archive such as this one, which is based on oral narratives, privileges the spoken word above the written word as its evidence or data. The recording itself is the original source and holds a wealth of detail unobtainable from written sources. For example, the accents of the interviewer and interviewee, hesitancies, stresses on certain words or statements, changes in tone, whispered or raised voices, all give more insight into the subject matter and interview dynamics than written words alone can convey. The oral interview, therefore, includes both substantive data and meta-information on the research process itself. As the interviewer and interviewee collaborate in the production of the life story, the conditions of this production are made more accessible by the opportunity to listen to the interviews themselves. Documenting historical and cultural memory brings with it questions, debates and responsibilities regarding process, standards, accessibility, representation and ethics (Gray 2008). The project tracked and recorded as much as possible about the research process and decisions made along the way and included this information and detailed fieldnotes in the library archive (Boole Library, University College Cork). Future researchers will, therefore, be able to locate their analysis in the context of the life story collection and archiving processes.

An archive of life stories embodies social relations and selective memories in its form, content and context of collection. It is evidence of relationships to the past, present and future at a particular moment in time and offers a point of reference with regard to how narratives of migration and staying-put are framed at different points in time and space and through particular contexts and practices of telling. The act of memorialising in narrating, collection and archiving tells us something about the relationship between the self and the social at the time of compilation as well as about the substantive topic of migration. The *Breaking the Silence* archive can be read as evidence of the impetus towards biographical autonomy in late modernity, but also reveals the deeply relational nature of all biographies and the particularly reflexive biographies of those whose lives are lived in a context of mass migration. The multiplicity of stories contained therein will facilitate constant re-interpretation and retellings and as the social context changes, so also will the questions that are brought to bear on these narratives.

Acknowledgements

Thank you to all who took part in this project as contributors to the archive and as researchers. I am also grateful to the three anonymous reviewers for their helpful feedback on an earlier version of this paper.

References

Adkins, L. (2002). *Revisions: gender & sexuality in late modernity*, Buckingham: Open University Press.

Alexander S. (1994). *Becoming a Woman and Other Essays in 19th and 20th Century Feminist History*, London: Virago Press.

Baudrillard, J. (1994). "'Holocaust' and 'History': A Retro Scenario", in J. Baudrillard, *Simulacra and Simulation*, Ann Arbor: University of Michigan Press.

Bauman, Z. (2001). *The Individualized Society*, Cambridge: Polity.

Beck and E. Beck-Gernsheim, (2002). *Individualization*, London: Sage.

Beck, U. (1994). "The reinvention of politics: towards a theory of reflexive modernization", in U. Beck, A. Giddens and S. Lash (eds.), *Reflexive Modernization: Politics, Tradition and Aesthetics in the Modern Social Order*, Cambridge: Polity.

Beck, U. (1992) .*Risk Society: Towards a New Modernity*, London: Sage.

Connerton, P. (1989). *How Societies Remember*, Cambridge: Cambridge University Press.

Coulter, C. (2003). "The End of Irish history? An introduction to the book", in Coulter and Coleman (eds.) *The End of Irish history? Critical reflections on the Celtic Tiger*, Manchester: Manchester University Press, pp. 1-33.

Foster, R. F. (2001). *The Irish Story. Telling Tales and Making it up in Ireland*, London: Allen Lane.

Foucault, M. (1982). "The Subject and Power", in H. Drefus and P. Rabinow, *Michel Foucault: Beyond Structuralism and Hermeneutics*, Chicago: University of Chicago Press.

Giddens, A. (1990). *The Consequences of Modernity*, Cambridge: Polity.

Giddens, A. (1991). *Modernity and Self-Identity*, Cambridge: Polity.

Gray (2008) 'Putting emotion and reflexivity to work in researching migration', *Sociology*, 42(4) 2008, pp. 919-936

Gray, B. (2007). "Breaking the Silence: emigration, gender and the making of Irish cultural memory", in L. Harte (ed.) *Modern Irish Autobiography: Self, Nation and Society*, Basingstoke: Palgrave, pp. 111-31.

Gray, B. (2003). "Global Modernities and the Gendered Epic of the Irish Empire", in S. Ahmed, C. Castaneda, A.M. Fortier and M. Sheller (eds.) *Uprootings/Reqroundings. Questions of Home and Migration*, Oxford: Berg, pp.157-78.

Gray, B. (2002) "Breaking the Silence" - Questions of staying and going in 1950s Ireland", *Irish Journal of Psychology* (Special Issue on Diaspora), 23(3-4), pp.158-83.

Huyssen, A. (1995). *Twilight Memories: Marking Time in a Culture of Amnesia*, New York: Routledge.

Kearney, R. (2002). *On Stories*, London: Routledge.

Kuhn, A (1997). "Memory and Textuality", paper presented at *Time and Value Conference*, Lancaster University, 10-13 April.

Lash, S. and Friedman, J. (1992). "Introduction: subjectivity and modernity's Other", in S. Lash and J. Friedman (eds.), *Modernity and Identity*, Oxford: Blackwell.

Lee, J. J. (1989). *Ireland 1912 - 1985: politics and society*, Cambridge: Cambridge University Press.

Lury, C. (1998). *Prosthetic Culture. Photography, Memory and Identity*, London: Routledge.

Marcus, G. (1992). "Past, present and emergent identities: requirements for ethnographies of late twentieth-century modernity worldwide" in Lash and Friedman (eds.), *Modernity and Identity,* Oxford: Blackwell, pp 309-27.

Miller, N. K. (2002). *But Enough About Me. Why We Read Other People's Lives,* New York: Columbia University Press.

Nora, P. (1994). "Between Memory and History: Les lieux de mémoire", in G. Fabre & R. O'Meally (Eds.), *History and Memory in African-American Culture*, Oxford: Oxford University Press, pp. 284-300.

Perks R. and A. Thomson, (1998). "Introduction", in R. Perks and A. Thomson (ed.) *The Oral History Reader*, London: Routledge, pp. viv-xiii

Plummer, K. (2001). *Documents of Life 2: An invitation to a critical humanism*, London: Sage.

Rabinow, P. (1984). "Introduction", in: *The Foucault Reader, An Introduction to Foucault's Thought*, London: Penguin.

Smart, C. (2007). *Personal Life. New Directions in Sociological Thinking*, Cambridge: Polity.

Summerfield, P. (2000). "Dis/composing the subject: intersubjectivities in oral history" in T. Cosslett, C. Lury and P. Summerfield (eds.), *Feminism and Autobiography. Texts, Theories and Methods*, London: Routledge, pp. 91-106.

CHAPTER 13

A MOBILE LIFE STORY: TRACING HOPEFULNESS IN THE LIFE AND DREAMS OF A YOUNG IVORIAN MIGRANT

Jesper Bjarnesen

Abstract

The analysis suggests an adaptation of the life history interview as a method in qualita-tive migration studies. By joining four analytical concepts into an overall methodologi-cal framework, the mobile life story is intended to guide the exploration of the subjec-tive experiences of migrants at various stages of a migrant trajectory. The notion of 'mobility' evokes a holistic orientation in the study of migrant biographies; the unpre-dictability that characterises the social practice of migrants is captured through the con-cept of 'hopefulness'; the concept of 'vital conjunctures' is argued to provide a tem-poral delimitation and a focus for the organising of a life history interview; and the spa-tial dimension of the methodology is delimited through the concept of 'emplacement'. As opposed to a migration history, the mobile life story explores the significant trans-formations that have characterised the migrant's past and relates these defining mo-ments to the broader migration history.

This chapter suggests an adaptation of the life history interview as a method in qualitative migration studies, based on the insights of anthropological studies of African youth and migration. As an illustration of the proposed method of the *mobile life story*, I draw on my own material from Korhogo, a regional town in northern Côte d'Ivoire, where I have conducted qualitative interviews and extended participant observation in an attempt to understand the aspirations, decision making processes, and practices surrounding young people's mobility in the wake of the country's recent political crisis[1].

A Conceptual Outline of the Method of the Mobile Life Story

By way of delimiting the method of the mobile life story, this section considers four analytical concepts that are fundamental to the approach; mobility, hope, vital conjunctures, and emplacement. In conjunction, these concepts delimit an interview method that includes formal interviews, casual conversations as well as (participant) observations within the same

[1] Since the following is a conceptual and methodological argument, and due to the restricted space, I include very sparse information about the field site and the socio-political context of the study. A fuller analysis of young people's mobility in Korhogo would obviously require a more detailed account of such information.

methodology, with the goal of pursuing the subjective experiences of migrants, with particular attention to their migrant trajectories. The method further illuminates not only the retrospective, as inherent in the life history interview, but also the prospective; the potentiality of the present, projected into the future.

Mobility: Towards a holistic appreciation of migration

A central premise of the project that I am conducting in northern Côte d'Ivoire[2] is that ethnography of migrant aspirations and practices requires a thorough appreciation of the broader socio-cultural context within which these aspirations are formulated, and these practices prepared and initiated[3]. In this vein, a recent edited volume (Nyberg Sørensen & Olwig 2002) suggests a more holistic approach in migration studies, captured in the concept of *mobile livelihoods*, which considers not only the entire migration spectrum of aspiration-preparation-realisation-return but also the experiences and influences of those who stay behind when a migrant departs. The editors argue that '… mobile populations do not necessarily migrate to start a new life elsewhere, but rather to search out new opportunities that may allow them to enhance and diversify livelihoods practiced and valued back home (Nyberg Sørensen & Olwig 2002:1)'. Mobile livelihoods, then, may be seen to encompass more than merely wage labour and include the broader socially and culturally embedded project of creating a meaningful life, or what Lisa Åkesson (2004) has called *life-making*. 'People say that the meaning of their migration project is to *fazé um vida* (make a life)', Åkesson explains. 'Life-making is associated with livelihood, but it also signifies the transformation of an unfulfilling life into a potentially fulfilled one. The desire to migrate and make a life is therefore intimately connected with local notions of what constitutes a good life' (Åkesson 2004:22).

Thinking of young West Africans' migration as a mobile livelihood achieves a broadening of our inquiry, to accommodate our understanding of migrant biographies at various stages in a migratory process. Retaining this holistic approach, the concept of life-making in itself implies that an individual migratory project makes little sense without an appreciation of the social context within which it is formulated, prepared, and put into practice.

As the following incorporation of the concept of *hope* into the analysis will clarify, the underlying premise for the opening up of the conventional life history interview is that neither aspirations nor trajectories remain stable and predictable over time – and neither do the retrospective accounts of past

[2] I have, so far, conducted two fieldwork periods of four weeks in Korhogo, the regional capital of northern Côte d'Ivoire, as a part of a PhD programme in cultural anthropology at Uppsala University. An additional fieldwork period of eleven months is planned to begin in January 2010.

[3] This has led me to formulate my research interest as a study of mobility rather than migration per se – an approach inspired by a recent literature with a similar subject matter (de Bruijn, van Dijk & Foeken 2001; e.g. Carling 2002; Lindquist 2002; see also Bjarnesen 2007; Langevang 2007).

stages in the migratory project.

Hope: Understanding aspirations in subjunctivity

When trying to understand the ways in which young people in Korhogo attempt to anticipate and influence their life trajectories, and how migration plans or practices figure into this broader project of life-making, the concept of hope might better capture the uncertainty and unpredictability that characterises these anticipations than, say, the notions of aspirations or agency, which tend to emphasise the capacity of the individual to steer a course through life; to envision a future and act in order to make it happen. As such, an attention to hope might better combine the active aspirations and practices of the hoper with the social (and metaphysical, cf. Crapanzano 2004:100) forces that are seen to influence the possible or past outcomes of specific hopes. In this way, an attention to hope aligns with Henrik Vigh's notion of *social navigation* which is inspired by the term "*dubriagem*" that young combatants in Guinea-Bissau used (see Vigh 2006:129) to express what was needed to manage in the difficult times that young people face in a country torn by war and poverty:

> *As we seek to move within a turbulent and unstable socio-political environment we are at the same time being moved by currents, shifts and tides, requiring that we constantly have to attune our action and trajectory to the movement of the environment we move through. Social navigation may thus involve detours, unwilling displacement, losing our way and, not least, redrawing trajectories and tactics. Social navigation in this perspective is the tactical movement of agents within a moving element. It is motion within motion (Vigh 2006:14)*

Vigh's transfer of the navigational metaphor from the map, and the solid terrain it represents, to the constantly moving sea provides a framework that is sensitive to the force of external influences on the possibilities of the individual. In this way, it highlights the unpredictability that faces the agent in social navigation: an aspect that points simultaneously to the predicaments of migrant itineraries and the ways in which they may be seen as akin to the more general existential challenges of life-making. As Susan Reynolds Whyte argues, 'where people are negotiating uncertainty and possibility, subjunctivity is an aspect of subjectivity' (Reynolds Whyte 2002:174-75).

In this understanding, uncertainty is not just a momentary doubt, but a fundamental premise of social life – that inspires action as much as it constrains it; '…it is not just doubt, but hope for a better future that hangs on the ifs and maybes' (Reynolds Whyte 2002:177; see also Weiss 2004:14). Although this sense of potentiality is characteristic of social life in general, I would argue that both the promise and uncertainty of subjunctivity is acutely felt by people on the move and should therefore form a cornerstone in the research of migrant biographies. As subjective experience this double-sided uncertainty may be seen as expressed through the ambiguity of *hopefulness*; we hope because we are at once trusting and fearful of what is to come. Finally, we should note that hoping takes on several different forms, with varying temporal horizons and varying degrees of specificity[4].

Having proposed a holistic orientation in the study of migrant biographies and argued for an attention to the underlying subjunctivity of a life-making project that characterises this broader context within which a migrant biography takes shape, I now turn to two concepts that might help delimit the investigation and orient the mobile life story. The first, the *vital conjuncture*, delimits a temporal dimension while the second, *emplacement*, suggests a spatial delimitation.

Vital Conjunctures: Deconstructing the Life Cycle in Life History Interviewing

As a number of recent anthropological studies[5] have argued, studying the social worlds of young people in Africa is a particularly illuminating prism for appreciating wider social dynamics, in part but not only because of the demographical dominance of people under the age of 25 years in Sub-Saharan Africa.

What these studies have shown is that being a young person in many African societies implies an inferior social status and a time of dependency and lack of influence. The anthropology of youth illustrates that achieving social adulthood is not a natural consequence of increased (biological) age but is rather related to the active achievement of social recognition (see Cole & Durham 2008:6 for an authoritative statement of this argument).

This understanding has methodological implications, since the use of the life history interview is in most cases – more or less consciously – structured chronologically, and in relation to the transitional landmarks of the life cycle, for example initiation, marriage, the birth of the first child, etc. Jennifer Johnson-Hanks (2002) found that, for her Cameroonian informants, this chronology of defining events in the life cycle could not be taken for granted and there seemed to be no significant overall correspondences in the sequence or timing of these events.

She argues instead that we think of a defining moment in a person's life as a *vital conjuncture*, which she defines as 'a socially structured zone of possibility that emerges around specific periods of potential transformation in a life or lives. It is a temporary configuration of possible change, a duration

[4] This is illustrated by Darren Webb who outlines an entire taxonomy of different 'modes of hoping' (see (Webb 2007)).

[5] Several edited volumes have been published in the past few years on this topic, (including Abbink & van Kessel 2005; Honwana & De Boeck 2005; Christiansen, Utas & Vigh 2006; Cole & Durham 2007), as well as a number of monographs applying a youth oriented approach to specific empirical fields, (e.g. Utas 2003; Vigh 2006). Furthermore, the anthropology of youth has been discussed in research articles, (most notably Durham 2000; Bucholtz 2002; Durham 2004; Cole 2005).

of uncertainty and potential' (Johnson-Hanks 2002:871). The significant point here is that the nature of these potential transformations cannot be taken for granted a priori, but are to be explored in each case. From a methodological point of view, a life history interview cannot simply fill in the blanks of a ready-made timeline but must explore which significant changes have characterised a person's life and what the nature of these transformations were.

It is here that the mobile life story may serve as a useful methodological tool for the study of migrant biographies. As opposed to a migration history, the mobile life story explores the significant transformations that have characterised the migrant's past and relates these vital conjunctures to the broader migration history. Some moves are often more significant, or transformative, than others and it requires the analyst's acute attention to appreciate these nuances – as opposed to simply mapping the various journeys or locations that have brought the migrant to the present moment. Furthermore, Johnson-Hanks' definition of a vital conjuncture should bring the previous discussion of the concept of *hope* to mind, since this latter notion is precisely suitable for analysing the subjunctive nature of social navigation. In this sense, both concepts point to the prospective; the *in potentia*; life in the making. They thereby open up the life history interview to include possible futures in a migrant biography.

Before proceeding to demonstrate the application of the mobile life story to a case from Korhogo, a final concept is necessary to specify the locus of vital conjunctures in migrant biographies, and to indicate a data collection technique that assures a sufficiently thorough appreciation of past vital conjunctures.

Emplacement: Locating Migrant Biographies

Conceptual discussions of the concept of place have dominated cultural geography and anthropology for the past two decades (cf. Casey 2001). In terms of methodology, this has made ethnographers uneasy about the delimitation of 'sites' in which to conduct fieldwork (see Gupta & Ferguson 1997) and about what significance to ascribe to the locality in which we encounter informants. In his (2002) article 'Ethnography after Globalism: Migration and Emplacement in Malawi', anthropologist Harri Englund suggests 'an approach to emplacement that discloses ethnographic subjects as *situated* in specific historical conditions that are as much embodied as they are discursively imagined' (Englund 2002:263). Drawing on insights from phenomenological anthropology, this approach challenges both the modernist conceptions of place as a bounded social unit and the strictly constructivist approaches that place all their emphasis on the ability of actors to imagine their position in the world, thereby neglecting the situatedness and historicity of these imaginations. Englund's solution to what he calls the 'ethnographic doubt about local-global distinctions' (Englund 2004:276) is to acknowledge 'the futility of disconnecting culture from place' (ibid.) and appreciate that the challenge of ethnography lies in focusing on the meanings ascribed to particular places and to further analyse the meanings ascribed to *the experience* of places, that is, to distinguish analytically between a place that the actor imagines and a place the actor is situated in.

In this way, Englund's appropriation of Edward Casey's (2001) concept of emplacement encompasses the dynamics between the everyday realities of the here-and-now, the imaginings of future life situations, and aspirations towards mobility, that characterise migrant biographies – in West Africa and probably beyond. When exploring migrant biographies through the mobile life story, we might therefore investigate the subject's account of *past emplacements*. This implies that, rather than simply mapping geographical locations, an appreciation of the migrant's subjective experiences requires us to probe the social contexts and individual emotions that characterised previous life situations.

Having outlined the four main concepts that orient the mobile life story, the following section illustrates its relevance to the study of migrant biographies by applying the method to the biography of an informant[6], Moudi, whom I met in Korhogo and followed for one month in April/May 2008 and another month in November/December. The account is based on continuous interviews and casual conversations, as well as participant observation during this time; techniques that are all standard to the ethnographic method and necessary for the collection of a mobile life story.

Moudi's Mobile Life Story

A Mobile Life in Retrospect

Moudi lives in a house that his maternal uncle, 'Big Moudi', rents for 50.000 franc CFA[7] per month in a neighbourhood called 'Quartier Quartorze (14)'. His mother lives in Abidjan where she sells vegetables at the market. His father is in France, where he has remarried and had two children, whom Moudi has never met. Big Moudi who rents the house, moved to Abidjan one year ago, following the bankruptcy of the cotton company that he was the regional director of. He does not seem to be planning a return to Korhogo but rather to be preparing to end the contract on the house. He now works for an Abidjan-based company that sells palm oil.

---

[6] The case is chosen from a sample that, so far, includes ten informants with whom I have had regular contact since April 2008. The data include fieldnotes from participant observation and casual conversations and fifteen recorded qualitative interviews of between one and three hours' duration. The sample will be expanded during following fieldwork periods. Although the ethnographic method does not warrant statistical representativity, I feel confident in arguing that the case of Moudi is far from unique in the region and that his example illustrates a more general phenomenon.

[7] Approximately 75 €.

When Big Moudi moved his family to Abidjan, he needed someone to look after the house in his absence. This task was given to Moudi, after a meeting between Moudi's mother and her older brother. Moudi divides his time between keeping the house in order and working as an apprentice at a nearby garage – a job that his uncle has ensured him as part of the agreement.

Moudi was born in the bété village of Kani, in the west. He never went to school – only Koranic school – because his parents did not want him to. Following the divorce of his parents, he was brought to his paternal grandmother in Gagnoa, with only him and another child in the family courtyard. His grandmother took good care of him, and helped him get an apprenticeship in a garage. She was the one who had encouraged him to take up that line of work, and she had meant very much to Moudi. When she passed away, he remained in her house in Gagnoa all by himself. He had no way of contacting his mother, and no money for the ticket to Abidjan, so he was stuck there for two years before he was able to save enough money for the ticket. The ticket was 3.000 franc CFA[8] and he would put money aside, one penny at a time: when he earned 200 franc CFA at the garage, one coin would go into his savings.

His mother had been shocked to see him when he first arrived: he was so thin and wearing only rags. He had enjoyed life in Abidjan. His family had arranged a job for him, and he had his own money to spend on clothes and girls and having fun. When his uncle had told him about his wish for Moudi to come to Korhogo, a smaller regional town, Moudi had been very disappointed: "*Non, il y'avait un grand parti de moi qui voulait rester là bas, vraiment, je n'était pas content, quoi*"[9], he told me. There was a great part of him that wanted to remain in Abidjan; he agreed to go but did not feel he had a choice in the matter.

Anticipating a Vital Conjuncture?

Moudi's girlfriend, Cristelle, also lives in the house in Quartier 14. Moudi was hesitant to bring her, since they were all men living there, but her parents had insisted that she move when they found out that she was pregnant. She is due in June.

Moudi would have liked to marry Cristelle and take responsibility for the child, but with the ways things are it is too tough – '*c'est dure!*'; and he has no means of making it by himself. If he goes to Abidjan, he would want to take Cristelle and the baby with him but he probably wouldn't be able to take care of them on his own. If Moudi was able to decide he would remain in Korhogo and establish himself there. But he does not think that likely: if Big Moudi ends the contract on the house Moudi would have to move

[8] Approximately 5 €.

[9] No, there was a great part of me that wanted to stay there, really, I wasn't happy, you know.

somewhere else and then he thinks he would prefer to go back to Abidjan.

During my stay in Moudi's house in Korhogo, Big Moudi gave word that he was preparing for Moudi to return to Abidjan to work in the same garage as before and eventually open his own when the time was right. Big Moudi would invest in the garage and Moudi would run it for him. Big Moudi would be ending the contract on the house in Quartier 14 within a few months. Moudi was told to send his ID papers to Abidjan by courier for renewal, and to be ready to leave when everything was ready.

Moudi's current emplacement in Korhogo was drawing to an end but his migrant trajectory remained uncertain until the last minute. Ahead of him were several minor and major moves; the journey to the capital to be installed as a mechanic under the continued patronage of his uncle or the move out of the house in Quartier 14, into a more independent but much less promising tomorrow – and several variations of these two basic alternatives over which he had some, but far from complete, influence. Both moves could potentially become vital conjunctures in that they could achieve a stable livelihood or the setting up of his own household, respectively. But by the time I rejoined Moudi in mid-November, his move to Abidjan had proved to be just another minor change in his life-making, since he had neither been able to begin work in the garage of his uncle nor to take responsibility for his girlfriend and their newborn son.

Conclusion: Tracing Hopefulness

Moudi's mobile life story reverberates with mobility, as well as with hopes and anxieties: his narrative is characterised by a sequence of emplacements that can be related to hopefulness, in the sense discussed above. When Moudi was suddenly left on his own in his grandmother's house in Gagnoa, he was forced to start articulating hopes for himself – in a sense an expression of his increasing maturity. It was the hope of seeing his mother again that kept him devoted to putting money aside over such a long time; an objective that needed no horizon beyond the point of its achievement. Reaching his mother in Abidjan seems to have been the end-goal of Moudi's hopes at that point in time – perhaps because of the destabilized social world he was emplaced in at the time[10]. It was only once this objective was achieved that he began to think ahead. His time in Abidjan gave him a chance to envision a more distant future, as he came to articulate his hope of making it on his own, possibly as the manager of a garage.

As we approach the present of Moudi's narrative, his hopes seem to centre on the patronage of Big Moudi. It is a more patient kind of hope that fluctuates between hoping that his uncle's promises will materialise on the one hand, and that Moudi would somehow be able to free himself from that

[10] We could think of de Certeau's (1984) distinction between *tactics* and *strategies* here: the less resourceful a person is, the shorter his horizon of possibilities.

dependency on the other.

The notion of a mobile life story emphasises that we should see Moudi's story as a *life history*, in the sense of being a narrated ordering of his past from a particular standpoint, and that this ordering projects itself into his possible futures. Both Moudi's hopes for the future and his reflections on his past reflect his orientations in the present[11]. As a *mobile* life story, Moudi's narrative is structured by significant moves; the move to his grandmother when his parents divorced; to Abidjan when he was able to save up money for the ticket; to Korhogo where he met his girlfriend Cristelle. In addition, another significant phase in Moudi's life story is marked by *immobility*; the time spent in his grandmother's house before he was able to leave. To put it differently, his vital conjunctures are characterised by moves and not by, say, when he left Koranic school; when he was circumcised, or initiated.

The mobile life story builds on existing approaches in cultural anthropology and related disciplines but is attuned to the detailed appreciation of migrant biographies. By tracing past and present emplacements in the lives of active or aspiring migrants, the mobile life story focuses the exploration of past and present moments of hopefulness, and projects them into possible futures. Such a holistic methodology requires a varied selection of data collection techniques, as well as the time and incentive to pursue the details that bring a migrant biography to life. The gain of such an effort is a richness of detail that allows for a more fine-grained and engaging analysis.

Acknowledgements

The fieldwork and literature studies that inform this paper have been conducted as a part of a PhD programme in cultural anthropology at Uppsala University. I am grateful to my supervisors, Sten Hagberg and Mats Utas for their encouragement and support, and to the Nordic Africa Institute (NAI) as well as the Göransson Sandviken foundation for the financial support that has made the fieldwork in Côte d'Ivoire possible. I particularly wish to thank Henrik Vigh for engaging with the ideas that have shaped this argument. Finally, I wish to thank the Guest Editors of this special issue, Theodoros Iosifides and Deborah Sporton, for the opportunity to contribute to an important theme in migration research, as well as to the Managing Editor of Migration Letters, Ibrahim Sirkeci, for his attentive and encouraging involvement.

References

Abbink, J. and van Kessel, I. (eds.) 2005. *Vanguard or Vandals. Youth, Politics and Conflict in Africa* Leiden: Brill.

Åkesson, L. 2004. *Making a Life. Meanings of Migration in Cape Verde.* Ph.D. Göteborg: Göteborg University.

Bjarnesen, J. 2007. *On the Move. Young Men Navigating Paths towards Adulthood in Gueule Tapée (Dakar).* MA Thesis. Copenhagen: University of Copenhagen.

Bucholtz, M. 2002. 'Youth and Cultural Practice', (p.525-52) in *Annual Review of Anthropology*,

[11] The methodological point here is that this ordering should not be understood as an unchangeable personal history.

Vol.31.

Carling, J. 2002. 'Migration in the Age of Involuntary Immobility: Theoretical Reflections and Cape Verdean Experiences', (p.5-42) in *Journal of Ethnic and Migration Studies*, Vol.28 (1).

Casey, E. S. 2001. 'Between Geography and Philosophy: What Does It Mean to Be in the Place-World?' (p.683-93) in *Annals of the Association of American Geographers*, Vol.91 (4).

Christiansen, C., Utas, M. and Vigh, H. E. (eds.) 2006. *Navigating Youth - Generating Adulthood. Social Becoming in an African Context.* Uppsala: Nordic Africa Institute.

Cole, J. 2005. 'The Jaombilo of Tamatave (Madagascar), 1992–2004: Reflections on Youth and Globalization', (p.1179-83) in *Journal of Social History*, Vol.38 (4).

Cole, J. and Durham, D. (eds.) 2007. *Generations and Globalization. Youth, Age, and Family in the New World Economy.* Bloomington IN: Indiana University Press.

_____ 2008. 'Introduction. Globalization and the Temporality of Children and Youth', (p.3-23) in Cole, J. and D. Durham (eds.), *Figuring the Future. Globalization and the Temporalities of Children and Youth.* SAR Press.

Crapanzano, V. 2004. *Imaginative Horizons. An Essay in Literary-Philosophical Anthropology.* Chicago IL: Chicago University Press.

de Bruijn, M., van Dijk, R. and Foeken, D. (eds.) 2001. *Mobile Africa. Changing Patterns of Movement in Africa and Beyond.* Leiden, Boston & Köln: Koninklijke Brill NV.

de Certeau, M. 1984. *The Practice of Everyday Life.* Berkeley, Los Angeles & London: University of California Press.

Durham, D. 2000. 'Youth and the Social Imagination in Africa: Introduction to parts 1 and 2', (p.113-20) in *Anthropological Quarterly*, Vol.73 (3).

--- 2004. 'Disappearing Youth: Youth as Social Shifter in Botswana', (p.589-605) in *American Ethnologist*, Vol.31 (4).

Englund, H. 2002. 'Ethnography after Globalism: Migration and Emplacement in Malawi', (p.261-86) in *American Ethnologist*, Vol.29 (2).

_____ 2004. 'Cosmopolitanism and the Devil in Malawi', (p.293-316) in *Ethnos*, Vol.69 (3).

Gupta, A. and Ferguson, J. (eds.) 1997. *Anthropological Locations. Boundaries and Grounds of a Field Science.* Berkeley, Los Angeles & London: University of California Press.

Honwana, A. and De Boeck, F. (eds.) 2005. *Makers & Breakers. Children & Youth in Postcolonial Africa.* Oxford: James Curry.

Johnson-Hanks, J. 2002. 'On the Limits of Life Stages in Ethnography: Toward a Theory of Vital Conjunctures', (p.865-80) in *American Anthropologist*, Vol.104 (3).

Langevang, T. 2007. *Youth in the City. Life Strategies of Young People in Accra, Ghana.* Ph.D. Thesis, Copenhagen: University of Copenhagen.

Lindquist, J. 2002. *The Anxieties of Mobility. Development, Migration, and Tourism in the Indonesian Borderlands.* PhD. Stockholm: Stockholm University.

Naila, K. 2000. 'Inter-Generational Contracts, Demographic Transitions and the 'Quantity-Quality' Tradeoff: Parents, Children and Investing in the Future', (p.463-82) in *Journal of International Development*, Vol.12 (4).

Nyberg Sørensen, N. and Olwig, K. F. (eds.) 2002. *Work and Migration. Life and Livelihoods in a Globalizing World.* London & New York: Routledge.

Reynolds Whyte, S. 2002. 'Subjectivity and Subjunctivity. Hoping for Health in Eastern Uganda', (p.171-90) in Werbner, R. (ed.), *Postcolonial Subjectivities in Africa.* London & New York: Zed Books.

Utas, M. 2003. *Sweet Battlefields. Youth and the Liberian Civil War.* PhD Thesis, Uppsala: Uppsala University.

Vigh, H. E. 2006. *Navigating Terrains of War. Youth and Soldiering in Guinea-Bissau.* New York & Oxford: Berghahn Books.

Webb, D. 2007. 'Modes of Hoping', (p.65-83) in *History of the Human Sciences*, Vol.20 (3).

Weiss, B. 2004. 'Contentious Futures: Past and Present', (p.1-20) in Weiss, B. (ed.), *Producing African Futures. Ritual and Reproduction in a Neoliberal Age.* Leiden: Brill.

CHAPTER 14

POWER AND POLITICS IN MIGRATION NARRATIVE METHODOLOGY: RESEARCH WITH YOUNG CONGOLESE MIGRANTS IN UGANDA

Christina Clark-Kazak

Abstract

This paper explores the power dynamics inherent in qualitative research involving mi-gration narratives. Drawing on the author's experiences collecting life histories and constructing narratives of Congolese young people in Uganda, this article addresses the ethical and methodological issues of representivity, ownership, anonymity and confi-dentiality. It also explores the importance of investment in relationships in migration narrative research, but also the difficulties that arise when professional and personal boundaries become blurred.

Introduction

Life stories and personal narratives are increasingly popular in migration studies as methods that capture migrants' 'lived experiences' (Eastmond 2007). The advantages of such an approach have been well articulated by other scholars (Eastmond 2007; Powles 2004). These include an understanding of complex migration processes through an interpretive approach; making such complex experiences more accessible to practitioners and academics who have not themselves experienced migration; counteracting homogenizing and essentializing discourses about migrants and their experiences; and, providing opportunities for migrants to directly share their experiences.

However, migration narratives also pose particular ethical and methodological challenges to researchers. This article attempts to expose some of these challenges through the lens of power relations. Drawing on my experiences with Congolese young people in Uganda, I argue that issues of representivity and representation arise in the use of migrants' narratives. Representivity refers to the degree to which individual migrant's stories can be deemed 'representative' of larger populations and thus generalized beyond the research subject(s). Representation is concerned with the differing ways in which migrants and researchers ascribe meaning to particular people and events. I thus also address the complex issues of ownership and editorial control over stories' content, as well as challenges of anonymity and confidentiality. The article concludes with a discussion of investing in research relationships as a way of addressing some of these challenges, but which also poses some of its own methodological and ethical issues.

While narrative methodology and its challenges are not unique to migration research, there are particularities that should be highlighted. As part of status determination processes and to access services, migrants are often required to 'tell their stories' many times in different contexts. Narratives are thus inherent to the migration experience, and research offers an additional set of circumstances in which migrants recount their experiences. Moreover, migration research takes place within politicized policy contexts, where findings can have tangible implications for migrants, whether or not this is the researcher's intention. As a result, issues of representation and representivity, discussed below, are particularly salient.

Similarly, this article draws on narrative research conducted with young people, but many of the arguments apply to migration narratives generally. This being said, the challenges may be exacerbated in research involving young people for two principal reasons. First, age hierarchies affect power relations and thus impact interactions between adult researchers and young research subjects. In particular, young people have historically been perceived as unreliable sources of information due to their immaturity (Christensen and James 2000; Qvortrup 1994). Second, dominant development discourses promote 'universal' notions of childhood and youth (Boyden 1997, 2001), thereby contributing to homogenizing notions of young migrants' experiences.

Context and methodological approach

This article draws on research with young Congolese migrants[1] in Uganda in 2004-2005. I spent 9 months in Kampala and Kyaka II refugee settlement over a 15-month period, during which a number of qualitative methods – including semi-structured interviews, focus group discussions, observation, and writing exercises – were used to collect data from over 400 research subjects[2]. Of the total research population, 15 young people in each research site became key research subjects, with whom I met at least once a week and, in some cases, daily. Research was also conducted with members of their social networks, including adults, to contextualize and cross-reference key research subjects' experiences. Over the course of my relationship with these Congolese young people, I collected life histories: "retrospective account[s] by the individual of his [or her] life in whole or in part, in written or oral form, *that [have] been elicited or prompted by another person*" (Watson and Watson-Franke 1985: 2); emphasis in original).

[1] In this paper, 'migrants' is used broadly to designate people of Congolese origin who have come to Uganda as refugees, immigrants and asylum seekers, as well as those living informally without legal status.

[2] I prefer the term 'research subject' to 'participant', given the limits to participation, discussed below.

Combining these life histories with the other research methods outlined above, I constructed narratives to contextualize research subjects' experiences as young migrants living in Uganda. I thus make a distinction between life histories, in which the research subject is central to the telling of her/his story, and narratives, in which the researcher takes a much more directive role in situating the individual's story in a broader social and historical context. In the latter, explanatory and contextual information is provided to facilitate understanding by readers unfamiliar with the particular context. "Put simply, narrative is a form in which activities and events are described as having a meaningful and coherent order, imposing on reality a unity which it does not inherently possess. Narrative also inevitably reduces experience which, in its vitality and richness, always far exceeds the expression which a person can give it." (Eastmond 2007: 250) Moreover, in the narrative approach, the researcher draws on other data to supplement the life story and, in some cases, highlight alternative interpretations of particular events. Such an approach presents particular challenges regarding ownership and representation, which will be explored below.

Representivity and representation

Narratives have been promoted in migration studies as a way to provide detailed and intimate insight into the everyday lived experiences of migrants, thereby counteracting essentialist and homogenizing discourses (Eastmond 2007; Powles 2004). However, due to the in-depth nature of narratives, and the time required to establish rapport, record lengthy stories and construct these into narratives, researchers are only able to draw on small sample sizes. Indeed, some studies rely solely on one individual's story (Behar 1993; Eggers 2006; Powles 2004) or collate individual narratives into collective 'panels' (Malkki 1995). Even in research using multiple narratives, representivity is limited. For example, in my research, I collected life stories from approximately 30 young people. However, this is still a small sample size, which is exacerbated by non-random sampling techniques. In my study, key research subjects were not randomly or purposefully 'selected'. Rather, our relationships evolved as young Congolese migrants expressed interest in my research and gradually invited me to share more of their lives. Because participation would involve young people contributing long periods of time regularly to the research process, voluntary involvement was important. However, gender, social age (Clark-Kazak Forthcoming) and socioeconomic biases in self-selection were consciously managed by dividing time and interactions among young people of different backgrounds, ages and sex. Despite these efforts, key research subjects are not representative of the broader Congolese migrant population. In particular, individuals from relatively wealthier socio-economic backgrounds are over-represented in my study.

Studies involving one or a small number of migrants provide rich, finely grained data. Statistical generalization is usually not the objective of such research, while analytical and theoretical generalizations are still possible and valuable. However, given the topical and policy-relevant nature of much migration research, findings may be misappropriated as indicative of 'the refugee experience', thereby contributing to the over-generalization that narrative methodology attempts to prevent. Limited representivity thus poses methodological and ethical challenges in migration research. "[A]ny telling of 'a story' may be affected by race, ethnicity, gender, class, age, sexual orientation, religious background, personal history, character – an infinite list of possible factors that form the scaffolding of relationships between people" (McLean Taylor, Gilligan, and Sullivan 1995: 14). There is "no single, authentic, indigenous voice or reality that the researcher can discover and present to the world" (Wilson 1993: 181). Even when researchers carefully qualify their findings, the politicized context in which migration research is undertaken creates particular dangers that information in narratives may be extrapolated to represent broader groups, with concrete consequences in terms of policy and programming (Boyden and Ennew 1997).

Issues of representivity and generalizability are also related to challenges of representation – the ways in which meanings are ascribed to particular people and events (Clark-Kazak 2009; Hall 1997). In telling their stories, research subjects choose to present themselves in particular ways at particular times (Rosenwald and Ochberg 1992). As such, the audience and context of the story-telling are important. Over the course of my interaction with Congolese young people, they told me about themselves and their circumstances in different ways, sometimes leading to internal contradictions in their narratives. For example, Paul[3], a young Congolese musician, explicitly promoted unity in his lyrics. In one song entitled "Identity", he attempted to "show people that we are all one. We are all children of the same father, whatever our morphology. Before, Africa was like one country, without borders, so we only had one single identity."[4] However, while recounting his story to me, and in discussions with his friends about politics in the African Great Lakes, Paul revealed extreme anti-Rwandese sentiments, including against Congolese of Rwandese origin, whom he believed should be excluded from Congolese citizenship. As a researcher gains rapport and trust, migrants may disclose information they had previously not shared. For example, only after I had known 16-year-old Salome for over a year did she tell me that she had been raped and given birth to a son. This corroborated information that her mother had shared with me several months earlier.

Migrants, particularly those seeking asylum, regularly have to tell their story to multiple government officials, refugee agency workers and service providers, who determine legal status and admissibility for programs and

[3] All names have been changed in an attempt to protect anonymity and confidentiality. See below.

[4] I have translated all young people's direct quotations from French or Swahili into English.

services. Given the resources at stake, migrants may have an incentive to present their circumstances in particular ways in order to qualify for programs or assistance. For example, in Uganda, many of the Congolese young people with whom I worked had adopted a discourse of vulnerability when interacting with government, United Nations (UN) and non-governmental organization (NGO) representatives (Clark 2007). They understood that priority assistance and resettlement to third countries was given to so-called 'vulnerables' and thus attempted to 'fit' their stories within these categories. However, over the course of my interaction with them, many young people admitted that they did not perceive themselves to be 'vulnerable' and, indeed, believed that the categorization denied their own coping strategies. As one young man explained, "Young people are not vulnerable, but they play the system because they are obliged to do so. I am a refugee, so I must play the game as refugees are expected to. I must act weak and humble."

While researchers may thus be able to piece together much more complex narratives, there are ethical implications of doing so. First, the discrepancy between these richer narratives and the more simplistic, 'cookie-cutter' stories told to officials may reinforce stereotypical notions of migrants as 'liars' who manipulate the system (Rousseau and Foxen 2006). Second, disclosing information that migrants have chosen to suppress publicly may put them in danger or jeopardize their legal status. For example, a young Congolese male told me that he had been jailed several times for his political advocacy. However, he had decided not to tell the Ugandan government and UN this part of this story because he was worried that they would send him to Special Branch, which assesses criminal responsibility, thus delaying and potentially prohibiting, his application for refugee status and resettlement. In these cases, confidentiality, discussed in more detail below, becomes particularly important, but also especially challenging.

Appropriating 'voices'? Issues of ownership and editorial control

This discussion of representation leads to another methodological and ethical challenge in migration narratives: issues of ownership. Migrants' stories are sometimes promoted as a way to "give a voice to the voiceless". However, as others have pointed out, "Behind the writing of any story is a writer. An obvious statement, perhaps, but researching life stories asks questions of the in/deliberate hand of the researcher." (Goodley et al. 2004: 79). Researchers must thus seriously consider our role in the editorial process of translating oral data into text (Eastmond 2007: 249).

In my research with Congolese migrants in Uganda, I chose an ethnographic, but non-participatory, approach:

While the mode is non-participatory – the researcher works from the position of final and perhaps constant ownership of raw material – the use of life story aims to emphasise the significance of a number of experiences of people [...]. In this sense, while our characters have no hand in the writing of their own stories, an ethnographic stance encourages the writer/researcher to try to authentically capture their stories in meaningful and accountable ways. (Goodley et al. 2004: 59)

I shared parts of the narratives with research subjects, who had opportunities to include additional information, but I retained editorial control (Powles 2004; Salazar 1991). Despite this non-participatory approach, compilation of life stories was an interactive, iterative process, in which young people presented themselves in contradictory ways at different times, omitting, including and revising information (Rosenwald and Ochberg 1992; Powles 2004).

Regardless of how participatory the data collection, analysis and presentation may be, power relations are such that it is likely that the researcher will benefit more than the migrant(s) from the finished product. As 'authors' of published works, we ultimately reap the academic, professional, social and economic benefits – which can be substantial for 'bestsellers' – of other people's stories (Myhre 2004). This then begs the question that Patai (1991) has so eloquently stated: "Of the frequent claim that [research] [...] is empowering in that it 'gives a voice' to those who might otherwise remain silent, one might well ask: is it empowerment or is it appropriation?" (Patai 1991: 147) Even when using verbatim transcripts, researchers project their own interpretations on events and choose particular sections to highlight or edit out.

Anonymity and confidentiality

A critical decision in the editing process is how much and what kinds of information to include in the narratives. Most western ethics boards place a premium on the principles of anonymity and confidentiality. For this reason, many researchers choose to use pseudonyms to obscure the identity of migrants whose narratives they publish. However, this poses a methodological contradiction between one of the stated aims of narratives – providing migrants with an opportunity to 'tell their stories' – and the reality that pseudonyms render the key protagonists 'invisible'. Indeed, many of the young people in my study wanted their real names to be used (see also (van der Geest 2003). However, after reflection, I decided to use pseudonyms for everyone. Because many young people in my study are part of overlapping networks, using real names for some could expose others who had requested anonymity. Moreover, neither my subjects nor I knew who would read the research findings and the potential impacts the study would have. Nevertheless, I struggled with this decision. Is it paternalistic to override research subjects' own preferences in the belief that I 'know best'? Am I appropriating young people's stories by obscuring their identity, and hence ownership of the narratives?

Even when pseudonyms are used, this is often not enough to protect anonymity. First, collecting life stories usually involves prolonged interaction with migrants in order to build trust and to record complex narratives over several sessions. In small communities, particularly those in which a researcher does not regularly live and work, others will likely know who was involved in the research. For example, in Kyaka II refugee settlement, where I was the only Caucasian and thus particularly conspicuous, some research subjects indicated that neighbours, local authorities and camp officials had commented on my interaction with them. I tried to alter the timing and routes I took to key research subjects' homes and also spent time with others who were not central to my study in order to provide a modicum of protection. In a more extreme case, another anthropologist chose to use pseudonyms not only for his key informants, but also himself and the village in which he worked in order to protect the identity of those who participated in his research (van der Geest 2003).

Second, narratives inherently contain detailed information about migrants' backgrounds, migration patterns and current circumstances. Given that officials often collect similar kinds of information for their case files and that migrants often belong to interconnected networks, data and 'markers' in narratives can easily be used to identify research subjects. In my own research, I chose to omit some personal details that would obviously identify a research subject. For example, Boniface's grandfather was chief of a small village in North Kivu. Even though he told me the name of this village, I did not include this information in his story, as this would clearly identify him. On the other hand, researchers have a scholarly responsibility not to suppress data that is crucial to the study's findings. Therefore, a balance must be struck between ethical obligations to migrants and academic integrity.

Investing in research relationships

When confronted with these ethical and methodological challenges in collecting and using narratives, researchers must rely on context-specific solutions to creatively weigh the richness of narrative research against the potential harm it may cause to research subjects. This context-specificity requires an in-depth knowledge of the circumstances in which migrants are living, as well as the particular strengths and vulnerabilities of individual research subjects. Nevertheless, we should be cognizant of the risks involved in blurred lines between personal and professional relationships and the conflation of research with social work.

The collection of life histories often involves sustained interaction with research subjects over long periods of time. Such interaction is necessary to establish rapport and gain trust, thereby providing an environment conducive to story-telling. However, these same circumstances can lead to ambiguous relationships, where friendships alongside professional relationships may emerge. While there is, of course, nothing wrong with friendship between researchers and the people with whom they are working, these personal relationships can pose methodological and ethical dilemmas. First, it may become difficult for the researcher to distinguish between information disclosed in the context of personal interaction, which the migrant does not intend to be recorded in the research, and information for research purposes gathered in ethnographic situations. In these cases, the ethical principle of informed consent is obscured.

Second, personal relationships between researchers and migrants may yield differential expectations of the research. As the researcher spends more and more time with migrants and shares in aspects of their lives, migrants may believe they have certain claims over the researcher, who should help them 'as their friend'. This is particularly significant in societies, such as those in Central Africa, where extended kinship forms the basis of social, economic and political roles and allegiances (de Boeck 2005; Clark 2006). A researcher can quite quickly be 'adopted' as a pseudokin (Southall 1955) with associated responsibilities to the migrant and her/his extended networks. These could include an expectation that the researcher will provide assistance and/or that she/he will advocate on the migrant's behalf.

Third, by researching the details of migrants' lived experiences, researchers may become aware of situations of abuse or danger posed to their research subjects. In these cases, should the ethical principle of 'do no harm' be extended to include an ethical imperative to intervene to prevent harm by others? For example, over the course of my interaction with 16-year-old Rose, she disclosed that she was subject to sexual harassment by the male head of household with whom she lived. She feared that she would be raped. I felt ethically and personally moved to intervene to prevent this from happening. However, when I raised her case with Ugandan and UN authorities and local NGOs, no one was willing to help her, because she was an 'illegal migrant'. Given the lack of social services available to Rose, and my limited stay in Uganda, one colleague warned me of the methodological and ethical perils of conflating research with social work. If I was perceived to be in Uganda to 'help' people, migrants would begin to see me as another service provider. This could then alter our research relationship, making them more likely to adhere to the 'vulnerability' discourses mentioned above. Moreover, as an individual, I did not have the financial, organizational and emotional means to help every research subject I encountered.

Conclusion: Towards reciprocity and sustainability

By investing in relationships based on principles of reciprocity (Alderson 1995) and sustainability, researchers can partially overcome some of the ethical and methodological challenges highlighted in this paper. Reciprocity is important to avoid the two extremes of exploitative, extractive research, and unequal donor-recipient power dynamics. In terms of sustainability, responses should contribute to research subjects' longer-term initiatives. For example, in order to recognize the contribution that many refugee youth leaders had made to my research, I organized a workshop for them on management issues. This workshop, during which they developed detailed strategic plans and budgets, contributed to their long-term goals of building effective organizations. It was also a reciprocal gesture: I was providing information in return for the data and access to their organizations that they had given me. When individuals confronted problems, we explored their limited options and sources of assistance within existing structures. Reciprocity involved responding to their requests for meetings or information with the same willingness and openness as they had engaged in my research: meeting them on their own terms and for their own reasons, at times and places fixed by them, even when it was inconvenient for me to do so.

The 'give and take' involved in reciprocal relationships also helped me to resolve some of the tensions related to ownership and editorial control, highlighted above. The rapport we developed over long-term relationships allowed me to query in a non-confrontational way contradictions and discrepancies in migrants' stories. The resulting narratives were thus a product of negotiated interactions, 'belonging' completely to neither my research subjects nor myself.

Narrative research with migrants offers key insights into the complex experiences of migration. However, this same complexity renders such research methodologically and ethically challenging. Researchers must be aware of these challenges before embarking on narrative research and should consciously seek to manage the risks our studies pose to migrants. Rather than assuming that our research inherently 'gives a voice' to migrants, we need to carefully consider the nature and extent of our mutual relationship and strive for reciprocity and sustainability.

References

Alderson, Priscilla. 1995. *Listening to Children: Children, Ethics and Social Research*. Ilford: Barnardo's.

Behar, Ruth. 1993. *Translated Woman: Crossing the Border with Esperanza's Story*. Boston: Beacon Press.

Boyden, Jo. 1997. Childhood and the Policy Makers: A Comparative Perspective on the Globalization of Childhood. In *Constructing and Reconstructing Childhood*, edited by A. James and A. Prout. London: Falmer Press.

———. 2001. Some Reflections on Scientific Conceptualisations of Childhood and Youth. In *Managing Reproductive Life: Cross-Cultural Themes in Fertility and Sexuality*, edited by S. Tremayne. Oxford: Berghahn Books.

Boyden, Jo, and Judith Ennew, eds. 1997. *Children in Focus: A Manual for Participatory Research with Children*. Stockholm: Radda Barnen.

Christensen, Pia, and Allison James. 2000. Researching Children and Childhood: Cultures of Communication. In *Research with Children: Perspectives and Practices*, edited by P. Christensen and A. James. London: Falmer Press.

Clark-Kazak, Christina. 2009. Representing Refugees in the Life Cycle: A Social Age Analysis of United Nations High Commissioner for Refugees Annual Reports and Appeals, 2000-2008. *Journal of Refugee Studies*.

———. Forthcoming. Towards a working definition and application of social age in international development studies. *Journal of Development Studies*.

Clark, Christina. 2006. Livelihood Networks and Decision-Making among Congolese Young People in Formal and Informal Refugee Contexts in Uganda. Brighton: Households in Conflict Network, Institute of Development Studies, University of Sussex.

———. 2007. Understanding vulnerability: From categories to experiences of Congolese young people in Uganda. *Children & Society* 21 (4):284-296.

de Boeck, Filip. 2005. The Divine Seed: Children, Gift and Witchcraft in the Democratic Republic of Congo. In *Makers and Breakers: Children and Youth in Postcolonial Africa*, edited by A. Honwana and F. De Boeck. Oxford: James Currey.

Eastmond, Marita. 2007. Stories as Lived Experience: Narratives in Forced Migration Research. *Journal of Refugee Studies* 20 (2):248-264.

Eggers, Dave. 2006. *What is the What*. San Francisco: McSweeney's.

Goodley, Dan, Rebecca Lawthom, Peter Clough, and Michele Moore. 2004. *Researching Life Stories: Method, Theory and Analyses in a Biographical Age*. London and New York: Routledge Falmer.

Hall, Stuart. 1997. The Work of Representation. In *Representation: Cultural Representations and Signifying Practices*, edited by S. Hall. London: Sage Publications.

Malkki, Liisa. 1995. *Purity and Exile: Violence, Memory and National Cosmology among Hutu Refugees in Tanzania*. London: University of Chicago Press.

McLean Taylor, Jill, Carol Gilligan, and Amy Sullivan. 1995. *Between Voice and Silence: Women and Girls, Race and Relationship*. Cambridge and London: Harvard University Press.

Myhre, Knut Christian. 2004. The Bookseller of Kabul and the Anthropologists of Norway. *Anthropology Today* 20 (3):19-22.

Patai, Daphne. 1991. U.S. Academics and Third World Women: Is Ethical Research Possible? In *Women's Words: The Feminist Practice of Oral History*, edited by S. B. Gluck and D. Patai. London: Routledge.

Powles, Julia. 2004. Life History and Personal Narrative: Theoretical and Methodological Issues Relevant to Research and Evaluation in Refugee Contexts. Paper read at Evaluating the Use of Research Methods in Humanitarian Contexts: Promoting Good Practice, April, 2004, at Geneva.

Qvortrup, Jens. 1994. Childhood Matters: An Introduction. In *Childhood Matters: Social Theory, Practice and Politics*, edited by J. Qvortrup, M. Bardy, G. Sgritta and H. Wintersberger. Hants: Avebury.

Rosenwald, George, and Richard Ochberg. 1992. Introduction: Life Stories, Cultural Politics, and Self-Understanding. In *Storied Lives: The Cultural Politics of Self-Understanding*, edited by G. Rosenwald and R. Ochberg. New Haven and London: Yale University Press.

Rousseau, Cécile, and Patricia Foxen. 2006. Le mythe du réfugié menteur: un mensonge indispensable? *L'évolution psychiatrique* 71:505-520.

Salazar, Claudia. 1991. A Third World Woman's Text: Between the Politics of Criticism and Cultural Politics. In *Women's Words: The Feminist Practice of Oral History*, edited by S. B. Gluck and D. Patai. London: Routledge.

Southall, Aidan. 1955. *Alur Society: A Study in the Processes and Types of Domination*. Cambridge: W. Heffer and Sons.

van der Geest, Sjaak. 2003. Confidentiality and Pseudonyms: A Fieldwork Dilemma from Ghana. *Anthropology Today* 19 (1):14-18.

Watson, Lawrence, and Maria-Barbara Watson-Franke. 1985. *Interpreting Life Histories: An Anthropological Inquiry*. New Brunswick, New Jersey: Rutgers University Press.

Wilson, Ken. 1993. Thinking about the Ethics of Fieldwork. In *Fieldwork in Developing Countries*, edited by S. Devereux and J. Hoddinott. Boulder: Lynne Rienner Publishers.

CHAPTER 15

TELLING DIASPORA STORIES: THEORETICAL AND METHODOLOGICAL REFLECTIONS ON NARRATIVES OF MIGRANCY AND BELONGINGNESS IN THE SECOND GENERATION

Anastasia Christou

Abstract

This article explores the theoretical and methodological implications of the study of sec-ond generation migration through the use of life stories, a narrative and biographical approach. It presents a theoretical contextualisation of life history research in addressing the direction it has taken in the study of migration and identity in order to problematise how the subject and subjectivities in narrative research have been framed by social cate-gorisations such as gender, ethnicity, class as well as social experiences such as trauma, exile, memory and imagination. The paper develops the analytical contribution of re-searching the biographicity of everyday migrant lives.

Stories of the self: narratives of identity and migration

We have been told that the 20th century marked the end of many things and we did bear witness to the demise of some including the collapse of grand narratives. However, this era is characterised by the emergence of new paradigms and the "rise of the life narrative" in the "age of small narratives" as the narrative paradigm is penetrating most domains of private and public life in our individualised societies, as it is finding its way in art, culture, politics, in the macro and micro spheres of sociality (Goodson, 2006).

Biographies are shaped by life decisions and trajectories such as migration which may offer or may deprive individuals of certain alternatives. Migration often becomes the centre of one's biography as a self-referential point of awareness of one's potential for autonomous action but also of limitations, often structural that become control mechanisms. Migration as a social phenomenon produces and is produced through multiple biographies that may be expressive of pain and joy, optimism and depression, instability and development and so on. Migrant stories are not only binaries of life events but the pieces that put together the fabric of mobility of memories, territories and people.

Narrative theorisation argues that narratives are the central device of identification processes and hence the crux of how we construct the self and how we give meaning to our lives (Bruner, 1990; Mishler, 1991; 2000). However, in reaching meaning we also need to scrutinise the wider social context of life narratives (Goodson, 2006) as we cannot ignore social context because we will then deprive ourselves and our collaborators of meaning and understanding (Andrews, 1991). In this respect, the *storied life* transforms into a catalyst that initiates the reassessment of a *lived life* in the exploration of meanings directed by constructions of culture, nation, ethnicity and place, in other words, where the *ethnos* meets the *topos* and where the stories are constructed around a perception of *self*, contextualised in past and present constructions of *home* and leading, in response, to a re-evaluation of the future (Christou, 2006).

Life stories have a "heuristic potential" (Chanfrault-Duchet, 1991: 79) which underscores the "hermeneutic potential" of the narrative approach (meanings as understandings that emerge when 'thinking through' and 'with' others to exemplify intersubjectivity). The driving force, as Plummer says, is that "we can see life stories working their way through a series of circles: self, others, community, the whole society" (2001: 243). The bridge between personal biography and cultural history connects the internal world to the external world, the subjective and the objective, while establishing boundaries of identities and collectivities as links across life phases and historical shifts in a culture (Plummer, 2001). Life stories illuminate lives and in doing so are very powerful because they capture the multi-dimensionality, richness and complexities of individual experiences, in particular socio-cultural contexts (Lawrence-Lightfoot and Hoffman-Davis, 1997).

The subject and (inter)subjectivities in life stories: gender, ethnicity and class

Life stories are constructed, negotiated and articulated subjectivities. They are contextually defined, socially situated and culturally mediated enactments of certain fragments of a life and of particular glimpses of time while they are saturated by social categorisations and marked by cultural experiences. Stories of the self cannot be anything but stories of a *gendered*, *ethnicised* and *classed* self.

Stories are not articulated in a vacuum but they are (re)constructed, recalled, (re)told, modified, expressed and narrated in a particular context which is also a space of collectives: events, past and shared memories, interrelationships of characters, configurations of experiences in specific temporal and spatial circumstances and intricate processes of identifications throughout. Hence, stories cannot stand in isolation but they are shaped by the very socio-cultural and politico-historical conditions that penetrate their narrative construction.

Here, we must see the subject as relationally, psycho-biographically, historically and culturally constituted (Chodorow, 1999). The individual, as a subject but also an active-actor, forms and develops the 'self' in response to specific 'others'. The life course of the individual takes place during social time and within social space as it is inscribed in and mediated by the subjectivity of the individual. This connection between individual and society is fundamental insofar as the individual and society cannot be understood other than intertwined in how people create personal meaning. Such meanings are subjective and they are grounded on the psychic realm, the biographical container, the historical context and the cultural platform of everyday life. These meanings are constructed but also acquired by the individual in a discursive and habitual manner.

The narrative discourse of trauma, exile, memory and imagination

The narrativisation of many deeply felt life experiences is most likely to be (re)constructed and expressed through the very filtering device of memory and imagination, notwithstanding the shaped outcome of time but also extreme conditions such as trauma and the feeling of alienation, exclusion and exile. That is because people "live their lives and tell their stories within socially constituted conditions but their actions and stories also have a potentially transformative impact on society" (Moriarty, 3.1: 2005) and this exemplifies a "sociology of stories" (Plummer, 1995).

The mnemonic distillation of stories is a process that occurs in everyday life but it usually requires external stimulation. As Passerini explains, "when someone is asked for his (sic) life-story, his memory draws on pre-existing story-lines and ways of telling stories, even if these are part modified by the circumstances" (1987: 28), which becomes meaningful when we realise that "we often narrate our lives according to a 'prior script', a script written elsewhere, by others, for other purposes" (Goodson, 1995: 97).

Memory is also a path of (re)discovery of the past through the present. Thus, it can be influenced by a variety of different factors and the past can be altered (Lowenthal, 1985: 193–210). In (re)constructing the past, the social arena acts as a context to unfold memories while inhabiting particular spaces.

Nevertheless, narratives are a testimony to the multiple interactive layers of subjectivity (Christou, 2006) or double subjectivity (Lentin, 2000) of people's lived experiences and offer the plurality of history, experience and perception as a small segment of interpretation of a complex social reality (Lentin, 2000). To illustrate then the counter-diasporic experience of second generation migrants and return migrants (Christou, 2006) we need to make sense of counter-narratives and auto/biographical accounts as acts of reckoning (Lentin, 2000) but also as transformative perfomative possibilities of the *self* in constructing the *other* and finally making sense of the collective. The varied ways in which migrants remember and tell their life stories are quite often illuminating about the very meanings of the migration experience and this raises questions about why some memories are more valuable than others and if specific memories serve particular purposes for migrants (Thomson, 2003).

The transformative power of biography

Only by embedding narratives in the unprecedented changes that have historically occurred on a global scale do we understand what Bauman (1991; 1995; 2000) means when he suggests that globalisation and postmodernity have exacerbated fragmentation, dislocation and uncertainty resulting in identity crises, fear and an ontological loss of security that comes with the fixity of identity and belonging. Hence, when one is narrating feelings of homeness and belongingness this unfolds in the temporal and spatial cultural redefinition of our era on a global scale. No matter how scripted the past is or how deep the structural limitations are of pre-scripted experiences, only living lives that are biographically explored and resisted can utilise this power of biography to its transformative and agential extent. These processes of transformation however, require social actors, active agents who can relate to their lifeworlds in a self-reflexive way in order to shape their social contexts and this is precisely the scope of *biographicity*.

But storytelling is a contingent process, a narrativisation of potential stories open to alteration and adaptation according to life stages, life circumstances and events that may have a profound effect on the life space, that particular insulated sense of personal space within the personal lifeworld which is open to self-interpretation, self-dispute, revision, exploration and finally self-coping. The more reflexively aware the individual is, the more critically evaluated the script becomes as the person delves into the depths of the self and the other. Inner dialogues in one's personal psychological space through reflexive acts of (re)membering are a doorway into the constitution of the self.

Methodological reflections on the biographicity of everyday (diaspora) returnee lives

The core empirical method of our research project entitled, "Cultural Geographies of Counter-Diasporic Migration: The Second Generation Returns 'Home'" – the collection of life narratives – is aimed at generating creative insights into the linked meanings of 'migration', 'diaspora', 'return' and 'home'. The narratives, 'authored' and 'authorised' by the migrants themselves, enable both 'authenticity' and great richness in the research material gathered. Part of this richness derives from the way that narratives of home, return and belonging will interplay between discourses of ethnicity, identity, race, class and gender (cf. Ahmed *et al.* 2003; Christou, 2006) in various diasporic spaces, each located within a particular social model of an evolving immigrant/multicultural society – the US, UK, Germany, Greece and Cyprus.

We appreciate that, in a world of accelerating mobility, individuals' narratives are complex and epicentred; movement is both real, across physical space, and imagined, across spaces of meaning and identification. We explore this idea that migrants develop *narrative capital* as they construct and author their accounts. In contrast to cultural capital, usually related to national social orders, narrative capital is both more personal and flexible, and related to the new global order (Goodson, 2006). If it is true that, in our current individualised society (Beck and Beck-Gernsheim, 2002), we live in an age of 'small' (as opposed to 'grand') narratives, the personal life-story emerges as a new socially-constructed genre providing the researcher with new scripts for analysis. In our case, the danger of a fragmenting individualisation of such life narratives is countered by their being anchored within the wider social scripts of the group (on migration, return, homeland, religion etc.) and within the cultural location and 'cohort time' of second-generation returnees to Greece and Cyprus. Furthermore, this methodological path in researching mobility and the varying expressions of migrants as agents of change and transformation, we also theoretically move from the otherwise stagnation of cultural capital to the intersectionality of *gender capital* through narrative capital in unveiling expressions of gendered embodied capital and the institutionalisation of power. Here, it is important to consider contemporary feminist analyses of the family and home life (Pratt, 2008) and their significance for a renewed theory of cultural capital. As the metaphor "capital" implies, it does not facilitate or cause action just because it exists but it must be mobilised and transacted in order to be utilised. This is a crucial theoretical point in how to problematise the very politics of our research.

Subsequently, the best methodological design to address our research questions is a multi-method approach built around our primary research technique, the life narrative. Personal narratives offer 'unique glimpses of the lived interior of migration processes' (Benmayor and Skotnes, 1994: 14); in more ways than one, they are *moving stories* (Thomson, 1999).

The choice of participants[1] for the life narratives is certainly crucial. Whilst in most cases the researcher's personal network offered one entry into the sampling process, we resisted the temptation of easy snowballing and aimed to ensure a diversity of participants by careful use of intermediaries and other access strategies such as digital ethnography.

In confirming our commitment to the production and excavation of

[1] The participants in our study are second-generation returnees. Usage of the term 'second generation' poses challenges both as a descriptive notion and as an analytic category. Researchers and others are rather free with their use of the term to connote a specific collective of people, but their definitions are blurred and often inadequate. In focusing on this rather intriguing term, we note the variable definitions used to circumscribe this population cohort, as well as the multiple understandings of the more general term 'generations'. For a detailed discussion on how we define the 'second generation', 'ancestral homeland return migrants' and 'diasporic subjects', refer to King and Christou, 2008.

personal narratives as realist social texts we are also aware of the dangerous syndrome of the ethnographer-voyeur "who comes back from the field with moving tales of the dispossessed" (Denzin, 1991: 2). But, on the other hand, second-generation returnees who have returned voluntarily (as opposed to being taken back as part of a family return) have considerable agency and control over their lives.

In the interview process the aspiration was personal elaboration and 'flow' with minimal interrogation in the first instance. It was as almost as if we tried to keep to a 'vow of silence' in the initial phases of the interview as we set these up. This is not to say that the interviews were unstructured, there was a narrative guide which was used in two ways, first as a 'fall-back' mechanism if the 'vow of silence' method did not work, and secondly even when the life story teller is in full flow there will be aspects of coverage which have not been fully explored. The aspiration is to have the life story teller in more control of the ordering and sequencing of data. This gives more insight into the *narrative map* of the life story teller. Letting the life story teller order and sequence the narrative tells us more important things about the narrative map. It creates appropriate context and space for flow to occur. This seeks to reduce issues of power (whilst we are aware that these can never be completely suspended).

We realise that people have different kinds of narrative intensity. By and large we feel that we lock into an eternal narrative flow when we have subjects who have high internal reflection. Conversely when that internal narrative activity is, for whatever reason, less frequent it is more difficult to achieve narrative flow in the interview. The interview process is highly contingent on the narrative intensity of each participant which in turn depends to a considerable extent on the degree of internal reflective activity.

We transcribe the interviews and then meet as an interdisciplinary team to discuss the themes. This in a sense is a first layer of analysis[2] but we bring in different disciplinary approaches to the analysis.

In terms of numbers, our target samples were to collect thirty life story narratives from second-generation Greek-American as well as thirty narratives from Greek-German (and British-born Greek-Cypriots as part of an ongoing PhD thesis) returnees along with written narratives plus focus-group and other ethnographic and visual material from a multi-sited field research period in urban, rural and seaside locations in Greece (Athens, Thessaloniki, Volos, Mytilene) with a pilot phase in Berlin and New York. We exceeded our target samples and achieved a grand total of 163 narrative voices, including 122 single narratives (all taped with a few self-written narratives). Specifically, as regards the samples of returnees we have collected

---

[2] Some of the preliminary results are presented in King and Christou, 2008; Christou and King, 2009; King and Christou, 2009a; King and Christou, 2009b.

thirty-two narratives of second-generation Greek-Americans of which twenty-four are females and eight are males and thirty-two narratives of second-generation Greek-Germans of which twenty are female and twelve are male. Their ages range from mid-twenties to mid-seventies while their lengthy of return stay in Greece varies from a few years to approximately forty-years. The fact that these particular groups are understudied underscored our interest in researching the lives of these particular returnees.

Some of the major analytic themes we are pursuing are:

Time / periodicity

Parental relationships

Narrativity / types of narration

Personal identity projects

Racism / Multiculturalism

Gender Relations

More specifically, as regards periodicity, we have begun to delineate three historical periods with regard to migrants' narratives:

Collective / Group Belongingness:

1950s, 1960s and early 1970s

This is largely modernist narratives with somewhat essentialised visions of the social order and Greek identity.

Transitional / Hybrid:

1970s-1990s

Some of the essentialised metanarratives seem to be breaking down in the face of the transformation with the economic world order and its associated narrative landscapes.

Flexible / Individualised:

mid 1990s-present day

Here narratives seem to be much more flexible and individualised. Instead of externally available metanarratives a good deal of self-scripting or internal narration seems to predominate in the presentation of narratives.

As well as social-structural influences to individual narratives a major component of refraction is the nature of relationships with parents. This is a micro-force that shapes narrative reflection in combination with the macro-forces of structural elements. For instance, the journey to the homeland can be seen as an act of reconciliation, redemption or rebellion depending on the nature of the parental relationship. Furthermore, parents' class origins and participants' conceptualisations of class are important parameters in the narrative analysis.

We are finding clusters of narrativity dependent not only on historical periods but also on personal identity projects. We have developed narrative portrayals of participants to define different kinds of narrativity. In the analytic process we follow one binary from essentialised scripted narrative to more flexible autonomy seeking narratives.

Personal identity projects are learning journeys into selfhood as classed, gendered and embodied experiences. The personal identity project is a point of arbitration between externally produced scripts and internally generated visions of selfhood. The space of selfhood is subject to appropriation by the forces we talk about, i.e. enforced gender dynamics, economic changes etc. but the personal identity project becomes a site of externally generated appropriation as well as self-generated re-appropriation.

The theme of racism / multiculturalism is an important factor in the analysis of portrayals. For one, it is interesting to view how participants from 'multicultural' societies view the changing homeland from a sending to a receiving society and on the other how they themselves (inter)act within this space. We seek to expose how racialised views and experiences shape the life narrative and how 'race' is embedded in the life story. In both the German and American (but also British context) case many participants had been brought up in an insulated micro-family environment of a Greek 'bubble' situated within the macro-social environment of a multicultural-multiracial context of the 'host' country. While it can be argued that the 'host' country surroundings do not represent an authentic multiculturalist space with all the racist ideologies (and practices) that exemplify this, there is a question of how racist ideologies embedded in everyday life in the diaspora find a more openly acceptable space of expression in the 'home' country or whether participants critically react to xenophobic discourses of ethnic purity, pride and superiority against the backdrop of issues of immigration in Greece and Cyprus. This will further illuminate the degree to which the family story of socio-cultural and moral values of essentialised Greekness is rejected by the participants or whether the homeland relocation strengthens the family narrative and xenophobic ideology.

Another theme that is emerging in the data is that of gender relations. We seek to move theoretically from cultural capital to *gender capital* through narrative capital and hence to extend the discussion of gendered embodied capital and the institutionalisation of power. Here, it is important to consider the narrativisation of family and home life and their significance for a renewed theory of gender capital. We therefore see femininities and masculinities not as single entities but as expressions of negotiated acts lodged in the structure of relationships among actors; i.e. the role of social structures in creating or maintaining inequality, exclusion, and hierarchy. We aim to interrogate the boundaries of gender relationships as fluid yet dynamic and lodged into the life narrative but also as a mediating force shaping the life narrative. We view migrant women and men as agents of change and resistance and their collective sense of belonging as not simply a community of fixedness but as multiple communities of gendered mobilities. We view migrant groups as collectivities of agency in order to understand gendered identities. We appreciate that migrancy is both a form and a forum of gendered cultural citizenship as women and men reflect on their identities as cultural citizens. For instance, women in migrant life are often regarded as the guardians and custodians of socio-cultural ties and traditions. Women migrants have been conventionally understood to be embedded in the cultural private world of the 'home' rather than the political public social world. Here we focus also on a third space that is emerging in the data which is around the psychic selfhood that is potentially agentic in new ways. It is against this conflating notion of gendered roles that we seek to question the lines between public and private drawn in migrant life, that is, where the boundaries are and who defines them. Furthermore, we investigate the ways in which the interplay between social networks and gender relationships might become a resource for migrant engagement and hence, unveil the types of gender relationships that potentially become sources of agency for migrants but also to uncover what may limit them. Finally, in the new flexible work order we seek to find out if there is a new emergent life politics space which is located around issues of identity and selfhood.

Our choice of portrayals is based on the 'thematic density' that participant narratives exemplify. Here, saturation is an important element in the selection of thematic density. We select portrayals that will elucidate as many as possible of these themes. We therefore select the core 'exemplary' portrayals to substantiate the discussion of themes listed previously but for reasons of writing limitations will not be able to present exemplifications on this occasion. Our narrative selections cover different regional relocation spaces as well as diverse generational biographies through which we illustrate dominant forms of second-generation storied lives but within each of these there are multiple layers of subjectivities and hence multifaceted layers of migrant narrativity, as we do not want to essentialise the very process of narration.

Acknowledgements

This paper derives from an on-going AHRC project on 'counter-diasporic migrations'. I gratefully acknowledge the financial backing of the AHRC under its 'Diasporas, Migration and Identities' programme (grant no. AH/E508601X/1), and the support of the programme director Professor

Kim Knott. I am particularly grateful to my project team colleagues, Prof. Russell King, Prof. Ivor Goodson and Janine Givati-Teerling, and to Dr Tracey Reynolds, who became a de facto team member during her secondment fellowship at the University of Sussex from London South Bank University. Special thanks go Dr D. Mentzeniotis for inspiration and encouragement. All subsequent omissions and errors remain my own.

References

Ahmed, S., Castañeda, C., Fortier, A.-M. and Sheller, M., eds., 2003, *Uprootings/Regroundings: Questions of Home and Migration*, Oxford, Berg.

Bauman, Z., 1991, *Modernity and Ambivalence*, Cambridge, Polity Press.

_____, 1995, "Searching for a Centre that Holds", in: Featherstone, M., Lash, S. and Robertson, R. eds., *Global Modernities: Theory, Culture and Society,* Sage, pp. 140-154.

_____, 2000, *Globalisation: The Human Consequences*, New York, Columbia University Press.

Beck, U. and E. Beck-Gernsheim, 2002, *Individualization*, London, Sage.

Benmayor, R. and Skotnes, A., eds., 1994, *Migration and Identity*, Oxford, OUP (International Yearbook of Oral History and Life Stories, vol. 3).

Bruner, J.S., 1990, Acts of Meaning, Cambridge, MA, Harvard University Press.

Chanfrault-Duchet, M-F. 1991, "Narrative structures, social models, and symbolic representation in the life story", in: S.B. Gluck &D. Patai eds., *Women's Words: The Feminist Practice of Oral History*, Routledge, pp. 77-92.

Chodorow, Nancy J., 1999, *The Power of Feelings. Personal Meaning in Psychoanalysis, Gender and Culture*, Yale University Press, New Haven & London.

Christou, A. 2006, *Narratives of place, culture and identity: second generation Greek-Americans return 'home'*, Amsterdam, Amsterdam University Press.

Christou, A. and King, R. 2009, "Movements between 'white' Europe and America: Greek migration to the United States", in Knott, K. and McLoughlin, S. eds. *Diasporas: Concepts, Identities, Intersections*, Zed Books, in press.

Denzin, N., 1991, "Deconstructing the Biographical Method", Paper to AERA Conference, Chicago, 9 April.

Goodson, I., 1995, "The story so far: personal knowledge and the political", *International Journal of Qualitative Studies in Education*, 8(1): 89–98.

_____, 2006, "The Rise of the Life Narrative", *Teacher Education Quarterly,* 33(4): 7-21.

King, R. and Christou, A. 2008, "Cultural Geographies of Counter-Diasporic Migration: The Second Generation Returns 'Home'", Sussex Migration Working Paper No 45, Sussex Centre for Migration Research, University of Sussex, UK.

_____, 2009, "Diaspora, Migration and Transnationalism: Insights from the Study of Second-Generation 'Returnees'", in Bauböck, R. and Faist, T. eds. *Diaspora and Transnationalism: Conceptual, Theoretical and Methodological Challenges*, Amsterdam: Amsterdam University Press, in press.

_____, 2009, "Cultural Geographies of Counter-Diasporic Migration: Perspectives from the Study of Second-Generation 'Returnees' to Greece", *Population, Space and Place*, Volume 15, in press.

Lawrence-Lightfoot, S. & J. Hoffman-Davis, 1997, *The Art of Science of Portraiture*, San Francisco, Jossey-Bass.

Lentin, R., 2000, *Israel and the Daughters of the Shoah: Reoccupying the Territories of Silence*, New York and Oxford, Berghahn Books.

Lowenthal, D., 1985, *The Past is a Foreign Country,* Cambridge, Cambridge University Press.

Mishler, E.G., 1991, *Research interviewing: Context and narrative*, Cambridge, MA, Harvard University Press.

_____, 2000, *Storylives: Craftartists narratives of identity*, Cambridge, MA, Harvard University Press.

Moriarty, E., 2005, "Telling Identity Stories: the Routinisation of Racialisation of Irishness", *Sociological Research Online*, 10(3): <http:// www.socresonline. org.uk/10/3/ moriarty.html>.

Passerini, L., 1987, *Fascism in Popular Memory: The Cultural Experience of the Turin Working Class*, Cambridge, Cambridge University Press.

Pratt, G. 2008, "Reflections on Postructuralism and Feminist Empirics, Theory and Practice, in Moss, P. and Falconer Al-Hindi, K. eds. *Feminisms in Geography: Rethinking Space, Place and Knowledges*, Lanham, Maryland: Rowman and Littlefield Publishers, pp. 49-59.

Plummer, K., 1995, *Telling Sexual Stories: Power, Change and Social Worlds*, London & New York, Routledge.

_____, 2001, *Documents of Life 2: An Invitation to a Critical Humanism,* London, Sage.

Thomson, A., 1999, "Moving stories: oral history and migration studies", *Oral History*, 27(1): 24-37.

_____, 2003, "I live on my memories: British return migrants and the possession of the past", *Oral History*, 31(2): pp 55-65.

CHAPTER 16

NATIONAL IDENTITY AND OTHERNESS IN GREEK SPEAKERS' TALK ABOUT IMMIGRATION: METHODOLOGICAL AND TRANSDISCIPLINARY REFLECTIONS

Maria Xenitidou

Abstract

The aim of the paper is to present the potential contribution of using Critical Discursive Psychology to study national identity and immigration. It draws upon a study on Greek national identity negotiations in relation to immigration. The study was guided by the perspective of banal nationalism which treats national identity as a form of life in a world divided into nation-states (Billig, 1995). In terms of Greek national identity and immigration, the study drew similarities between the perspective of banal nationalism and the critique of methodological nationalism (Wimmer and Schiller, 2002).

Introduction

Since the collapse of the communist regimes in Eastern Europe and the Balkans, Southern European countries have been regarded as experiencing a shift from migration senders to host societies. This shift, as a context of 'otherness' in Greece, has been theorised as contributing to re-opening the negotiation of Greek national identity, incurring a 'redefinition' to it. Inspired by this context, the aim of this study was to contribute to the exploration of the ways in which Greek identity discourse and discursive practices might have taken on board the presence of 'new' immigrant populations from the Balkans. This paper discusses two patterns identified in this study and considers the implications of the methodological choices and theoretical assumptions made.

Identity in the current study was treated as resource, discourse, topic and construct: all these manifestations were studied and analysed in the study from transcriptions using discourse analysis. Employing premises in Critical Discursive Psychology (Wetherell 1998), the study sought to explore the ways in which identity is both resourced in invoking constituted positions and practiced in participants' own orientations in talk, identifying both rhetorical (as ideological) and conversational (as situated) consequences.

Immigration in the current study was treated as a context for redefinition, amongst others - and redefinition itself was treated as a constant process - in the sense that it involves discourse on space - treated as national within nation-states (Wimmer and Schiller, 2002: 310-11). It is in this context that immigration - translocation in spaces which are treated as national - is seen as an issue of concern, provoking political and social negotiation.

Overall, the argument examined in this study was that Greek national identity is not a static phenomenon but a dynamic process, dependant on both context and on conversational pragmatics, rather than on axiomatic, resistant, solid and internally consistent definitions. When Greek national identity is constructed with reference to recent immigration from the Balkans, it is re-opened and re-defined in terms of the group of immigrants in question, constructing the national category and immigrant categories with reference to each other while attending to accountability and moral charges.

Methodology

The target population for the current study was Greek citizens and ethnic Greeks (see Petronotti and Triandafyllidou, 2003) who were born and raised in Greece. The parameters considered relevant in the sampling process were locality and age[1]. The age groups selected were 18-21 (as having grown up alongside 'new' immigration) and 35-45 (as recipients of 'new' immigration in the sense of not coexisting in compulsory forms of socialisation such as primary education). A distinction was made between urban and rural areas as it was hypothesised that they would diverge in terms of the percentage concentration, the origin and type[2] of immigrants as well as their effect on everyday life. The research area was set in the Prefecture of Central Macedonia (Central Northern Greece) on the grounds that the percentage concentration of immigrants from Balkan states in the total population of the area is considered as significantly high. The municipalities selected were Thessaloniki (with 6.5% alien[3] concentrations), Halkidiki (8.5%) and Serres (2.4%) (see Potter, 1996 on the use of statistics).

Participants were selected using snowball sampling. Snowball sampling "is based on the assumption that a 'bond' or 'link' exists between the initial sample and others in the same target population, allowing a series of referrals to be made within a circle of acquaintance" (Atkinson and Flint, 2001: 1). This has been selected since focus groups work better with participants who know one another, as naturally emerging groups (Billig, 1992).

[1] It should be noted that, while different age groups were sampled, the particular research context did not reveal patterns in participants' lines of argument which were age specific. However, the urban/rural distinction followed in the sampling process was treated in participants' talk in terms of scale. When talking about urban areas immigration was treated as a phenomenon, whereas in the context of rural areas immigrants were treated as people and talked about in terms of (low) numbers (as too few) and in terms of integration (as quite assimilated).

[2] This refers to categories constructed with reference to the purpose of mobility, such as economic/labour immigrants, ethnic Greek immigrants, refugees, and returnees as citizens of non-EU countries who are of Greek origin in that they derive from Greece or regions beyond the borders of the Greek state which were formerly influenced by Greek culture.

[3] Translation of term used by the National Statistics Service of Greece, 2001.

Overall, eight semi-structured focus group sessions were held with 39 participants. Focus groups were used in order to enable intersubjectivity (see Billig, 1989; Sacks, 1992; Tusting *et al.*, 2002), which personal interviews do not enable. Attention was paid to holding these group discussions in 'familiar' settings and to minimising the moderator's role in order for interaction to develop in a similar way as it does in everyday social encounters. Focus groups were typically held in what the researcher took to be 'neutral' places of socialisation, such as a coffee shop, a living room or a community hall.

National disinterestedness and categorical accounting practices

Participants' talk in this study treated national identity as commonsensical to 'have'. The main lines of argument which treated national identity as natural appeared to be the rhetorical denouncing of uniqueness, exceptionality and superiority, in their essentialist form as automatic, biological characteristics of Greeks by nationality. This is instantiated in the extract below.

Extract 1 - Focus Group 2 (Urban area, 35-45 years old)

754 Pavlos: what does it mean to you that you are Greek? How do you see yourself in?

755 Costas: e:h I will answer this question generally

756 Fotis: =what do you feel?

757 Costas: eh?

758 Fotis: what do you feel? German?

759 Costas: no (.) I feel Greek, but I believe that this is a label, e:h and

760 Fotis: =you don't believe in the distinctiveness of the race?

761 Costas: exactly. yes >that is to say< e:h I don't believe that as a Greek I have

762 something more: than the others [...] that I am Greek is clearly a matter of a:

763 coincidence (.) I was born by specific parents [...] anyway I believe that

764 what makes me be Greek is that I had Greek education, right? Namely that I

765 grew up with the books e:h of the: Ministry of Education in Greece

766 Vaggelis: [maths ((inaudible)) remember?

767 Costas: [EVERYTHING, EVERYTHING. This makes me stand

out say and

768 from then on the Greek language

769 Fotis: =the first

770 Costas: e:h (.) religion does not touch me much so I don't take this into

771 account but for many people it is quite important right as orthodoxy

772 Fotis: =religion for Hellenism is the burial of Hellenism

773 Costas: anyway e:h

774 Fotis: no I mean this

775 Costas: yes a:nd which means that even if I was born by Greek parents ok? And

776 was brought up for 5 years with them, if I then left and went to some other parents

777 and had Albanian education right? Albanian e:h an environment to influence me

778 right? A person constantly receives (.) then I would be completely different

779 to what I a:m now. Neither superior nor inferior but I would be: different

780 this is what I believe that makes me Greek in inverted commas right? Because I

781 believe that it is a label so to say it i:sn't (.) this is my opinion

The above extract evolves in response to the question on the meaning of being Greek. To this question, Costas' denial to respond specifically (line 755) seems interpreted by Fotis as a denial of 'feeling' Greek. This indicates that the speaker orients to the meaning of being Greek as automatically implying sentiment (line 758). In other words, national sentiment constitutes the definitional framework of Greek national identity in this context. Costas joins in the emotional discourse but his utterance is contrast-ridden as he then claims that feeling Greek is a 'label'. While this appears paradoxical at first glance, it is reflective of 'dilemmatic' argumentation indicated in a readiness to justify feeling Greek. Emotional discourse is tied into the discourse of nationalism, from which the speaker wishes to detach himself for the identity implications it may have in terms of rationality and objectivity (see Billig *et al.*, 1988).

Participants appear to acknowledge and disclaim for themselves distinctiveness, exceptionality and superiority. Thus, being Greek is a label, a formal category, in the sense that no exceptionality is or should be immediately attached to it. Participants' responses here, therefore, seem to indicate that attaching exceptionality and superiority to a national category commonly connotes a negative identity for the speaker, acknowledged as complying with nationalist discourse, which is commonly condemned (see Billig, 1995). This automatic association of national identity with making claims to superiority is explicitly then stated by Costas in lines 761-2. Costas reiterates that nationality is accidental and presents the criteria which compose Greek nationality, namely genealogical origin, education, language and religion – the latter seen as within the definitional discourse but resisted by participants (lines 762-774) (see Tsoucalas, 1983).

Finally, in lines 775-781, Costas formulates a personal hypothesis, as a common technique of fact construction, to argue that acquired criteria such as upbringing, education and social environment are determinants of national identification while genealogical origin and brief exposure to a culture are rendered insufficient to cultivate national identity. Prioritising acquired criteria of national identification functions to undermine origin for having negative connotations, while sustaining national identification as a formalised process. This enables Costas to argue that it is due to the accidental nature of nationality and its compromised role in national identity building that national hierarchies are irrelevant. In other words, he seems to subscribe to the view that talking about difference as an automatic understanding of national identities is relevant, while automatic positive or negative evaluations *per se* are not. The readiness to disavow claims to national superiority appears to have led Costas to an outward-looking account about the meaning of being Greek as a nationality rather than to an inward-looking account as an identity (see Billig, 1995). This may be indicative of a concern on the part of the speaker to 'present' a rational account of national categorisation, as internationally prescribed (see Billig, 1995). The main critique of such discourse has been that it retains national categories and national divisions as normative (ibid).

In view of the social norm against biological categorisation and classification (see Billig *et al.*, 1988), this may be taken to constitute the discursive act of 'disclaiming superiority' as an integral part of definitional accounts of the meaning of being Greek. In other words, this study has suggested that in Greek identity talk arguing becomes infused in the argument (see Billig, 1987; 1989; 1991), as in the context of talking about Greek national identity with reference to immigration from the Balkans reflexivity appeared to constitute an integral part of definitional accounts.

It was in the afore-mentioned context that the negotiation of the boundaries of the Greek category with reference to immigrants in Greece became relevant. This negotiation emerged as a main pattern of discursive activity in talking about Greekness with reference to the presence of immigrants in Greece. This negotiation indicated a seeming readiness on the part of participants to categorise particulars along the national category (see Billig, 1987) by negotiating sets of criteria. The criteria of inclusion were presented as rational and inclusion was extended to various groups whose exclusion might have provoked the charge of prejudice. Nevertheless, central to this process was an implicit and explicit hierarchical arrangement of these categories. This is instantiated in the following extract.

Extract 2 - Focus Group 6 (Rural area, 18-21 years old)

359 Alex: what does it mean to you for someone to be Greek? [...]

360 Costas: they have to feel it

361 Alex: they have to feel it

362 May: that's what we concluded (.) that's right

363 Alex: regardless of whether he is an immigrant regardless if (.) he has to feel

364 Greek (.) to observe traditions

365 May: his parents may not be Greek they may live in Greece for years (.)

366 nevertheless he may feel Greek

367 Dina: a child who was born in Greece, who has never left for Albania or Bulgaria

368 or whatever his country is (.) and Greek is his first language

369 May: yes

370 Dina: who has learned to love Greece, who has learned to think in the Greek

371 mentality >if such a thing exists<

372 Costas: yes yes

373 Dina: how are you going to tell him that "you know you are not Greek" since he

374 doesn't have relations with his biological homeland (.) it's like

375 excommunicating him like telling him that "you have no homeland"

376 Alex: he is considered Greek Dina

377 May: yes

378 Dina: good (.) we agree

379 Alex: more or less all of whom you are talking about now are considered Greek

380 May: who? (...)

381 Costas: those who have been born here

382 Dina: yes

383 May: you may not have been born here (.) you may have come he may

384 have come when he was little he may live ((here)) many years (...)

385 Dina: it has do though with were you grew up

386 Alex: yes sure (.) it plays an important role (..) but also the one who didn't grow

387 up here and his father and his mother were here and left is considered Greek (.) he

388 will come he will do this that

389 May: with a different meaning

390 Alex: yes with a different meaning

An extensive negotiation of Greekness preceded this extract in which national feeling was constructed as the most important criterion of Greekness (lines 360-2). Extension to immigrants is "regardless" made by Alex (line 363) who also adds Greekness as a daily lived practice in the form of 'observing traditions' (line 364). Therefore, participants extend the construction of the category of Greeks, to include immigrants in general. May alludes to biological origin to compare it to long term residence, as 'nevertheless' potentially developing national feeling. Dina then lists three criteria (Jefferson, 1990) - place of birth, permanent residence and (first) language – followed by another two - love for Greece and Greek mentality - as factual reasoning for an extension of the boundaries. While these criteria are presented as normal and rational, their combination underlines the strictness with which this extension of Greekness is conducted, which also corresponds to Greek immigration policy directives. Speaking from a category of Greeks as entitled (see Edwards and Potter, 1992) to classify the Greekness of others (line 376 – "considered"), Dina adopts a distant footing (Potter, 1996) and uses active voicing (Wooffitt, 1992) to vividly construct this extension as an endowment as a matter of principle. At the same time full inclusion of these categories is mitigated by 'biological' origin, explicitly included in this line of argumentation (line 374). Thus, she seems to manage accountability both in terms of content and rhetoric (lines 367-375) (see Edwards and Potter, 1992, Potter, 1996, Billig, 1987).

It is, thus, revealed that an extension of Greekness is negotiated for moral reasons, which endows immigrants with formal Greekness. The formal, 'out-there' (see Potter, 1996) extension is co-constructed and extended to include first generation immigrants on the basis of this status (lines 383-385). In this negotiation of the inclusion of immigrants in the wider national group, constructing Greekness as prioritising the criteria of place of nurture and upbringing combined with the previous acquired criteria implicitly excludes Greek emigrants abroad from the national group. In the flow of argument though, and with the addition of origin and contact with Greece as criteria, the boundaries are extended - implicitly constructing a subcategory of Greeks "with a different meaning" as formal status for Greek emigrants abroad (lines 386-390).

This negotiation indicates a readiness on the part of participants to extend the boundaries of Greekness and 'nationalise' 'others' on the basis of complying with particular sets of criteria. Nationalisation is negotiated in terms of a hierarchical arrangement in categories of Greeks, speaking from a category of Greeks, as complying with all of the central criteria of Greekness. This initially functions to reveal a 'contract' suggested for immigration in Greece as being in line with the thesis of integration through nationalising immigrants in relation to host norms and expectations. This corresponds to a strategy of assimilation. Nevertheless, this nationalisation is conditional (see White, 1999) and does not imply a super-ordinate category of Greeks but a split into different peripheral categories hierarchically arranged by extending the boundaries of Greekness, yet prioritising some values over others. These categories are included into the wider national group but are excluded from the central category of Greeks.

Evaluating transdisciplinarity, approach and method

In terms of theoretical assumptions the current study was guided by the perspective of banal nationalism in its understanding of national identity as a form of life in a world divided into nation-states (Billig, 1995). This perspective has also been applied in the current study as an approach to understanding national otherness and as a theoretical context to studying national identity and immigration. In terms of Greekness (and immigration) as topic, the current study drew similarities between the perspective of banal nationalism articulated from a social psychological position and the critique of methodological nationalism (Wimmer and Schiller, 2002) articulated from an anthropological position on the basis that both forward critiques of the penetration of nationalism - the former with reference to everyday life and the latter with reference to the role of the social sciences - sociology in particular - in this penetration. The assumptions and conclusions of the current study supported the critique of methodological nationalism on traditional (sociological) migration research and aimed to contribute to a shift in perspective away from methodological nationalism.

This was done, firstly by exploring the complexity of Greek national identity in talk and challenging the fixity and homogeneity of Greek national culture with reference to immigrants (cf. Triandafyllidou, 2000; Triandafyllidou and Veikou, 2002). The findings that this approach enabled led to the argument that in talking about Greek national identity with reference to immigrants arguing becomes infused in the argument (Billig, 1987; 1989; and 1991): reflexivity and content appear as inseparable aspects of Greek national identification and immigrant otherness.

Secondly, the shift in perspective was attempted by focusing on the interconnectedness between traditions of argumentation of Greek nation-building and discourse on immigrant integration, which has been identified as a major shortcoming of migration research (see critiques by Brubaker, 1992; Castles, 1995; Favell, 2001a; 2001b; 2005). By challenging the assumption of homogeneity in Greek national identity, relational definitions of national identity were enabled, which seemed to contradict taken-for-granted assumptions that immigrants *de facto* reduce cultural homogeneity. In the context of people positioned and addressed as Greek, born, raised and living in Northern Greece talking about immigrants from the Balkans in focus group sessions, Greek national identity was constructed as assimilatory. Taking the interconnectedness argument on board, this could be explained in terms of the prominence of aspects of ethnic nationalism in Greek nation-building, reflected in Greek lay actors' talk. However, whereas previous research claimed that on this basis Greek national identity is constructed as exclusionary (see Triandafyllidou, 2000; Ventura, 2001), in the context of the current study findings supported a more complex argument. In particular, the argument put forward is that in talking about Greek national identity with reference to immigrants, participants in the current research orient to an ethno-genealogical sense-making of the nation and organise immigrants hierarchically around this construction (see Triandafyllidou and Veikou, 2002; Pavlou, 2004).

These findings both indicated and responded to the need to trace shifts in context and argument as regards Greek national identity with reference to immigrants (Figgou, 2002). For example, Figgou's research on Greek people talking about refugees from Albania and the former Soviet Union, and the Muslim minority in Thrace indicated that for her participants "assimilation of groups from distinct cultural backgrounds into a common super-ordinate category is undesirable, illegitimate and even racist" (Figgou, 2002: 349). However, the current study identified and explored a relative 'openness' in the negotiation of Greek national identity - to the extent that assimilationist lines enable such an openness.

This could be explained in two ways: firstly, in terms of moving beyond the process of identity construction as undertaken by immigrants and locals as two distinct categories (see Favell, 2001a and 2001b) constructing two distinct identity narratives and towards arguing for the co-construction of identity in everyday social encounters; secondly, in terms of supporting the argument that context matters (Potter and Wetherell, 1987) in conditioning understandings of national identity and otherness. The first explanation necessitates a periodic exploration of social actors' understandings of national identity and otherness, in this case Greek national identity and immigration in local contexts. The second explanation necessitates local and modest in-depth research (see Figgou, 2002) and indicates that further research should focus on the interaction of social and policy discourse in their understandings of integration and their construction of categories of hosts and others (see White, 1999). As such, it cautions against attitudinal, survey-type research which makes claims to generalisability and universal application of its findings without taking into account the macro-social and local-interactional contexts in which these findings are produced.

Overall, therefore, the theoretical assumptions and conclusions of the current study indicated that the combination of banal and methodological nationalism, which has not been addressed by researchers or by a dialogue between social psychology and sociology, appears useful in providing alternative understandings of identity and immigration to the ones provided by attitudinal, anthropological or ethnographic type of research.

In terms of methodological implications in particular, while employing a reflexive approach in the sense of transcending the nation-state/immigrant nexus and treating national identity and otherness as topics, the current study focused, nevertheless, on 'national' identity, rather than on identities and immigration 'in general'. The focus group schedule in particular 'positioned' participants in national terms and conditioned the ways in which national identification and immigration were talked about. This might have interfered with both the conclusions of this study and their generalisability beyond the particular focus group contexts. In particular, considering the conclusions of the current study beyond the focus group schedule and outside the emergent conversational activities that intra focus group dynamics conditioned, would be countering the argument on which the research was based and sought to examine: namely, that Greek national identity is not a static, unidimensional phenomenon but a dynamic and complex process, dependant on context and conversational pragmatics rather than on axiomatic, resistant, solid and internally consistent definitions.

The significance of the findings presented in the current study - as revealed during the analytic process – is found at identifying the potentials of opting for a relational approach to identification as well as at foregrounding the complexities of identification. In many respects participants transcended the 'conditions' of the focus group schedule by formulating reflexive accounts of national identification and by negotiating the boundaries of Greekness with reference to immigrants, which may have been overshadowed by a methodological emphasis on matching content to categories and making evaluations on it.

References

Antaki, C. and Widdicombe, S. (Eds.) (1998). *Identities in Talk*. London: Sage.

Atkinson, R. and Flint, J. (2001). Accessing Hidden and Hard-to-Reach Populations: Snowball Research Strategies. *Social Research Update*. 33: 1-4.

Berg, S. (1988). Snowball sampling. In: S. Kotz and N. L. Johnson (Eds.) *Encyclopaedia of Statistical Sciences,* Vol. 8.

Billig, M. (1987). *Arguing and Thinking. A rhetorical approach to social psychology.* Cambridge: Cambridge University Press.

Billig, M. (1989). The argumentative nature of holding strong views: A case study. *European Journal of Social Psychology*, 19: 203-223.

Billig, M. (1991). *Ideology and Opinions. Studies in Rhetorical Psychology*. London: Sage

Billig, M. (1992). *Talking of the royal family*. London: Routledge.

Billig, M. (1995). *Banal Nationalism*. London: Sage.

Billig, M. (1997). Discursive, Rhetorical and Ideological Messages. In: C. McGarty and A. Haslam (Eds.) *The Message of Social Psychology.* Oxford: Blackwell Publishers.

Billig, M. (2001). Discursive, Rhetorical and Ideological Messages. In: M. Wetherell, S. Taylor & S. J. Yates (Eds.) *Discourse Theory and Practice: A Reader.* London: Sage, pp. 211-221.

Billig, M. (2002). Henri Tajfel's 'Cognitive aspects of prejudice' and the psychology of bigotry. *British Journal of Social Psychology*, 41: 171-188.

Billig M., Condor S., Edwards D., Gane M., Middleton D. and Radley A. (1988). *Ideological Dilemmas: a social psychology of everyday thinking*. London: Sage.

Bozatzis, N. (1999). *Greek National Identity in Talk: The Rhetorical Articulation of an Ideological Dilemma.* Unpublished Ph.D. thesis. Lancaster: Lancaster University.

Brubaker, R. (1992). *Citizenship and Nationhood in France and Germany.* Cambridge. Massachusetts- London, England: Harvard University Press.

Castles, S. (1995). How nation-states respond immigration and ethnic diversity. *New Community,* 21: 293-308.

Edwards, D. and Potter, J. (1992). *Discursive Psychology.* London: SAGE.

Favell, A. (2001a). Integration policy and integration research in Europe: a review and critique. In: T. A. Aleinikoff and D. Klusmeyer (Eds.) *Citizenship Today: Global Perspectives and Practices.* Washington, DC: Brookings Institute/Carnegie Endowment for International Peace, pp. 349-399.

Favell, A. (2001b). Multicultural nation-building: 'integration' as public philosophy and research paradigm in Western Europe. *Swiss Political Science Review.* 7(2): 116-124.

Favell, A. (2005). Assimilation/Integration. In M. Gibneyand R. Hansen (Eds.) *Immigration and Asylum: From 1900 to the Present.* Santa Barbara, CA: Clio.

Figgou, L (2002). *Social Psychological and lay understandings of prejudice, racism and discrimination: an exploration of their dilemmatic aspects.* Unpublished Ph.D. thesis. Lancaster: Lancaster University.

Gourgouris, S. (1996). *Dream Nation: Enlightenment, Colonization and the Institution of Modern Greece.* Stanford: Stanford University Press.

Jefferson, G. (1990). List contruction as a task and resource. In: G. Psathas (Ed.) *Interaction Competence.* Washington, DC: University Press of America.

Pavlou, M. (2004). Οι μετανάστες «σαν κι εμάς»: όψεις της απόκρισης στο μεταναστευτικό φαινόμενο στην Ελλάδα και την Ευρώπη. [The immigrants "like us": aspects of responses to the phenomenon of immigration in Greece and Europe]. In: M. Pavlou and D.

Christopoulos (Eds.) *Η Ελλάδα της μετανάστευσης. Κοινωνική συμμετοχή, δικαιώματα και ιδιότητα του πολίτη.* [Greece of migration. Social participation, rights and citizen status]. Athens: Ekdoseis Kritiki AE & KEMO.

Petronoti, M. and Triandafyllidou, A. (2003). *Recent Immigration Flows to Greece.* Bibliography of Social Sciences in Modern Greek Society. Athens: National Centre for Social Research.

Potter, J. (1996). *Representing Reality. Discourse, Rhetoric and Social Construction.* London: Sage.

Potter, J. (2004). Discourse analysis as a way of analysing naturally occurring talk. In: D. Silverman (Ed) *Qualitative Research: Theory, Method and Practice.* (2nd ed). London: Sage.

Potter, J. and Wetherell, M. (1987). *Discourse and Social Psychology.* London: Sage.

Sacks, H. (1992). *Lectures on Conversation. Vols. I & II.* (Edited by Jefferson, G.). Oxford: Blackwell Publishers.

Triandafyllidou, A. (2000). 'Racists? Us? Are You Joking?' The Discourse of Social Exclusion of Immigrants in Greece and Italy. In: R. King (Ed.) *Eldorado or Fortress?: Migration in Southern Europe.* Basingstoke: Macmillan, pp. 186-206.

Triandafyllidou, A. and Veikou, M. (2002). The hierarchy of Greekness – ethnic and national identity consideration in Greek immigration policy. *Ethnicities,* Vol. 2, No. 2, pp. 189-208.

Tsoucalas, C. (1983). Παράδοση και Εκσυγχρονισμός: Μερικά γενικότερα ερωτήματα. [Tradition and Modernization: Some general questions]. In: D. G. Tsaousis (Ed.) *Ελληνισμός και ελληνικότητα: Ιδεολογικοί και βιωματικοί άξονες της νεοελληνικής κοινωνίας [Hellenism – Greekness: Ideological and experiential axes of modern Greek society].* Athens: Estia, pp. 37-49.

Tusting K., Crawshaw, R. and Callen B. (2001). 'I know, cos I was there': how residence abroad students use personal experience to legitimate cultural generalizations. *Discourse & Society,* 13(5): 651-672.

Ventura, L. (2001). Εθνικισμός, ρατσισμός και μετανάστευση στη σύγχρονη Ελλάδα. [Nationalism, racism and immigration in contemporary Greece]. In: M. Pavlou and D. Christopoulos (Eds.) *Η Ελλάδα της μετανάστευσης. Κοινωνική συμμετοχή, δικαιώματα και ιδιότητα του πολίτη.* [Greece of migration. Social participation, rights and citizen status]. Athens: Ekdoseis Kritiki AE & KEMO.

Wetherell, M. (1998). Positioning and interpretative repertoires: Conversation analysis and post-structuralism in dialogue. *Discourse & Society,* 9(3): 387-412.

White, P. (1999). Ethnicity, racialization and citizenship as divisive elements in Europe. In: R. Hudson and A. Williams (Eds.) *Divided Europe: Society and Territory.* London: SAGE, pp. 210-230.

Wimmer, A. and Schiller, N. G. (2002). Methodological nationalism and beyond: nation-state building, migration and the social sciences. *Global Networks,* 2(4): 302-334.

Wooffitt, R. (1992). *Telling Tales of the Unexpected: The Organisation of Factual Accounts.* Hemel Hempstead: Harvester Wheatscheaf

www.ingramcontent.com/pod-product-compliance
Lightning Source LLC
LaVergne TN
LVHW020046110826
845155LV00029B/642

* 9 7 8 1 9 1 2 9 9 7 1 0 7 *